Hopes n Hats

Tears through Laughter and Laughter through Tears

Cheryl O'Brien Huber

authorHOUSE®

AuthorHouse™ UK Ltd.
500 Avebury Boulevard
Central Milton Keynes, MK9 2BE
www.authorhouse.co.uk
Phone: 08001974150

First published by AuthorHouse   4/22/2009

ISBN: 978-1-4389-3070-1 (sc)
ISBN: 978-1-4389-3071-8 (hc)

This book is printed on acid-free paper.

Special Thanks:

Paul,
Thank you for making all things possible and believing in me, as much as I believe in you.

Billy O'Brien,
Thank you for allowing me to add some of your beautiful poetry to this book.

For my Children, Kelly, Mike and Dan
In memory of my parents, Ed and Alva whose love will endure forever
in the memories of their
Children and grandchildren.

Contents

Pictures are available online at: http://HopesnHats.com

Preface

With a career as an engineer in the oil industry, Paul's job has necessitated several moves over the past thirty years of our marriage. Many of these played out like slapstick comedy with the calamity of errors and constant obstacles in the way. Now he works as an executive for *Lloyds Register of Shipping*, a classification society, in *London, England*.

I was raised in a tight community in *Tulsa, Oklahoma*. I was lucky number seven of eleven children born to Ed and Alva O'Brien. I was born in 1957, toward the end of the baby boom era. I had nineteen aunts and twenty uncles. When my grandmother O'Brien turned eighty-years-old, she had 101 offspring. In a Catholic community, volunteer work is expected, and social injustice is not.

I learned to love volunteering. I coached, taught music and Sunday school, was on various committees, involved in theater, opera and choir. I worked with parents of children with learning disabilities and volunteered as a County Master Gardener in *Fort Bend, Texas*, and I was a patient advocate at the *Katy Memorial Hermann Hospital*. Most dear to me, I volunteered for hospice.

I found that when we would pack the house and move to another state or country, I could never recreate what I left behind. I tend to be passionate about my work, whatever it is. I look ahead and not back and wait for an opportunity to present itself. As I tell my children, "If a door opens you must walk through. I call it trying on hats!"

Often I started out a bit green, but I would give it my all. Some things I was better at than I was others. I was constantly learning. All of these hats helped to lead me here, to write *Hopes n Hats*.

I tend to allow my instincts to lead me. When I moved to *London*, I immediately felt as though I was a character in someone else's book. I was one of many personalities in a big city; I recognized characters all around me.

Within the first three months, I made friends with two different published authors by coincidence. One had taken the self-publishing route, and the other was solicited by her publisher. The more I began to learn about writing, the more I thought that perhaps this is where I am being led.

For several years, many of my friends were convinced I had a message to share. They were often encouraging me to put it down on paper. Perhaps living in a foreign country without distraction would give me the time that is necessary to do just that.

In this book, I wish to share with the reader an O'Brien culture, a culture of our own. These are the rules that we lived by, using humor to get us through the toughest times. We learned to laugh at ourselves in the face of terror, in the face of evil, in the face of danger and at our own misgivings.

Still, it is impossible to find humor in some things. Waiting for a diagnosis is the toughest time for families. Once you know what you are dealing with, you can get on with life. The waiting is hell! Looking for that cure is hell! Feeling like there is nothing in your life that you can control is hell! Stress helps no one. Let it go.

This book offers something for a broad range of people. Looking back over the Sixties and Seventies through rose-colored glasses, I have to allow the truth to enter in on occasion, exposing a large cast of characters. We lived in a simpler time; we still underwent massive changes in our culture.

In the Eighties and Nineties, we raised our own children using the faith and values bestowed upon us by our parents, with some modifications. Our children are now on their own; given all that we had to give, not monetarily but from the head and heart.

My introduction to death and dying came about through my own personal experience with my brother, Danny, when I was a teenager. As a result, our family went through its own metamorphosis. Each of us in our own unique way was changed forever. Yet sharing the experience brought the family even closer together.

The community came together to get through the toughest times. Years later, I lost my father when I was 22-years-old. I realized that experiencing grief without someone who understands what you are going through would be terrifying. Until you experience losing a loved one yourself, you can't understand what it's like. Sharing tears is as important as sharing the good times.

The strength of the women in this book is an inspiration for all women. The dedication of the men to their families and their community is an example for all who need to stand proud in recognition of their determination and perseverance.

When Aint Jo was dying, my momma was present at her bedside. Hospice was there to help care for her and to deal with the uncomfortable details. Momma was in awe at the difference that a presence could make.

I began to look at what hospice really was. I wanted to make a difference. What I found is that I had a special gift dealing with death and dying. The dying experience doesn't have to be painful for the person dying, and the families can cherish the experience, like rocking a baby to sleep.

Using laughter through tears and tears through laughter, we sang our mother to sleep to end her battle with cancer. Hospice was a humane system of care for Momma and the rest of the family. I would choose volunteering in hospice care for my new hat.

The purpose of this book is twofold; I want to share my experience volunteering with those who have limited life expectancy. These people accepted their fate, no longer looking for a cure, but still had a message they wanted to share.

Dying is a personal experience, never the same for any two people, and it is much more than just a medical experience. I hope there is something that I can communicate to the reader through this book, which can enhance the experience for families and friends of the dying. Don't miss the experience because of fear or anxiety. You don't want to miss the message they are communicating in their last hours.

There's a great connection, which comes from just holding someone's hand and walking through it with him or her. In addition, I hope that perhaps, others will volunteer to work with the terminally ill and elderly because of something I communicated to them. Offer to give a primary caregiver a day off every once in awhile. Families need our help, and the medical community needs our assistance as well. They have more work than they can effectively handle. If you can lend a hand, you will be rewarded for your efforts in more ways than you can imagine.

For my family, this is our history through my eyes. It's not to be relived through you, but the strengths can be taken forward. You will persevere and I hope you will never feel like you are alone in your endeavors.

Introduction

Do you have a unique culture in your family? Do the children revert to their childhood characters when they gather for the holidays? Do your siblings constantly look at you as the person that you were when you were hormonal and going through the tumultuous teens? Do you see yourself as an eighteen-year-old, always?

When you visit your parents or grandparents are you relating to the one that was, or the one that is? Are you constantly trying to read into what people are saying, instead of just listening to what they say? Do you listen to how they feel?

Seldom should people listen to anything I say. They should be listening to how I feel, keep that in mind as you read the book. The words are not as important as the emotion. Don't get stuck on the details. Follow the message carried through the feeling.

Prepare yourself for a huge cast of characters. Feel free to stop and look to the back of the book to see who belongs to which family, acknowledging that, some of the names will repeat from generation to generation. I try to keep the story moving forward, but I jump back to an earlier time often. Look over your cast of characters before you start the next chapter, if you have to take a pause.

Though this book carries some valuable lessons, not all of them will you agree with. They may just give you food for thought. It's important that you enjoy the book and allow yourself to laugh and cry at the stupidest things. Sometimes in my honesty, I may offend someone, but that is not my intent. You may find yourself saying; "Did she just say what I thought she said?"

There is a family tree for the first generation, my parents and their siblings, which follows this introduction. My family tree follows them.

In the back of the book is my husband Paul's family tree, followed by my siblings and their children and children's children.

THE FAMILY TREE – DADDY'S FAMILY
TJ- Grandpa/ Mabel -Granny
1. Uncle Dick/ Aunt Dorothy
2. Aunt Norma/ Uncle Ray
3. Uncle Bill/ Aunt Mary
4. Daddy(Ed)/ Momma(Alva)
5. Uncle Les/ Aunt Donna
6. Uncle Pete/ Aunt Kathy
7. Aunt Lettie/ Uncle Johnny
8. Aunt Bea/ Uncle Bob
9. Aunt Rosie/ Uncle Jerry
10. Aunt Dodie/ Uncle Larry

THE FAMILY TREE-MOMMA'S FAMILY
(If you're from *Louisiana*, you're an Aint)
(If you're from anywhere else, you're an Aunt)
Sam- Grandpa/Katie -Grandma
1. Aint Jo/Uncle George
2. Uncle Gus/Aunt Vi
3. Uncle Bo/Aint Jenny Sue
4. Uncle Jack/Aint Evelyn
5. Uncle SJ/~~Aint Pauline~~/Janelle
6. Uncle Possum
7. Aint Leona/Uncle Steve
8. Uncle Jody/ Aint Jackie
9. (Momma) Alva / (Daddy) Ed
10. Aint Sue /~~Uncle Red~~/ Johnny

THE FAMILY TREE- MY FAMILY
Ed- Daddy/ Alva - Momma
Bryan
Danny
Christy (Dit)
Ray
Kitty
Billy
Cheryl (Me)
Bo
Sarah
Patsy
Punkin

MY BRANCH ON THE TREE
<u>Cheryl/Paul</u>
Kelly/Aaron
Mike
Dan

CHAPTER ONE

THE LONG GOODBYE

My big brother, Danny, looked healthy. He was six foot tall, proud and he smiled all of the time. He was extremely popular and well liked. Danny played football and wrestled in high school. He was lean and strong, yet his smile showed the kindness in him. He got up early every morning and threw a paper route before school. After he graduated from high school, he spent time in the United States Marine Corps.

The year was 1969, and the country was in the midst of the *Vietnam War*. We were fortunate with the draft still in effect, that none of the boys in our family went to war. My cousin Stan spent time in *Korea*. It was very difficult for his family to cope with him being so far from home. I saw it from their perspective, but I can't possibly imagine what the experience was like for Stan.

Danny was on leave. He finally had some time off from the Marines. The entire family couldn't wait for him to come home. He was bringing with him a couple of his friends whom he couldn't wait to introduce to his family. They felt they already knew each of us because Danny would share his letters from home. They were driving in from *California*, all the way to our home in *Tulsa, Oklahoma*. The trip is about 1,500 miles. It would give the guys several days to bond even tighter to share stories of their childhood.

We were a proud family. We were especially proud of Danny, because he was in the Marines. Patriotism was big in the O'Brien family. I'm sure that we drove our friends crazy talking about family all of the time. There was always someone's accomplishment to focus on, so I'm sure that it sounded like we were braggers. Our letters would fill him in on who won what wrestling match or spelling bee. He was anxious for his friends to meet all of us! There were eleven of us!

Everyone pitched in, cleaned the house, and we even made the beds. That didn't happen upstairs very often. We wanted to make our company feel at home. The children marched like soldiers when we knew that visitors were coming.

Daddy would bark out the orders in his deepest, loudest voice, "Momma wants the house to be company clean!" *(As opposed to looking lived in.)*

"No blankets on the floor! Somebody pick up those orange peels! This upstairs looks like a pig pen!"

We stepped in line and got it done. The oldest sister, Christy, made the work fun for us. We would pretend to be robots and she would give us jobs to do. When we completed the work, we would report for another assignment.

The master bedroom was downstairs, and it had a bathroom with a shower. It was the only bathroom downstairs. There was a set of French doors between the dining room and the master bedroom, toward the rear of the house. It then, had an exit to the backyard, a patio converted to a half size basketball court and a back apartment. There was a lot of traffic going in and out of the master bedroom. Momma always had her bed made and she worked hard every day, trying to keep the downstairs clean. It seemed as though she was always running the dust mop on the wooden floors, with a cigarette in one hand and the elongated dust mop in the other.

Our house on Newport was a two-story house, within walking distance of downtown *Tulsa*. From the street, looking up at the house, it looked big. There were two trees in the front yard and little grass growing beneath them. They were gigantic elm trees, one tree on each side of the walkway. Our house was raised somewhat.

From the street there was easement, then, a four-foot cinder ledge embankment that held the soil back from the sidewalk that paralleled the street. Our front yard was at the top of four stairs that you climbed, leading from the sidewalk. Then, there was a second set of stairs, which took you to our front porch from the yard. The porch was often a gathering place for our family and friends.

Our house had a large porch with stairs on the front and stairs on the right side, near the driveway. Tall brick columns held the roof up, and between the columns was the railing. On the same side, near the driveway, was a huge picture window. It was a perfect place to put the Christmas tree during the proper season. The house had a brick exterior painted light green, a pukie color, like smashed peas, in the front. There was green siding, on the sides and back of the house.

There was an apartment in the back, behind the house, and attached to it, was a workshop that they originally built to be a garage. We had it enclosed so we could use it for storage.

Momma and Daddy rented the apartment out, back in 1960, when we first moved in. The Penix's moved in as our tenants. Edith and Jimmy needed the place to be wheelchair accessible. My daddy and brothers built a ramp to the porch and a ramp through the door of the apartment.

Some may have considered Mr. Penix to be disabled, but his inability to walk did not keep him from getting around. He was a strong man and could lift himself from the car. He had his car modified, so he could drive with his hands and without the use of his feet. Then, he could lift himself from the car to the wheelchair and from the wheelchair to the couch relatively easy. He never complained or acted as if he had a disability.

Edith and Jimmy had no children, but Edith had a cat, named Sammy. She talked to it in baby talk and looked after it like a child. Sometimes Edith would pay my brother, Billy, to crawl into the sewer to get the cat if she couldn't find it. If a storm was coming in you could hear her yelling for Sammy in the night, and we would join her in the search.

In the late Sixties, our family needed more space as the big kids began to require more room and more privacy. Edith and Jimmy moved across town and we cleaned up the apartment to prepare it for the new tenants. Momma and Daddy moved the four older brothers, Bryan, Danny, Ray and Billy to the back apartment and left the five girls and youngest boy, Bo, in the house.

Danny and his friends arrived at our home at 3:00 a.m. Momma always left the porch light on and we never locked the door. The guys could have easily sneaked in, but that wasn't the O'Brien way. The call went out as soon as they pulled up to the curb. "They're here!" We all got up to greet them when they arrived. "Danny's home"! It sounded like thunder rumbling as all of the little kids came running down the two flights of stairs in their little footie pajamas. Then, they waited in line to get their hug.

The entire family stayed up the rest of the night listening to stories about the military and tales of their friends on the base. Everyone was so excited that we didn't think about the time. We chatted until the sun came up. Billy and Ray would have to go throw the paper route and the rest of us needed sleep.

Daddy declared, "Today is an O'Brien Holiday! No school!" I'm certain that the school would have disapproved. O'Brien Holidays didn't happen often, but it put emphasis on the fact that this was a special occasion.

While Danny was home on leave, he caught a strep throat. He got a shot of antibiotic before he went back to the service. Then, flu followed the strep throat; he never seemed to get any better! The faces of my parents told a true story. It was a story that we didn't want to hear, something we were not supposed to talk about, an unspoken truth. Danny, my big brother, was not going to get better.

I learned to recognize the face of despair in the early years of my developmental growth. I was thirteen-years-old. Momma's eyes looked tired. They were puffy, as if she spent a lot of time crying, but I never saw her cry. Sometimes I would see her lying face down on her bed. She would say that she was napping, or that she had a headache and needed a rest. She was a very strong woman.

My daddy, I did not see him cry, yet I heard him wailing in the night, and it broke my heart. The doctors diagnosed my big brother, Danny, with idiopathic dilated cardiomyopathy. (In simple terms, this meant that he had an enlarged sick heart for no known reason.) At the young age of twenty-two, this was not a common affliction. We were going to need a lot of strength to get through this dance with reality, for there was no known cure.

They performed the first heart transplant in 1967. The man lived 18 days, caught pneumonia and died, that was in *South Africa*. By 1968, there had been ten heart transplants worldwide. The first one in the *United Kingdom* was in 1968. That man lived 46 days. There would be many attempts in the early Seventies, but none of them lived beyond a year. When the doctors offered to put Danny on the transplant list, he declined. He said he didn't want to put the family through the surgery and all of the worry that would follow.

Many family members begged him to have the surgery. Perhaps it would prolong his life long enough to give science a chance to develop something which would work. In hindsight, I believe that Danny was correct in the decision he made. It wasn't until the 1980's and cyclosporine came into play that heart transplant recipients began to achieve a longer life span.

"Your heart is enlarged to the size of a football", the doctors told him. "The sack around your heart is leaking fluid. Death is inevitable. It's just a matter of time before your lungs will fill with fluid."

Heart transplants would provide hope for another day and another time, but there would be no hope for Danny.

I realized that regardless of how complicated life becomes for someone you care for, the race is still on for you. You have to keep up with your daily chores, because time does not hold still to give one time to grieve.

My parents sacrificed a great deal of their resources monetarily, to send all eleven of us to Catholic schools. They felt the guidance given by the sisters and the Lasallian Christian Brothers, would help to mold us morally. I'm certain through example, that they did just that.

From the time, that they reached their twelfth birthdays Bryan, Danny, Ray and Billy, the older brothers, would throw paper routes in the morning before school to help supplement our education and give them a little spending money. In all reality, it added to the family income, thus allowing for a little spending money. We were not wealthy, but children didn't know who had money and who didn't. We all wore the same checkered uniform every day and ate in the same cafeteria. We played the same sports and shared the same car pool. There were no designer tennis shoes or designer purses at that time.

Father Mayfield would drop in on the family from time to time and check on things. The sisters at *Marquette School* were supportive and were well aware of the situation at home. They also looked after us in a special way, which I have not forgotten. They were kind and generous with their time. I appreciated their prayers and concern then, as I do now. We would pray before class for Danny. Not necessarily for healing but for the family, that we would be at peace with whatever God had laid before us and we would be free from anxiety.

One of my daddy's brothers, my uncle Bill, needed heart surgery. The last words he said to his children before he went in to surgery were "Keep the faith!" Then he shot them the finger. O'Brien's are always trying to lighten up the more serious moments. Uncle Bill had not even reached his 50th birthday. He suffered a massive heart attack while on the operating table. His death was a shock for the whole O'Brien family. Aunt Mary would have to continue to raise their five children on her own.

That very summer, Uncle Bill's family would suffer another loss. Mary and Bill's son, Tommy, died in a motorcycle accident. Tommy's friend ran a stop sign at 31st and Mingo, and my cousin was riding on the back. He was only fifteen-years-old.

This only compounded the sorrow that the family was already going through with Uncle Bill's death and Danny's illness.

My school, *Marquette*, had a Christian service program. This was a program designed to encourage us at a young age to be socially involved and aware of social injustice. We would help people without consideration of race, religion or country affiliation. We could volunteer at various places.

On the very first Earth Day ever, we walked down 15th, Street, picking up trash along the sidewalk. Service to your fellow man was highly encouraged in the Catholic Church. It still is.

As a Christian service project, our eighth grade class chose to go to the nursing home every Friday. Hospitals were not foreign to me, and I love old people!

We would visit the elderly. Sometimes we would sing songs or do arts and crafts. This seemed perfectly natural to me. I always looked forward to Friday.

After school, when Danny had a bad spell, my younger brother, Bo, and I would walk to the hospital. St. John's was a Catholic, non-profit hospital, founded in 1926, and the hospital was run by Benedictine Sisters. It was only about a mile walk from Marquette School to the hospital for us. This was the first year that my brother, Danny, was ill.

The intensive care waiting room was like a second home for us that year. The waiting room was not very big. It had a table and chairs on one end and a desk with a phone on the other, with a couple of couches in the middle. I would bring my books and do my homework at the hospital.

It was very quiet, but you could here the machines beeping from the small rooms outside our door. Too much activity outside the door, sometimes made me feel a little uncomfortable. The family wanted someone to be there, in case of an emergency, but also once every three hours Danny could have two visitors for 15 minutes. Bo and I wanted to get our 15 minutes before our siblings got out of school, or my parents came up to the hospital after Daddy got off work.

Danny was in and out of the hospital a lot that year. He had a reputation of being a bit of a playboy. Danny was very popular with the nurses. When he would leave the hospital, he always sent candy to the nurse's station, and he often dated the nurses he met when he was in the hospital. He was a nice looking young man, with sandy brown hair. He was clean cut and quite masculine in his build. Danny had a great personality. He was also a big flirt. We used to tease him because he was constantly fixing his hair in the mirror. He also had that **Clark Gable** smile.

Danny was a volunteer for the Big Brothers Organization. They helped kids from divorced homes by giving them a male roll model. Danny had two young boys he was responsible for visiting and being their mentor. They were cousins from two separate homes.

Danny took one of the kids, Eddie, to get his eyes tested and bought him some glasses. I remember him taking both of the boys shopping for new tennis shoes. Danny helped Eddie's family move into a two-story apartment and brought them a Thanksgiving turkey with all of the fixings. Both families got a turkey, and he delivered a big basket of fruit. I thought; this is cool, Danny takes the time to do for others even though he knows he has little time left.

We received a call from Momma's family in *Louisiana*. Momma's mother had a series of strokes and she was dying. Momma and Daddy went to say goodbye. Momma flew in from *Tulsa*, and Daddy flew in from *Chicago*, where he had been out of town on business. My sister, Kitty, was the eldest of the siblings still living at home. Momma and

11

Daddy left Kitty in charge. She was very trust worthy and responsible, but she could be a little bossy when she was in charge.

In later years, we would have fights over who was the "*Sheriff of the House*", an old **Bill Cosby** line. "Let it be understood, before Momma died, she made me the Sheriff!" I'm sure Kitty will still make me leg wrestle her for the position. That's often how we had to settle our disputes.

Kitty was as beautiful on the outside as she was on the inside. She had long blonde hair and Daddy's blue eyes. She spent as much time fixing her hair in the mirror as Danny did, and she primped twice as long on her makeup, but you never saw anything that was out of place. She easily could have been a model, but she was shy in front of a crowd.

Danny had something they called a "code blue", his heart stopped and he nearly died during that time. Kitty gathered the kids together she headed us to the church, where we prayed. There was little else, which we could do at the time.

Kitty and Christy headed up to the hospital, where one of my daddy's brothers, Uncle Les and his wife, my aunt Donna, greeted them. They were always there for added support when we needed it the most.

The hospital rules would not allow visitors in the Intensive Cardiac Care Unit until they stabilized Danny. We had to call Momma and Daddy home with the emergency. It must have been a long flight home.

Kitty and Christy had the opportunity to go in and see him in ICU, once the doctors had him stabilized. The first thing that came out of his mouth was, "Where's my fudge?" It seems that Danny had made a request of Kitty the last time he had seen her and he wasn't going to let her forget. It was his way of keeping the moment light.

Danny pulled through, but asked Momma and Daddy to make a promise, "Please, understand I don't want to live on a respirator. It was unnatural to have the machine breathing for me. You're just prolonging the inevitable. Next time don't let them bring me back. Let me go!"

In those days, things were different around the house, but we kids were still happy most of the time. There was no dark cloud hanging over us as one might think. With Danny's illness, the family stayed closer to home. On the weekends, every Friday and Saturday night the folks would have card parties. They played Spades or Pitch most of the time, sometimes until 1:00 or 2:00 in the morning. We could hear them laughing and hollering from the tables downstairs, from our rooms upstairs.

Aunt Dodie and Uncle Larry would come for most of the card parties. Dodie was my daddy's youngest sister. She was close to the same age as my older siblings. Uncle Larry was so much fun to be around because he was funny but not in a sophomoric way. He had a quick wit and silly antics, which would get us tickled. Aunt Dodie was jolly and had a lot of personality. She was great at leading Uncle Larry into his jokes. The laughter could rock the house.

Our eldest sister, Christy and Dink, her husband, Kathie Sullivan, and Tom Burton, Christy's best friends, Bryan the oldest and his wife, Debbie, Momma and, and the Gilpin's, Momma and Daddy's friends would all gather. Then, Danny and his girlfriend Judy, his best friend Russell Otterstrom and other fillers would challenge the winner or start another table. There were so many of the adults and big kids playing cards, sometimes they would get as many as four tables going at a time.

The cigarette smoke was thick on most nights. We didn't know about the dangers of second hand smoke back then. Most of the adult family members were smokers. Daddy smoked cigars, so his smoke had a different scent, one I would miss in later years.

While the adults were playing cards, we kids were playing games of our own, with our cousins and friends. We played a game called Kick the Can, or we played Hide and Seek. We would play upstairs when it was cold outside. Sometimes we could be quite destructive; we certainly did have fun.

One game we played, we called Quick sand! The idea of this creative little game "never touch the floor", or you would drown in the quick sand. We would actually jump from the dresser to the bed. From the end of the bed, we would stand on the doorknob. We would kick the wall and swing the door so that you could go from room to room by hanging on the doors and trim. Super Mario, before video games were even invented! We were clever little monkeys! I wonder if Momma and Daddy ever knew why the doorknobs were falling off the doors, or why there were footprints on the walls and trim between the doors.

Momma and Daddy played cards for years prior to Danny being ill. It was cheap entertainment for a family with so many children. The Gilpin's had eight children. The last one, they named Ed, after my daddy.

One summer, back in the 1960's, we children had a secret project going in one of the bedrooms upstairs which had been going on for months. It started with a small stenciling at the top of the wall. My brother, Billy, began it one day in his boredom. Then, the magic markers and colored sidewalk chalk began to come out. It became an entire room of art projects for all ages. I think Momma suspected something for a long while.

Our graffiti project kept us especially quiet and busy. We kept the door shut and it encouraged us to have our dirty laundry out in the center hallway at the top of the stairs, where it was supposed to be, as opposed to Momma having to climb under the beds looking for under ware and socks on laundry days.

Ray and his friend Ronnie from across the street would use a ladder for the ceiling. Near the light switch, it said, "Shed a little light on the subject." On the ceiling it said, "Good morning son."They spelled it "son", not "sun" and had a large picture of the sun. Then, in a big dialogue balloon, it said, "That's so punny." There were many puns. It was very colorful, witty and amusing.

Then, one day, it was a little too quiet. Daddy went upstairs and opened the door. He never just opened the door. He would turn the doorknob and then kick the door open, so it would make a big sound and scare the heck out of us. "What are you doing?" He yelled!

He pretended to be mad, but I think he really thought it was funny. I suspect he and Momma knew what was going on up there. It was just time to get it under control.

Momma and Daddy allowed us to leave our project on the wall for several months. They had the boys paint over anything they felt was a little inappropriate. They told us not to deface any other rooms!

Then, they explained in no uncertain terms, "Eventually this room will have to be repainted. We'll buy the supplies, but you kids are the labor. We won't stop with just that room either. You will be repainting the entire house, from the top to the bottom!"

Daddy would barbeque on the weekend and Sunday afternoon, we usually had a basketball game on the back patio. Danny was not supposed to exert himself, so we played a lot of Around the World and Horse. These are games of shooting skill with no real running or exertion. When Danny got tired, the rest of us would kick up a real basketball game. Then, the rules were no blood no foul! Danny would watch, and he could make the call if we needed someone to referee.

The following year, I started at *Bishop Kelley High School*. The Christian brothers ran *Bishop Kelley*. It had recently become co-ed. When Bryan and Danny went there, the Christian brothers ran the boys' school, and the sisters ran the girls' school, where Christy went.

I was a freshman, and I was not old enough to drive. After school, I would get a ride with a family friend, Mrs. McCarthy, to *Marquette* and walk with my youngest brother, Bo, to *St. Johns Hospital*. If the weather were bad, Mrs. McCarthy would give us a ride to the hospital. Bo and I would spend a great deal of time together that year.

Bo was smart, and he was so cute. He was a little big for his age so our cousin Carlton, who was much smaller than Bo, would annoy people on purpose and try to get Bo into fights. Bo made good grades and his teachers loved him. He would read encyclopedias at night to help him fall asleep.

Bo and I were forever competing in some way or another. Who could do the most pushups, which could do the most sit-ups or pull-ups? We loved exploring the neighborhood together when we were younger. I hated when I had to start school in the first grade. My first day of school, I cried because I didn't want to leave Bo alone. He wasn't alone. There were three younger sisters at who followed him.

There was nothing demanding about Bo. We loved spoiling him because he was the baby boy. There was nothing pretentious about Bo. He was a good soul. I once compared him to *Rocky Balboa*, from the movie, *Rocky* (1976). Daddy got mad at me because he thought I was calling Bo stupid. Bo definitely wasn't stupid. It was the gentle heart that Bo had which drew me to make the comparison.

When Bo got older, we girls would fight over who was going to make him a sandwich or who was going to fix his breakfast in the morning. We were all clamoring for his attention. He was a sweet kid and always appreciative.

Bo was the only boy who slept upstairs, where the girls were, since the other brothers moved to the back apartment in 1969. This really opened up the house for the rest of us. We girls had three of the rooms and Bo had room number four, upstairs. In the morning, we girls would commandeer the bathroom. There were six girls. One of us would go in, another would go out, and there was never a break. Momma said we had to invent a new house rule; "When Bo has to go to the bathroom in the morning, everybody out!"

Sometimes, at the hospital, Bo and I would play cards. We brought Danny a Jigsaw Puzzle with 1,000 pieces on a large board. He would work on it when he was feeling up to it. We would work on his puzzle in the waiting room when he was not feeling well. Once he would get out of ICCU (Intensive Cardiac Care Unit) and into a room, the puzzle would go to him. We kept it under the bed until he was ready to work on it, or we could work on the puzzle together.

You should understand with a family our size it was like having a party in the Intensive Cardiac Care Unit waiting room, with laughing and carrying on. I'm sure other folks thought we were crazy or disrespectful for being so noisy. This was our way of life for a long while.

We knew where to find the coffee and how to fill the pot. We all knew how to find the cafeteria and the vending machines, what time the cafeteria and chapel opened and closed.

Once they stabilized Danny and they would get his medication the way they wanted it, the doctors would send him to a regular room. There, he would have to be on a special diet, but he could watch TV and work on puzzles. In this room, he could have more visitors and the visiting hours were longer. He usually had a roommate. Not even one of the roommates was young like Danny. They were usually old men in the unit with the heart patients.

Danny would call the house and ask for Kitty. She was the second to the oldest girl, or child number five. He would try to talk her into sneaking up something that wasn't on his diet. I suspect it worked a time or two, but Kitty was someone who could say no if she thought he was being ridiculous in his request. She could hold her ground with anyone. I do know she brought up some fried chicken once.

Danny talked Christy, the oldest sister, into sneaking something up to his room once, as well. The hospital had rules. Children could not visit unless they were over the age of twelve. Danny was afraid he would never get to see the little girls, Sarah, Patsy and Punkin ever again before he died. Christy took the three little ones up the back staircase and the nurses turned their heads long enough to allow Christy to sneak them into Danny's room for a visit.

Then, one time when Danny came home from the hospital, he enrolled in *Tulsa Junior College*. It was a two-year college at the time. It later became a four-year college. Danny took a creative writing course. He had hopes of writing about what it was like to know you are dying. What he found was it was too difficult for him to think in detail about his own mortality. He changed his life direction.

Danny decided instead, to travel. He said, "I want to live until I die." He claimed this would be a good time to visit old girlfriends in *California*. He could visit his old Marine buddies at their homes, as they did with him the previous year.

Momma and Daddy were not excited about Danny traveling when he was so ill, but Danny had his mind made up. He bought a trust worthy vehicle, a yellow 1969 Pontiac Le Mans. Danny took my brother, Billy, with him on his vacation. Billy would be the second driver, and someone to look after Danny, if he began to decline in health while traveling. It was the only thing Momma and Daddy could do, they had no options. Danny was going to travel!

Billy was only sixteen-years-old at the time. I can tell you that Billy was conscientious and trustworthy for someone his age. He had his first job when he was ten-years-old, shining shoes at the barbershop for a dime. I think often that the patrons would forget a young man was there and they would tell some good jokes. Then, Billy, with his great memory, would come home and tell us the jokes he heard at the barbershop. Billy definitely knew how to deliver a joke. It's a gift, which he still has today.

Then Billy began working at a filling station pumping gas and washing windows. The *Bill Lepley's Gulf Station* he worked at had a small clock in the window and he had 15 seconds to greet the customers. It kept him jumping. He did all of this and threw the paper route in the morning before school as well.

Danny and Billy spent several weeks of the summer traveling across the *United States*, from *Oklahoma*, to *California*. I have never heard stories about the trip in any detail. Perhaps it's just too hard for Billy to talk about the trip.

Danny never told his friends from the past why he was visiting. He wanted to be around people who were not aware he was dying. He wanted to have fun and he did not want to have any reminders of the illness he was running from. Danny could no longer see the pain in his mothers face when she looked at her pale and failing son. He would look into the eyes of those friends who knew him only as Danny.

Danny tried to deny his illness. He ran from it for as long as his body would allow. Everyday he was growing weaker.

Reality does eventually have to present itself. No longer in denial, Danny decided it was time to return home. If he was depressed, he never showed it. If he was angry, he never showed it. All we saw was acceptance. (Alternatively, perhaps it was denial.)

When Danny and Billy returned, I could see Billy had changed a great deal. He was a tall lanky, awkward looking teenager when he left. He was at the age when a boy's body changed a lot in a short period. His face had filled in and he had put on some needed weight; he was good looking. He had also changed in other ways. Billy was carrying a large load on his shoulders that summer. Billy had bonded with Danny and was preparing himself emotionally for what was inevitably going to come.

Billy spent many days alone, writing. He was in my mind, a very good poet. His poems revealed the depths of his soul and his inner most personal thoughts. I think it's just too difficult for some men to put their feelings out for the world to see. He knows I wish that he would publish his poetry. He has shared a few poems with me for the purpose of this book.

Danny did not move back in to the house or the back apartment when he returned home. He didn't think it was healthy for Momma to have to worry about him all of the time. She and Daddy would jump every time he coughed, and he was coughing a lot at this point. He courageously wanted to lead a normal life, for as long as possible.

He found a roommate through the *Tulsa Junior College Newsletter*, a guy by the name of Kevin. Danny would move into the brand new

Barcelona Apartments, across the street from *LaFortune Park* and very close to the hospital. It was close enough to Momma and Daddy to visit, but he was not so close that they would see his constant decline. The apartment was a very nice two-bedroom place with plush, white, wall-to-wall carpeting, an open kitchen and white walls.

It was not long after Danny moved into his apartment that he purchased himself a brown leather recliner for the living room to watch TV. Then, he would sleep at night in the recliner because he could breathe better sitting up.

His heart was failing and his lungs were filling with fluid, as the doctors had predicted. He knew what was happening. It was just happening much faster than he had anticipated.

Danny became friends with a cardiologist, Dr. Mark, who lived in the same apartment complex. He would visit the doctor when he needed to talk about his illness. It was Dr. Marks recommendation that Danny enter the hospital, when he could no longer sleep well, even sitting up.

Bo and I happened to be the ones who were at the hospital when Danny had the code blue! This was one of many but, the one that finally took his life. "Code blue" was hospital jargon called out on the intercom when someone's heart stopped beating.

I heard them call out a code blue. Activity in the hallway drew my eye to Danny's room. I didn't need to wait for a doctor to tell me what was happening before making my phone calls. In my school notebook, I had written down all of the phone numbers I needed to call. Momma and Daddy, Granny and Grandpa, Danny's girlfriend Judy and various others were to receive a call if there was any change in Danny's condition.

I needed to call to let them know that Danny was in trouble! Most of the phone numbers I had memorized, but I knew under pressure I would need to look them up.

Momma and Daddy, my brothers and sisters, my aunts and uncles, we all filled the hospitals ICCU waiting room. The adults present, concluded it would be best if we would split into shifts. There were more of us there than the hospital waiting room could handle. I went home with Billy and Kitty and waited for a phone call, but there was never a second shift.

Momma and Daddy had to honor the promise, which they previously made to Danny. They gave the doctors permission to turn the machines off, and they let him go. There would be no more card parties in the waiting room.

CHAPTER TWO

JUST COPING

✝

Our aunts and uncles filled our house on Newport. They helped clean the house before guests began arriving. The housework had been somewhat neglected, with all of the coming and going to and from the hospital.

Momma was running the dust mop downstairs on the wooden floors and cleaning the mirrors in the living room and dining room. The aunts were cleaning the upstairs. That's not an easy job. Things could be messy up there because Momma and Daddy seldom climbed the stairs. If you closed your door and had your laundry in the center hallway Momma didn't see in when she collected the laundry.

"They threw away my collection of shaving cream cans!" I protested.

I had cans from my cousins weddings lined up on my dresser. We had decorated the cars at Pat and Rhonda's wedding and Ricky and Vicki's wedding the summer before. They were my Uncle Les's boys. I had the shaving cream cans from my older sister, Christy and Dinks wedding, when we decorated their car, and one of the nurses Danny dated, Barbara, had married one of the Peshka boys, from *Saints' Peter and Paul Parish* that same summer. I was at their wedding as well and collected a can from the car décor, to add to my fast growing collection.

"I guess it was difficult to tell that it was a collection of anything other than trash." I admitted. Still, I felt that my room had been violated.

I made the bed in my room. I purchased a pink Victorian floral bedspread at a garage sale. I also purchased my bedroom furniture from a garage sale. I stripped it and antiqued it myself. I tried very hard to make my room a special place. When my friends came over, it's where we hung out.

My room had a phone (that didn't work) and a record player in the walk in closet. The record player worked, but it was very old, and again, something that I purchased from a garage sale. I only owned three albums, **The Monkees** and **Bread** (a *Tulsa* band that had made it big). I also had a **Leon Russell** album that I won on the radio by answering a quiz question. He was another local who had made it to the big time.

I had a desk in the walk-in closet and a small lamp. I had a lock, hook and eye, on the inside of the closet, so that I could lock myself away from the rest of the world and write poetry. I would write in my journal and sometimes do homework. This was my private place.

There was constant traffic in and out of our house. Neighbors, friends and family made there way to and from the house dropping off meals and visiting at the dining room table. We were all grateful for the support. Sometimes, those people who were offering condolences to us, needed support from us in return.

The vans were pulling up delivering flowers about every 30-minutes or so. The little kids would run out of the door, onto the porch and jump four stairs. They would race down the walkway to a second set of stairs bound them and screech to a halt at the curb. There they would greet the driver and bring the flowers to the dining room table, placing them under the chandelier proudly.

I tend to divide the children into two groups. There are the big kids and there are the little kids. The big kids were those of my siblings who were older than me, Bryan, Danny, Christy, Ray, Kitty, Billy, in that order, with Bryan being the oldest. I was number seven. Then, there were the little kids, those younger than me, Bo, Sarah, Patsy and Punkin. There were not even twenty years between the eldest, Bryan, and the youngest we called Punkin.

This list of names, in this order is necessary for anyone who associates with the O'Brien family.

Bryan, 1947	(the Teacher)
Danny	(the Marine)
Christy	(the Nurse, later known as Dit)
Ray	(a clown, and later a Marine)
Kitty	(our conscience)
Billy	(our poet, replacement clown, and later a Marine)
Cheryl, 1957	(wearer of many hats)
Bo	(our baby boy, Engineer)
Sarah	(the domestic procreator)
Patsy	(a lion, later a cheerleader and anesthetist)
Punkin, 1964	(baby girl, entertainer, Teacher)

We used to quiz our friends to see if they had the order memorized and straight in their heads. "How else will you be able to understand and follow along with our stories? Believe me there are many factual and fictional stories which we share from day to day, year to year and decade to decade!" I will warn you though, the snow gets deeper, the miles get longer, and the fish get bigger over the years.

As I got older, I realized it sounded sometimes like I was trying to one up my friends. They would bring up a story about a friend or family member and I would always have one to come back with. Cute baby stories, funny baby stories, children's logic, or a troubled teen, you name it! You're never out of informative or funny events to talk about.

When Granny O'Brien, my daddy's Momma, turned 80, she had 101 offspring. We were the stereotypical Irish Catholic family. I contend that I have a list of stories about every one of these relatives. Some of those stories I suspect they would rather I didn't share.

One could not imagine the number of people who came to give condolences to our family. Momma saved all of the cards and letters in one of Daddy's old King Edward Cigar boxes. It's a funny thing though, even on this sad occasion, we still found things to laugh about.

We would sit around the dining room table and tell our stories. Over the years, the stories became even funnier, as they became exaggerated. As with any Irish wake, there was a scent of bourbon in the air. I'm sure this helped with the hilarity in our tales as well.

Christ the King was our parish. The church was beautiful. Its famous stained glass windows are some of the best representation of stained glass in the *United States*. One side of the church has stained glass windows of the kings of the Old Testament and the other side has kings of the New Testament. Behind the altar is a mosaic of Christ. There were statues of Mary and Joseph on each side of the altar, outside of the marble communion rail. They filled our church with flowers. Danny's casket was adorned with the American Flag, because of his service to our country.

People contributed to the *Bishop Kelley High School*, Adopt a Student Program, in Danny's name. This was a program, which made Catholic school education affordable for children from low-income families.

Some people contributed to the Big Brother Organization, the organization that Danny belonged to, which helped Eddie and his cousin. Eddie was at the funeral, and I saw him push his glasses up onto his nose, as he wiped away his tears.

There was standing room only in the church. I could not believe how one person could have touched so many lives. A choir of *Bishop Kelley* students sang at the funeral. I felt blessed because they were there. It meant a great deal to me then, and it still does.

They released as many as a hundred children from the schools for the funeral. *Marquette Grade School* had students there to represent the classes of each of the siblings who were going to *Marquette* at the time. The community came together to give support to my family in a way I had never seen before.

It was a beautiful service. Mamma was especially touched by the music. Music had a way of touching Momma's soul. Sometimes, music would bring a tear to her eye. Rarely did Momma's eyes water. She was a strong woman who showed very little emotion. Daddy was usually the softie in our family. He would cry during The Brady Bunch. I suspect the reason Momma held up so well, was to ensure she would not get Daddy to start crying.

Shortly after the funeral, we got a call from Danny's roommate Kevin. He was wondering where Danny was because he had not seen him for a while. When we told him what had happened, he was stunned. Danny had never told his roommate that he had a heart problem. When Kevin heard him coughing in the night, he thought Danny must have had a cold or flu.

We explained that Danny didn't want people to treat him as if he was different. He just wanted to be a normal 23-year-old. The folks paid Danny's share of the rent until his roommate could find someone else to share the bills.

I think we were all a little numb. It took a few weeks for reality to sink in. Every one of us had to deal with our sadness in our own unique way. There are steps each of us would go through in time to deal with our sorrow.

Bryan was the oldest child. He was nearly exactly ten-years-older than I was. Both of us were born in the month of April. I was born on the 12th. Bryan was born on the 21st.

Bryan felt as though he had lost his twin. There were actually 15 months between them. They didn't look alike, but he and Danny were close in age, and they had the same brown eyes. Bryan had dark hair and Danny's was more of a light ash brown. For years, the stories were Bryan and Danny this and Bryan and Danny that. Now, new stories beginning in the fall of October 1971 would no longer run the two names together in the same sentence.

There are many accounts of events pertaining to Bryan and Danny as babies. For instance, one where they're riding naked on their tricycles, while church was letting out and Momma was too embarrassed to go and get them. She sent Daddy!

When Danny started kindergarten, he told the teacher his name was Danny O'Danny. I guess if Bryan could be Bryan O'Brien, why couldn't he be Danny O'Danny?

Some stories date back to the 1950's and the big kids playing in the field which Daddy would mow near the old house on Vandalia. Daddy made a baseball diamond, just to give the kids a place to play. This was on the north side of town, before the move to our house on Newport.

Bryan lettered four years in football and wrestling at *Bishop Kelley* and was the most valuable player on his football team his junior year. He was built like a wrestler, with short legs and large chest and shoulders. He was also a very good student. Bryan started in the *Air Force Academy* straight out of high school. He got homesick and had a difficult time at the Academy. He transferred to *Southwest Missouri State College* on a wrestling scholarship, where he broke records for most wins and pins. Then, he graduated with a degree in science, and he was a member of the National Guard when he moved back to our home in *Tulsa, Oklahoma.*

Bryan taught science in *Tulsa,* at *Booker T. Washington High School* on the north side of town and he coached wrestling. The north side of *Tulsa* housed the poor and underprivileged. Bryan wanted to work there because he truly wanted "to make a difference in the world."

"Education is hope for the next generation of children being raised in poverty on the north side of *Tulsa.*" Bryan would say.

Booker T. Washington became a magnet school and brought in the best teachers from all over the city. Bryan was a new teacher, so he was transferred instead to a different school but still on the north side, *Cleveland Junior High.* He worked there until he retired after thirty years of teaching. My aunt Norma worked at the same school. She was a cook in the cafeteria. There are not many places in *Tulsa* where you could go or work that you didn't run into family or a close friend.

Bryan married a girl he met when he was in college in *Springfield, Missouri.* Her name was Debbie Grover. She was a nurse's aide. They were newlyweds and had no children at the time that Danny died. I'm certain they leaned hard on each other for comfort during those dark days.

Christy, she was the oldest girl. She was a good athlete and was very active in the few girl sports that were available when she was in school. She appeared to be confident and self-assured, but it was a mask. Down deep inside she was just as insecure as the rest of us. She just didn't want anyone to see weakness.

Her reaction to Danny's death resulted in anger. She could not stand to see anything that even reminded her of Danny, yet she was married to Danny's best friend in grade school, Dink. Dink is a strange name, but his real name was Delbert! I guess that's why he kept his childhood nickname.

When Christy and Dink were newlyweds, they lived in an apartment close to our home. Then, they moved into a house that they were renting which was across the street from Granny and Grandpa at 1st and Lewis. It was the same old house our aunt Dodie and uncle Larry had rented for several years prior to Christy and Dink.

Christy came over to our house shortly after Danny's death. When she drove up and saw the 1969 La Mans, Danny's car, she had a fit. I didn't understand her anger. She wanted the car gone. I'm glad she didn't get her way, because that yellow La Mans with the black vinyl top and bucket seats was our ride to school for several years after that. I don't know what we would have done without it.

My sister, Kitty, and a couple of her friends were driving the other car, our blue Catalina and smoking cigarettes, trying to be cool. One of the girls threw their cigarette out the window, and it must have blown back into the car. I guess they didn't realize it.

In the middle of the night, someone off the street knocked on the door. Kitty was the one who answered the door. The stranger told Kitty the car had smoke pouring out of the windows.

The car was on fire! Kitty acted quickly...*I guess*... she ran to get Billy from the back apartment. He put the fire out using the water hose on the side of the house, near the driveway, while Kitty supervised.

They put the fire out completely, or so they thought! It's never that easy.

The next morning, when we got up for school, the seats had burned out of the car. This would be our ride!

I was so embarrassed. There was no possible way to wash the smell of the smoke off my clothing or out of my hair. The entire day I smelled as if I had been in a fire. If *Bishop Kelley* still had a "bomb of the month club", I'm sure that we would have won. I'm thankful the honorary society for the trashiest car was no longer a fad. They abolished the bomb of the month the year before. I would not have to endure the embarrassment of a picture of our fried car in the school paper.

Ray was in the Marine Corp. at the time Danny died. His plane ride to *Tulsa* was difficult enough. I'm certain he was expecting the same kind of homecoming we gave to Danny or Bryan when they came home, with hugs and tears.

When he stepped off the plane and entered off the ramp into the *Tulsa International Airport*, the only person there to receive him was my uncle Pete. We were all so tired and busy nursing our own wounds that we neglected to be there for him emotionally. Perhaps there was nothing left of us to give.

Still, that's no excuse. We should have been thinking of him as well. Ray only had time to stay for the funeral. There was no time for bereavement for him. Once again, "Time doesn't hold still to give one time to grieve."

Ray actually made a career of the Marines, and he retired at twenty years. It must have been very difficult for him to be so far from family during a time of crisis. He would have to fly home again for a funeral, some ten years later, but that's another chapter.

Ray was married to De. She was a beautiful girl, who looked like **Sally Fields**. She was like a celebrity to me. She had traveled with Up with People. Up with People was a group of students from 18 to 23-years-old. They traveled all over the world, sharing their music. When Up with People was in *Tulsa*, they put on a concert at *Marquette*, my grade school, when I was in the eighth grade. They were an educational, non-profit, organization, without religious political affiliation that performed for communities globally. My new sister-in-law, De wore a high school ring that had a globe on it.

De had done a great deal of traveling. She moved a lot in her lifetime and military life was not going to be a shock for her. She was a great blessing for our family and for Ray. I know she made a huge impact on my life. De understood how important education was, and she was constantly learning something new, eagerly sharing it with us.

We could have used a bit more of Ray and De around in those tough days. Ray's sense of humor could keep heavy moments light. He was the family prankster. Punkin's first words were "Raaaaay don't!" He was an equal opportunity prankster. He picked on all of us and it was not always funny, but he was always laughing! De's pragmatic outlook on life and her ability to look forward and not back, would have been a blessing as well.

One story from years past, which we tell frequently at our family gatherings, is when Ray was chasing Christy with a snake. Christy made him eat it. That's how the story is told! She really just shoved it in his mouth. She was a tough cookie and with two older brothers, you can bet she knew how to defend herself. Daddy raised us all to be tough and she was the toughest. Another time, Ray chased her with dog fesses on a stick. Well, she sat on him, and he ate that too.

Kitty, she took the rest of us under her wing, like a mother bird protecting her young. She helped us to deal with Danny's death through our faith. She saw to it that we went to Mass on Sunday and prayed. She inherited Mommas strength and helped keep things running smoothly until the rest of the household got back into our routines.

Kitty was aspiring always to be a saint, but every once in awhile she slipped and a wild side came out. She introduced me to my first cigarette in the eighth grade. This was after a weekend at the lake with our cousins. It was always dangerous to get us together in a large group once we hit those teenage years. Uncle Les's daughter, Joanne, was the same age as Kitty. They sneaked cigarettes together at the lake and Kitty brought them home and shared one with me. We were bonding, in the TV room downstairs, after Momma and Daddy had gone to bed. Daddy must have heard us because he came in and you never saw two girls move so fast in your life.

Suddenly, we were practicing our cheerleading and Kitty was flapping her arms around and swinging that long blonde mane, trying to get rid of the smoke...Stupid girls!

Kitty also introduced me to my first double date at fourteen. Kitty and Denny Peska had tried to set me up. We went to a drive in movie together. This is my first date mind you. Kitty and her date were in the front seat, and I was with my date in the back. The guy was my age, but we were from totally different worlds. The guy tried to French kiss me and that was way ahead of this fourteen-year-old Catholic girl.

I told Kitty to meet me in the bathroom and I told her what had happened. She said to fake sick and we would ask to go home. Then, she kept trying to teach me how to gag myself to make myself sick.

She said; "It would be more convincing if you smell like vomit."

I did not learn how to make myself sick. I tried! She's the one that got sick and threw up in Denny's car on the way home. I think she had tried too hard to teach me how to gag myself.

My brother, Billy, spent a lot of time alone in those days. I'm sure he was remembering the time he and Danny spent together over the summer. He was processing in his brain, every word, every day every moment. His was a long healing process.

I believe Billy was going through depression that could be helped with medication by today's standards, but we didn't know enough back then to identify the symptoms. Billy was not motivated to play football anymore. He wanted to quit wrestling, but Daddy would not let him.

It caused a great deal of strain in their relationship as a result. I doubt if his grades slipped because Billy was really smart and loved math. He was in Brother Bernadine's class, and everyone knows, "you had to be really smart to be in Brother "B's" class."

Daddy was trying hard to be Billy's friend. It wasn't a position a father could fill. Still, I think Daddy understood what Billy was going through and tried his best to help.

Billy was dating my good friend Dina. She and I spent a lot of time together in the pep club, at the football games. Then she would go out with us for pizza after the game.

We hung out with Billy and his friends all of the time my freshman year. They named their group the KBI, "Kid Brotherhood International." Billy, we called "Kid". Their signature logo was a puppy dog, drawn like a cartoon character, by one of the gang. "Bobus", Jim Bowman. One guy, Billy Taylor, we called "Ace". Ace was a small quiet guy compared to the rest of the gang. Billy's best friend was "Willie", Mike Smith. Mike and Billy went all the way back to grade school together. Billy and Willie both loved to dance. Dina and I always had a dance partner at the school dances. Left standing at the start of a song, anyone of the KBI would fill a slot.

Dina was strikingly beautiful. She was thin, had naturally curly hair, and she had really big green eyes. Dina's father didn't like her dating Billy, because he was a couple of years older than she was. I didn't understand because Billy treated her really well. It was all about the age difference. How could two years make such a big difference? … I have a better understanding now.

Daddy leaned a little too hard on the bottle when Danny was sick and in the years, which followed. He tried to hide it from us, but we knew. His siblings intervened at one point. Daddy did stop drinking, for a while.

My daddy wasn't mean when he drank; he was just mellow. I suspect he was looking for something that would help him cope. Daddy was always up in the night with insomnia.

One evening, when we were living in the house on Newport, Daddy heard a noise in the night.

"It's after 2 a.m.! What the hell!" He had already made sure that all of the kids were in.

Daddy got out of bed to see what the noise may have been. No one was in the kitchen or utility room. The lights were all out. He didn't see anyone in the dining room, so he entered the living room. It sounded like someone came through the front door, but all the children are in. He peered outside through the picture window… "There are no lights on in the cars"…

Suddenly, he heard movement and caught something out of the corner of his eye. Sitting on our couch in his birthday suit, little Jamie, from across the street. He was four-years-old and cute as could be. Jamie was wearing nothing but his cowboy boots. Jamie had taken a seat in the living room and was waiting for action.

"Hey, I'm waiting for some pancakes." Jamie said.

Daddy took Jamie back to his home. His mother was mortified. She had put him down for bed in his room, with the house locked up tight.

His bedroom window was open. Jamie found his way over, all by himself.

I have no recollection of how the younger siblings dealt with Danny's death. I'm sure their lives have been impacted as much as the rest of us. No one in the family was the same after Danny died. I remember thinking; "How many people would come to my funeral, if I died tomorrow?"

It is impossible to explain to anyone what it feels like to loose someone you love. Ask any parent who has lost a child. Ask any child who has lost a parent. Ask any man who has lost his wife or any wife who has lost her husband. There are no words! Yet, death is something we all must learn to cope with, in time.

Danny's funeral was going to be Monday. I remember going to see Mrs. McCarthy. Her daughter, Jill, was a friend of mine and in my class at *Bishop Kelley*. They were my ride to and from school. I walked up the street to their house, which was just a couple of blocks from us, across 15th Street. I wanted to let them know what had happened, and I would not need a ride to school on Monday.

I could not telephone from the house because there were too many phone calls coming in. There was no call waiting in those days. The calls were continuous. When phone calls were not coming in, there were calls going out to family and Danny's friends from out of town, giving details of the funeral arrangements and sleeping arrangements for incoming guests.

Many people needed to make special arrangements in order to come to the funeral. They would be coming from *Louisiana* and *Great Bend, Kansas.* Momma had nine siblings and Daddy had nine siblings. When I said that I come from a big family, I wasn't kidding. I had a whole slew of cousins.

Word got around fast in our community. Mrs. McCarthy already knew about Danny. She was very kind. We talked for a while about how things were going at the house. I kept my chin up, but I could feel my eyes welling up a couple of times.

When I left to go back home, I ran into a friend of mine from school. He was an afternoon paperboy. James McCullough was sitting at the northeast corner of Fifteenth and Newport, folding newspapers, left side over, right side over and then putting a rubber band around them. Then he would stack them in his cotton bag. I had helped my brothers on the route enough to know the routine.

James gave me several of his leftover copies of the newspaper with the obituary about Danny in them. I opened one and began to read the article on the way home. It was time for me to let go of the tears I had been holding back. I began to cry uncontrollably.

A stranger on the street, I think maybe God sent her, because this heavyset woman allowed me to collapse in her arms and I sobbed like a baby. I will never forget the relief I felt when I finally had a good cry.

Punkin wishes she had memories of Danny. She was only five-years-old when Danny died. She can't remember him and feels as though she missed out.

She did miss out. We carry him with us through our memories, which we need to share with her. We also need to share our pain with her. When Punkin told me this, I wondered, what does this tell us about our lives? Sharing pain is as important as sharing happiness. Punkin, she wants to share our love, our memories, hope and, she wants to share our pain.

That's it! It's this sharing, which helps us cope! I think it's the idea that as long as someone remembers those who have gone before us they are never totally gone. Christ is with us and it's been 2,000 years since he died. We share his story, but we also share the sorrow of the crucifixion. We Christians also believe that Christ shares our sorrow and pain.

I love getting together with family and friends and talking about the old days. It's important also, that we are still sharing good times together, creating new memories. Our shared memories of the good and the bad times bring us closer together as a family and as a community.

Pen without Ink By: Wm H. O'Brien

I wish that I could find the words
To describe his funny face
I wish that I could share the warmth
I felt in his embrace.
Whenever I guide my thoughts to him
I feel a strong sensation:
But when I try to put it into words
It suffers in translation.
If only I could word my thoughts
In ways that are appealing;
Then maybe you would understand
The emptiness I'm feeling.

CHAPTER THREE

COMMUNITY SPIRIT

☺

My daddy was a works manager at *Oklahoma Steel Castings Company,* in *Tulsa, Oklahoma.* He began working there when he was sixteen-years-old. Daddy's family moved to *Tulsa,* from their farm in *Great Bend, Kansas,* after a long struggle during, what Granny called, "the *Kansas* version of the dust bowl." Everyone was looking for work.

They were losing their farm in *Kansas* after years of drought and two hail outs, so Grandpa found a job in *Oklahoma* working for an ice cream company. Later that year, Granny locked onto a job at *Hillcrest Hospital* and the rest of the family traveled to *Oklahoma* with her. They had to leave all of their furniture and traveled only with linens and the clothes on their back. They bought a broken down house and fixed it up.

My daddy lied about his age in order to get the job at *Oklahoma Steel* and helped to support the family. He left during WWII, and he joined the *United States Navy.* He would write home to his folks often. Each time he wrote to them, he talked about his best friend Al.

"Al and I played tennis together." "Al and I stopped by the bar after work." Then he wrote home, "Al and I are getting married!"

They roared with laughter, "Al's a girl!" The entire time my daddy was writing home to his family, they had assumed that Ed's friend Al was a guy.

My daddy returned to *Tulsa* when the war was over, bringing back with him, his new bride. He went back to work at *Oklahoma Steel* and worked his way up the ladder, along with my uncle Les and Uncle Jerry. We were never far from our family.

I visited *Oklahoma Steel* one day. Daddy showed me around the foundry first, then, he took me to his office. It was impressive. He had a large wooden desk that sat up high. He had his own secretary who sat in the office, just outside of his door.

I thought, someday I might like to be a secretary.

They called him "Big Ed" at work. He prided himself on always having an open door if the employees wanted to speak to him. He made good money, but as you can imagine, the money does not go very far when you have eleven mouths to feed.

Making money was never the driving force for Daddy. Family was the driving force in his life, always. Many times, Daddy had offers for jobs in other states. *Chicago* was where most of the steel industry was and he had very tempting job offers there over the years. If money had been important to him we would have moved, but our home was in *Tulsa*. That's where Daddy's family was. We were tight.

Historically, the steel industry was being hurt in the late Sixties and 1970's. I was not old enough to understand everything that was going on, but I know *Oklahoma Steel* didn't have a union. The union was trying to form and Daddy was not for it. The steel industry had many union strikes in the 1970's. I cannot imagine how the family would have survived if the union had existed and Daddy had to strike.

After work, in the fall, Daddy volunteered as football coach for *Marquette*, along with his friend, Pat Gilpin. They usually didn't get home until after 8:00 p.m. most nights of the week. Often they would stop at *Arnie's Bar* for a beer before coming home. They would sometimes stop to visit with my uncle Les and Uncle Jerry. My uncles coached one of the other football teams. Football was so popular at that time, every boy in my grade played football, with the exception of maybe one. Each school had a seventh grade team and an eighth grade team.

Some people would think a woman who had eleven children in the house would be angry if her husband didn't come home right after work, but not my momma. My parents believed that sports and community kept kids out of trouble. They wanted us involved and they stayed involved as well.

My uncle Les was once a running back for *Tulsa University.* He was a good athlete. Then, he volunteered to coach for fifteen years at *Sts.*

Peter and Paul, Holy Family and *Marquette*. In 1966, he coached *Holy Family* and led them to the Catholic State Championship. I would imagine this brought him a great deal of satisfaction and the rest of the family a great deal of pride.

My daddy and uncles were tough coaches and pushed the young men to be the best they could be. Their hard work and dedication paid big rewards when they saw the young men they coached become productive citizens. The boys were grateful for the attention they received from selfless volunteers, willing to give so much of their time.

There were several children in the neighborhood that lost a parent when they were young and still living at home. Daddy would always open our home to them. As far as Daddy and Momma were concerned, they were family.

Ronnie Hunt, across the street, was one of those who lost his father at a young age. Ronnie was like a brother to me. He was very much a part of my childhood.

Ronnie and Ray taught me how to ride a bicycle. They would get me balanced, and then they would get me going downhill from the top of Fourteenth, Street; then let go. I didn't know how to use the brakes, so I would jump the curb on the right and wreck in the grass at the bottom of the hill. Then, we would do it again, until I could do it myself.

Ronnie would play catch with me when no one else seemed interested. Once, I stepped on a honeybee in the clover while playing catch. Ronnie carried me into the house so Momma could pull out the stinger and put meat tenderizer on it.

I still have scars on my knees from a bicycle incident with Ronnie. We were playing chicken. He came at me full speed, we both jumped the same direction and he mowed me down. I had scabs on both knees for a while.

Ronnie's mom did a great job raising him. He spent a lot of time at our house from the time school let out, until his mom came home from work. Summers, he spent more time at our house than he did at his own home. We liked it that way.

My best friend, Jenny Hawkins, lost her father when she was in the third grade. Her mom busted her tail. She had six children, three still living at home. It's difficult to emphasize just how organized she was.

Mrs. Hawkins would call from her job at Flintco and remind the children to put something out to thaw for dinner every day. Then, she came home and you could set your clock by the time she would show up in the driveway.

At one time, I remember Mrs. Hawkins was working two jobs, because she sold Sara Coventry jewelry on the side. I wonder how she did it, because I don't ever remember her house being messy or anything out of place. There was laundry folded in stacks at the bottom of the stairs for the kids to carry up to their rooms.

Jenny's mom wore rhinestone eyeglasses. Mostly I remember them on her head. She had a chain that kept them from falling off. She had black hair, with a little silver mixed in. When she took us places in the car, she had elevator music playing softly in the background, on the radio. Jenny would complain and ask for KAKC or KELI. Those were the rock stations in *Tulsa*. I actually enjoyed listening to the elevator music.

One evening, I remember my daddy going over to have a talk with Jenny's mom. He offered to be there for the kids in any way he could. My daddy took it upon himself to be there for both Ronnie and Jenny. He did his best to make them feel like they had someone whom they could look to as a father. There is no substitute for the real thing, but I know they appreciated Daddy's efforts and loved him as a result.

Jenny and I enjoyed spending Saturday morning and afternoons at football games, played at *Cascia Hall Catholic School*. We had hot dogs and snow cones for lunch. If we picked up one hundred paper cups under the bleachers and turned them in, we could get a free Pepsi!

The little kids didn't see much of Daddy in the fall. They would be asleep before he returned home in the evenings. We saw him instead, pacing the sidelines of the football field, smoking his cigar and sometimes running the chains. Sometimes, we paced with him.

Daddy, Uncle Les, Uncle Bill and Uncle Jerry were all founding members of the Knights of Columbus, (whatever chapter they were in), near *Mohawk Park* and the *Tulsa Zoo*. Later, my Uncle Larry would join, as well. We would have huge barbeques at the *Knights of Columbus Hall*.

While the dads were having their meeting, the kids would be outside catching lightning bugs or chasing frogs. The mothers watched the kids and made all of the side dishes. The dads cooked the meat.

The Knights of Columbus is a fraternity of men in the Catholic Church, which formed to benefit the members and their families. There were many chapters of the knights throughout the city of *Tulsa*. They also would get involved in community affairs. They adopted a nursing home where members mowed the lawn and trimmed the hedges.

Marquette School went from kindergarten through eighth grade. We had two of each grade with class sizes near thirty students per class, with one teacher and no teacher's aids. Nearly half of the teachers were nuns and the principal was a nun.

I hear horror stories from people who grew up in the 1960's and went to Catholic school. I never experienced anything but love and respect from the Benedictine Sisters who looked after us at *Marquette*. There were a few times that I was disciplined with a paddle. Even though I'm sure I didn't deserve it, (tongue in cheek), I never felt like it was done in anger.

The sisters were very good to me. In first grade, Sister Antoinette would let me stay after school and help her erase the chalkboard. When I was in the second grade, she let me go with her and teach church songs to the first graders. I had two cousins in first grade, Kay and Owen. It made me feel special, like a big kid.

Sister Mary Williams was our basketball coach when I was in the fourth grade. She was very athletic, but you never forgot that she was a nun. She always wore the black robe, even when she was pivoting and making chest passes across the court. Some of the denominations of sisters quit wearing the black robes in the 1960's. I hated that. In their black robes, it gave me the same feeling I got when I would see a bride coming down the isle in her white dress. I viewed them in awe. It's hard to explain!

The pastor in the parish was the administrator of the school. There were other priests in the parish, but they had other duties. The other priests and the school council made suggestions, but the ultimate power was in the possession of the parish pastor, in our case, Monsignor Finn.

He was a gray haired priest, soft spoken and holy. He had some very good insight into the way we kids thought. I remember several of his sermons, even today. He would go to extra lengths to try to relate to us in terms we could understand, for example, using lyrics to **Beatles**, songs "*Mother McKinsey, leaving her face in a jar that she kept by the door*", when talking about hypocrisy. Once he used the words to a song from *Jesus Christ Superstar* (1973). I wonder how many other children might remember his sermons.

The cost of educating your children is and was expensive. There are no tax breaks for those who choose not to use the public school system. The result is teachers, underpaid and overworked textbooks that are falling apart and no funding for the arts.

Still, the nuns found a way to be sure we were ready for *Bishop Kelley High School*. *Bishop Kelley* was a college preparatory school. They had no problems with discipline they couldn't handle, even with the large class sizes. In those days, if you got in trouble at school, you were going to get it twice as bad when you got home. The parents would always back the teachers. I know my parents did!

We had several fundraisers every year to help with expenditures. They were always looking for ways to supplement the income, in order to keep the school tuition manageable for families. Brother Bernadine, in particular, made it his mission, to make Catholic school education available to anyone who truly wanted it.

The Knights of Columbus made it their mission to bring sports to the junior high children of the Catholic community where I lived. The schools could not afford coaches. To this day, the junior high coaches for Catholic schools in *Tulsa* are strictly volunteer positions. Knights chalked the field, ran the chains at the football games, mowed the grass and ran the scoreboard.

Marquette School participated in a track meet every year, which was strictly for the Catholic schools. The track meet was at *Cascia Hall*. *Cascia* had the reputation of being an elitist school. The other Catholic schools couldn't wait to beat them on the field. Our track meets and home football games were at *Cascia*. Even *Bishop Kelley High School* didn't have a football field in the 1960's and 1970's, just "the dust bowl", a name we gave the practice field, because it was in such terrible condition. I went to a freshman football scrimmage at the "dust bowl"

39

but there were no bleachers. I sat on the grass at the side of the field getting stickers in my bottom every time I moved. There were more weeds with stickers and burrs than there was any grass. The practice field was as hard as a rock.

There were about eight different Catholic schools back in the 1960's. A couple of those have shut down due to lack of enrollment in their neighborhoods over the past fifty years. Other schools have opened further south, as the city of *Tulsa* grew in that direction.

Oklahoma was once a missionary country. This is why it had two Catholic hospitals and several different orders of nuns present in such a small city. The poverty level was very high, especially during the great depression, followed by the dust bowl. The church sent missionaries to help with the poor.

The schools and hospitals were generally up and running before we built the churches. The church is a community of people, not a building. There was a strong foundation in the hierarchy of the church. Back breaking labor of the nuns and Christian brothers engineered and saw the projects through, with the cooperation of the families in the parish.

Priests we treated as God's representative on earth, with great respect. When a priest entered the room, everyone stood up immediately. "Only the priests can turn the bread into the Body of Christ." It's what we believe! The word of God is the motivation.

The Knights of Columbus were responsible for bringing girls sports to our schools. I played basketball and softball. Then, I also participated in the track meet. I loved high jump and the softball throw. Camille Quinn, a girl in my class I practically grew up with, would beat me in the softball throw. There was only one threat in high jump. Every year it came down to Susan Highland or me. We were both tall and lanky. I think that maybe the long legs were what made us good jumpers. We traded the first place ribbon back and forth for years. Susan came from a big family too. We would have an audience when we jumped.

There were several big families in the parish, and three of them had the name O'Brien, our family, my uncle Les' family and an O'Brien family that is no relation.

The Sposatos, McGraths, Highlands, O'Connors, Sullivans, Heckenkempers, Murpheys and Sheehans are tied to the school if not the parish and are known throughout the Catholic community of *Tulsa*, much like the Krafts and Peska's are tied to *Saints' Peter and Paul* or the De Bolts, and the Clarks are tied to *The Madalene* parish. If you weren't one of them, you knew one of them. There was nowhere in *Tulsa* that you could go that you didn't see someone you knew.

In our lives, emphasis was always on sharing time and talent. That's what love is. It's what the sisters and Christian brothers did. It's what the Knights of Columbus did. It's what my parents tried to teach us from birth.

This was my mother's favorite Bible verse: "God is love, and he who abides in love abides in God and God in him." (John). Anyone can say I love you. It is those who act, who make this point, understood, or as Momma would say, "Actions speak louder …"

I remember Daddy taking the brothers on a fishing trip and camp out. I wanted to go, but Daddy said I could not go, because I could not pee on a tree. This was his crude way of saying; "you are not a boy. You're not invited. This was a man thing."

I understand now, when Daddy took the boys on a fishing trip, he would buddy up with them and give them a beer. He would be their friend and listen carefully to what their thought processes were. Then, Daddy would "fish for more than fish" as Billy put it. This is where, they would open up to him and he could offer them fatherly advice. This is the importance of just being there in case they wanted to talk.

I'm glad Daddy did not try the fishing trip with me. The first time he wanted to give me the sex talk, I was in the fifth grade. I was riding with him to pick up the boys at *Henthorne Recreation Center*, after wrestling practice. I bet he spent 15 minutes talking to me about not letting a boy lay me. When I got home, I had to ask Momma,

"Momma what does lay mean?"

Momma laughed. She knew what Daddy and I were supposed to talk about that day. We had seen a movie at school about reproduction. The parents had to come to the movie too. Then, the parents were supposed to reinforce what we were learning, at school, at home.

Momma and I went out to *Kips Big Boy Burgers* and had a talk of our own. We ate warm apple pie and ice cream, while Momma spoke to me in a language, which was easier for me to understand. Still, I saved all of my toughest questions for my big sisters, Kitty and Christy.

Daddy and I were always speaking a different language. Kids now days are a little smarter than I was. I don't think my kids would have had any problem at all figuring out what we were talking about when we had our sex talk. I think I was just embarrassed enough I didn't want to interrupt my daddy.

I was afraid to say, "Daddy, I don't know what you're trying to say! Could you run that one by me again? "I was afraid he might keep talking about a subject matter, which made me uncomfortable.

My poor children, Kelly, Mike and Dan, had their mom tell them everything as blunt as possible. There was not going to be any misunderstanding what I was talking about when it came to reproduction.

"Boys, keep your peter in your pants." Once they became teenagers, I would end most phone calls with this line. Their friends would here it often as well. As crude as it sounds, I think they needed to hear it often, so it had a chance to sink in. Our children, berated by television and movies with the opposite influence, they needed absolute understanding.

"Kelly, boys think the green light is always on. You have to be clear when you say, "no"! If the red light is on, it means stop! Make sure they understand that there is no amber light." There is no question on where your father and I stand on this matter.

CHAPTER FOUR

HOSPITALITY

♥

My momma was the "queen of hospitality". Ray dubbed her so. We all agree. She knew how to make everyone feel welcome in our home.

"She was good company whether watching TV or playing cards. No one came in that she didn't offer food or drink." My cousin Charley would say, "She taught us best through example."

There was a story we would tell over the years of an evening, when Momma hollered that dinner was ready. In came all of the children, who had been playing outdoors, fighting for their space at the table.

When the meal ended, one of the children sitting at the dining room table comfortably walked through the master bedroom and out the back door.

Momma said, "Who was that?" We all shrugged our shoulders. No one knew! The kid was shagging balls for us in the street. It was a total stranger who shared our meal that evening. He must have heard the call to dinner and figured, why not?

Aunt Dorothy, my uncle Dick's wife, dropped by one evening, we were all sitting down to dinner, Daddy at the head of the table and the rest of us scattered about.

Momma generously offered her a place at the table.

"Dorothy, please sit down. We have plenty. Let me fix you a plate".

Aunt Dorothy was reluctant at first, saying "only if you have enough".

Momma, of course, insisted!

Momma went in the kitchen and fixed a plate for her guest with steak, green beans and a baked potato. She brought it out and sat it down at the table.

Then Momma went in the kitchen and fixed herself a green bean sandwich. Aunt Dorothy knew Momma well enough to know she would sacrifice her own meal to make someone else feel welcome. She snuck in the kitchen and caught Momma eating green beans between two pieces of bread.

"I caught ya!" Dorothy laughed aloud. "Alva, I knew it! I knew you would give up your own meal before you would tell me you didn't have enough!"

Momma and Daddy taught us that it's all about making the fish and the bread go a long way. They shared it with us and we are still sharing it with friends, family and strangers. A little hospitality goes a long way.

My brother, Bo, and I brought home a homeless man we found near the railroad tracks for breakfast and coffee. I thought; St. Francis of Assisi sold all of his goods in order to take care of the lepers. It was the least we could do. The man was hungry and it was cold out. Momma fed him outside on the front porch, and he was grateful for the meal. Momma had a talk with us about strangers that day.

The anti-establishment hippies were protesting the war and causing havoc downtown. There was talk of bussing and race riots. One of the largest race riots in US History happened less than a mile from our house, back in 1921. The majority of the victims from the race riots are buried only three blocks from our front door, right across the street from *Tracy Park*.

The *Tulsa* I grew up in wasn't very safe anymore! When I read The Outsiders, by, S.E. Hinton, I thought, "it's hard to believe this setting is *Tulsa*. Oh Crap, we're going to have to put a lock on the door".

We didn't. We were lucky if the front door would stay shut when the wind blew. Momma would not let me go anywhere with big groups of kids, she felt it was asking for trouble. I spoke my mind readily, I was argumentative, and I enjoyed a good debate. Most of my opinions didn't match the status quo. I was pro military, pro bussing, anti drug, anti hippie, anti "long hair" (on boys) and I didn't mind saying so!

During my eighth grade year, some kids at school wanted me to join their band. I loved to sing. "Momma said; "no"! Years later, I asked, Momma, why did you keep me closer to home?" The older brothers and sisters had so much more freedom than I did. I never got in any real trouble. Her answer was perfect.

"Maybe, that is why you never got into any trouble" she said, with a laugh.

Momma told me, "Actually, I think because Danny was ill in your early teenage years, you were all kept close in case of an emergency, Daddy and I wouldn't have to round you all up."

"Then again; Cheryl, you were a bleeding heart and trusted everyone. You fell for every sad story kids would tell you, and you thought any acquaintance was your best friend."

I couldn't argue with that logic. Momma was right! She knew me well. I still have the same problem today. I love people, the stranger the person, the more I like them. I cannot distinguish the good from the bad. I trust people even when I know they are lying to my face. I get hurt when they are not who they pretend to be.

I'm grateful Momma didn't try to treat us the same. I was easily deceived and didn't see things the way they really were. She was right. I needed protecting. Paul's the one looking out for me today (Paul, and my overworked guardian angel.)

In all reality, I think I enjoyed the time I spent at home, more than time I spent away. Friends would have me spend the night at their house, and it was eerie. It was much too quiet. I preferred my friends come to my house instead. I didn't want to miss anything going on at home.

Jenny was my best friend. She still is. She will always be my best friend. We are kindred spirits. She loved to come to my house, even though my brothers tormented her. We walked to school together. Jenny and I listened to the **Monkees** and **Three Dog Night**. We roller-skated and rode bicycles together. We would go to the park and play tennis. We loved to go to the movies and in the summer, her mom would take us to the drive-in. I miss her now. We do e-mail from time to time.

Jenny, and another girl Neva, who was visiting her grandmother for the summer, asked me to the movies when I was about thirteen-years-old. Momma said no, but she didn't give a reason. Jenny and I used to go to the movies all of the time together. We would see the *Bangladesh Concert*, (1971), three times in one day.

The rule was Momma does not need to give a reason. I didn't question it. I accepted "no" as an answer, but it puzzled me.

I questioned Momma about it years later and she did have a reason. She said, "I would never choose your friends for you, but if I felt there might be a bad influence among them, then you needed to just find something to do closer to home."

You know, that is what we did. She was smart. Maybe she had just experienced enough with the six kids before me to know what she was doing.

To this day, I think I'm one of the only children raised in the Sixties and Seventies who never smoked weed or tried illegal drugs. I take pride in the fact that I didn't. My friends respected how I felt, and they didn't try to push it on me.

One evening, during the late 1960's, Danny brought a couple of hitchhikers to our home. He picked them up on the *Turner Turnpike*. They stayed for dinner. We shared a meal and a room overnight. Then, Danny took them back to the turnpike gate, so they could hitch another ride. (I believe Christy unknowingly shared her watch with one of them.)

The beauty of our big family is feeling like you don't know a stranger. I suppose that sometimes that left us vulnerable. Even today, I talk to strangers as though they are family. It's not a bad quality to have if you move every few years.

Granny O'Brien shared a story with me, about a homeless man who showed up at her door, hungry and looking for food. He reminded her of her brother, during the great depression, jumping trains from town to town, looking for a job. She said, "I fed the stranger well and packed him a lunch for later in the day".

Momma's family was no different. There was no lack of hospitality on either side of our family. We would travel to *Louisiana* to see Mommas folks as often as possible. It wasn't easy in the years when all thirteen of us were living at home. Those of us who could make it to *Cheneyville, Louisiana* would make the effort. There was going to be a fish fry in the "*Old Possum Hollow!*"

On the old homestead where Momma and all of her siblings grew up is an old country store, about the size of a barn, with running water, a kitchen area and it has a bathroom. We call it *Possum Hollow*. *Possum Hollow* is located near old HWY 71. They erected it when the grocery store that my uncles built on a neighboring road, burned down. It served the family well over the years and later became a meeting place for various youth groups, thanks to the generous nature of Uncle Possum and now, my cousins, Charley and George.

Now, as a reader, you need to know that we have "Aunts" and Uncles on my daddy's side of the family and "Aints" and Uncles on my momma's side of the family. They are from *Louisiana*, and people from *Louisiana* talk funny. If you're from *Louisiana*, you think people from *Oklahoma* talk funny.

There was a tradition, which began when Uncle Jody, Mommas brother, returned from his service in the military, during WWII. Uncle Jody was born on the 4th of July.

Joseph L. Hoyt, my uncle Jody "was awarded the Bronze Star for heroic achievement in connection with military operations against the enemy in *France*, on November 19, 1944. He was seriously wounded, but he continued to fire his machine gun effectively supporting the advance of the platoon and contributing substantially to the success of the entire operation." (This is a quote from the Town Talk, *Alexandria-Pineville, Louisiana*'s local newspaper.)

My Aint Leona wrote in her memoirs of WWII, "Jody was transferred to a halftrack armored position, near *Birmingham, England*. After D-Day, he was with General Patton's 61st Armored Infantry of the 10th Armored Division. He swam the *Moselle River* with an overcoat and Walkie-Talkie on his back, scouting in advance of the main outfit. They stopped to check out a farmhouse. About ten crewmembers went into the house while Uncle Jody stayed in the tank to make coffee.

Uncle Jody saw German soldiers creeping up on the house, so he did the necessary thing and killed all of them, thus saving his crew members and him." She said, "Within five hours from that time, he was wounded twice by hundreds of shrapnel in the back and part of the halftrack in his knee. His fellow Marines carried him into a house where he had no medical attention or anesthetic for 48 hours, while Patton's Third Army Battalion disputed the town back and forth.

He was lying in bed, gun in hand, guarding a roomful of prisoners during all this time. This was near *Metz*; he was wounded at *Chateau-Terry*. He didn't remember how he got to a field hospital and later to a hospital in *Paris* for treatment of an infected leg and removing of more than two hundred pieces of shrapnel from his back.

Uncle Jody was a hometown hero. Aint Leona said, "He was awarded a Bronze Star, Purple Heart, and he received a Croix de Guerre from the American and French governments."

Uncle Possum had a fish fry to welcome his brother home. The fish fry became a family tradition. Every year on Uncle Jody's birthday, the 4th of July, our family and friends would gather in thanksgiving. Half of the people from *Rapides Parish* would show up for the event. The place was decorated in red, white and blue, with old glory flapping in the breeze. Everyone brought something to share, for a potluck dinner in *Possum Hollow*. We all knew certain items to expect.

We raved over Aint Evelyn's hush puppies. Aint Jenny Sue had a chocolate cake that was to die for, it melted in your mouth. She would make several desserts for the occasion. Her lemon cake is well known to us as well. Kitty has all of the recipes and never forgets to tell us whose recipe it is, when she treats us in *Tulsa* for special occasions.

If you check the refrigerator in Possums house, you will find Punkin's plate of deserts. While everyone else hits the food first, Punkin takes tiny pieces of each dessert and puts them away before it's too late, and sneaks them into the house. …We know her secret, so she may have to find a new hiding place.

Uncle Bo had an old whisky barrel, which he filled with lemonade and stirred with a boat paddle. It had a spout on it, where you could turn the knob and the lemonade would come out. Some years it was hot enough outside, we finished the barrel. We also would do damage to a stack of soda pop cans in the refrigerator in the *Possum Hollow*. Uncle Possum stocked it well in our honor. Then, we would use a can crusher and put the cans in a special bag for recycle.

When we were in *Louisiana*, we would often spend time playing in the fields. We would strike up baseball games in the front lawn with our cousins. Sometimes we would put our chairs in a circle under the huge pecan trees on the front lawn and just visit.

No alcohol! They didn't even allow beer on the property. That was against Grandma Katie's rules. After she died, they kept the rule, out of respect for Grandma. She didn't allow cussing either. I guess that's why my momma never cussed. The harshest thing I ever heard come out of my mother's mouth was "Hells Bells". If she were very, very mad, she would threaten you by saying, "I'm going to box your ears".

The uncles caught all of the fish for the fish fry and all of the crawdads for gumbo. I suspect the fishing was a lot more fun than cutting, scaling and flaying. The fish smelled a lot better cooking too!

My uncles converted an old washing machine, which somehow managed to scale the fish for you. There was no lack of imagination in my momma's family when it came to getting a job done.

Uncle Possum's health was failing as he reached closer and closer to his eightieth birthday. I often wondered how things would be able to continue in the tradition of old when the generation of Mommas siblings were gone.

Possum's doctor told him not to fish alone. He took his 84-year-old brother with him. His brother was in worse shape than he was in. It wasn't as if they were carrying cell phones either, in the 1990's.

There's a sign in front of the old *Possum Hollow* that says "old fisherman Xing". Inside the hollow, there are various other gifts that my uncle has received over the years, to decorate the abode. The décor of the house and the hollow was simple. There were pictures of family, friends and various gifts for the walls over the years. Once something made it on the wall, it didn't come down no matter how old it was. They didn't replace lamps until we broke them. I can remember two that we shattered over the years. One was a revamped hurricane lamp in one of the bedrooms, decorated with antique furniture. The other was floor lamp in the living room. We broke the legs on the couch a time or two as well. I never saw my uncle Possum look the slightest bit upset over anything that we did. He was as laid back as they come.

Uncle Jody and Uncle Bo would sit for hours and cut potatoes for the homemade chips. They used a cornmeal batter and deep-fried the potatoes until they were crispy. The crappie was crispy too. The best part was the crunchy tail. The catfish, flayed and cooked crispy on the outside and perfectly cooked on the inside, they place in ice chests for the insulation, until it's ready to adorn the table.

We kids were not a lot of help. We would stand around and watch, while the adults did all of the cooking, in hopes that we might need to be a "taster". We did try to take lessons on how to prepare our favorite things and we began helping sweep out the hollow in order to set things up the day before the big happening.

Uncle George and Grandma would sit on the front porch and snap the peas in the old days. Then, they would put them in a stainless steel bowl, until the bowl was full. We would help shuck the corn and pluck the little hairs out of the space between the kernels. I hated the little worms that you would find in the corn. If I ran across one, I would toss the ear of corn across the room in disgust.

Most of the vegetables grow right there on the farm or nearby. I can tell you there is nothing that tastes better than homegrown okra and tomatoes.

To be honest, I'm not sure we always knew what kind of meat we were eating. If you smoked it long enough, you could make a raccoon taste like chicken. Nothing would go to waste. It would feed the compost pile. The compost pile supplied some big juicy worms for the fishing.

It was time to eat, when Uncle Possum rang the big dinner bell, which was just outside the door to the hollow. We would all gather in front and wait for the blessing of the feast. The eldest generation of Hoyt's would go first, and then a line would form down both sides of the tables, which lined the old building. We would fill our plates and find a place to sit, usually outside under one of the large pecan trees.

We always hoped there would be enough left over, that we could snack on catfish, homemade chips and drink lemonade while we watched fireworks, which we kids would set off on the country road in front of the farmhouse.

That old country road was gravel at one time. Then, they tarred it. We never wore shoes in the country. That was not always wise. The road would get really hot with black tar. That old black tar would stick to the bottoms of your callous feet and was difficult to get off. Uncle Possum took us to the barn and used a little diesel fuel from the tractor, to remove the tar from the souls of our feet.

You would think we would have been smart enough to wear our shoes, especially in the wide-open spaces. In *Louisiana*, they had red fire ants. If they bite you, they sting. Fire ants leave a little blister, which will hurt, then, itch for days. You would not have any idea you had them on you, until it was too late. They would be all up and down your legs. The more you swatted them, the more they would sting you!

The mosquitoes in that part of the country are as big as wasps. Once the sun began to make its descent, the bottles of Off, mosquito repellant, would suddenly appear. There could never be enough to keep you totally bite free.

We lined the folding chairs up just before sundown, along the country road. Some of the smaller children were afraid of the noise that the fireworks made. They would watch from the window in the living room. Within a couple of years, they would be among the noise makers filling the road with debris.

The fireworks would get more extravagant as the years progressed. Sparklers and stink bombs with the little kids preceded the real show. The older kids would shoot off the fountains and artillery shells for the younger ones. They had flashlights to help them find their way to light the wick. There were no city lights out there in the country, just the stars and the moon. The only noise was the frogs, locust and an occasional nearby train. We changed that, one night a year, with the boom of the fireworks!

My kids, Kelly, Mike and Danny, especially loved that part of the trip when they would get to set off the fireworks. The next morning, we would make them go pick up the trash, which they left in the road, everything they could not see to pick up the night before.

When I was young, we went swimming at Uncle Clyde's, (He wasn't really our uncle) on the day after the 4th. My children would go to the French's house, which was just up the road, across *Turtle Creek* on Hwy 71, going toward *LeCompte*.

One year I had thirteen children filling my van as we approached the turn off HWY 71. I took the left turn too fast from the highway onto a gravel road. It was something that this city girl had not had much experience with and hopefully won't again. We slid off into a ditch. We were fortunate that the van didn't flip. A highway patrol officer and a man with a tractor pulled us out of the ditch and the children were still able to go swimming.

Aint Jo and Uncle George lived next door to Momma's folks near *Cheneyville, Louisiana*. They never had children of their own. My Aint Jenny Sue and Uncle Bo shared their children with Aint Jo. When Aint Jo and Uncle George died, they left their home to my cousin Charley, Uncle Bo's son and his wife Rose Marie.

Possum would leave the homestead to my cousin George. We called him "Shorty", though he probably stands about 6ft 4in. George was also one of Uncle Bo's children. They were the ones who spent the majority of their time helping on the farm and sharing their lives with Possum, especially in his later years.

Charley and Rose are still keeping things up on the old homestead. George is living in *Texas* and goes to help Charley get things ready before the 4th of July. Hospitality has passed to the next generation through Charley, Rose and George. Aint Jenny Sue is still healthy and does more than her fair share to feed the masses.

There's a pathway, which you can follow from one house to the other. It is where the grass is worn to nothing from people walking back and forth across the lawn between Grandma and Grandpas' house and, Aint Jo and Uncle George's house. When we would come to visit, we divide between three homes.

Some of us would stay at Grandma and Grandpa's on the old homestead. Some of us would stay at Aint Jo and Uncle George's, and the rest would stay with Uncle Bo and Aint Jenny Sue. They all lived close enough together, that we could spend most of our time playing in the fields with our cousins, and still be within yelling distance for meals.

Uncle Possum would make biscuits on Sunday and take them to church for many years, to have with homemade jellies provided by the women of his church. Then, he began taking them to the nursing home and having coffee with friends that were no longer active. When he could no longer drive, Possum would make the biscuits and Charley would take him to the nursing home in *LeCompte*.

The time finally came, when Uncle Possum became a resident in the nursing home himself. Charley and Rose looked after him daily. Charley would take Possum the paper and a cup of coffee first thing in the morning, on his way to work.

My Uncle Bo would mow the lawn at his churchyard well into his eighties. He would use his riding lawn mower on his lawn, Charley's and Uncle Possum's lawns as well, even in the summer heat. Doing for others was a way of life there.

We never went hungry when we went to *Cheneyville*. Uncle Possum knew what we liked to eat. Crawfish gumbo, served over rice was my favorite. Uncle SJ would make a spicy version from time to time.

Uncle SJ was the brother who looked the most like my momma. He had brown eyes and thick black hair that never turned gray. His skin was a little darker than the rest of the family, like Momma, Aint Leona, Bryan and Me. I always felt close to him as a result. It's hard to understand, but when you're one of the only brown-haired people in a family of blonde's, it's nice to know that you shared something unique with someone. My brother, Bryan, still has a full head of hair now and he's 60-years-old.

My brothers usually had first claim on staying at Uncle Bo and Aint Jenny Sue's house. They had all boys at their house. They lived in a large two story home that was over one-hundred years -old.

Uncle Bo always had pancakes for the boys in the morning. He would have the batter already mixed and when you came downstairs and the griddle was hot. You could pour the batter and cook your own pancakes so that they would be fresh and plenty hot, no matter what time of the morning you woke up.

Aint Jenny Sue has kept this tradition alive. I had the pleasure of staying with her the last couple of times I traveled to *Louisiana*. Her home is beautifully decorated with antiques and she has several collections. Most impressive to me are the beautiful quilts that she has sewn by hand over the years.

When you stayed with Uncle Possum, you were going to have biscuits and homemade jelly with a good strong cup of Community coffee. His coffee was strong enough to put hair on your chest. You never needed to worry about waking up before Possum. He was up before sunrise every year when I visited. You could also expect a cookie jar full of homemade tea biscuits on the dining room table, with a radio playing country music, softly in the background.

My daddy recalled the first time he visited *Cheneyville*. Momma brought a cup of black coffee to his bed. He wanted my husband, Paul and me to share the same memory. The first time Paul and I went to *Cheneyville* with the family, I'm guessing was about 1976. Paul and I were engaged and Paul was coming to meet Momma's side of the family for the first time. Daddy wouldn't let Paul get out of bed until I brought him a cup of coffee.

Paul slept on a fold out couch overnight. I stayed at Aint Jo's house next door. By the time I showered, dressed, and put on my makeup, Paul was definitely ready for his coffee. Daddy was standing guard over Paul, who was still in bed. The fold out bed was in the dining room and the dining room was full of people at this point. You can't imagine Paul's embarrassment. Paul is usually the first one out of bed.

Grandma and Grandpa's dining room had a china hutch. Inside the china hutch, were boxes of letters and pictures, which were sent to Momma's folks over the years. We loved to go through it and find letters we sent to Grandma and Grandpa when we were younger. We could find letters that Momma sent back home in her early years of marriage. There would be newspaper articles about births, football and wrestling.

There were also letters in the china hutch about Danny's diagnosis. Each letter gave insight into what was going through Momma's mind with the escalation of the disease. Her letters were usually very informative. She was keeping her parents posted on what their grandchildren were up to from week to week.

One of the letters I came across was the letter Daddy wrote to Momma's family, asking for her hand in marriage. What a wonderful thing to have hung on to for all of these years. Who knows what other treasures are hidden deep within the confines of the china hutch?

Uncle SJ and Aint Pauline, Uncle Jack and Aint Evelyn, would come in from *LeCompte* for the fish fry with their children. Aint Leona and Uncle Steve would bring their family from *Alexandria*, we called it *"Alec"*, and Aint Sue and Uncle Red came from *Texas*. There were years when Uncle Gus would come with his family, all the way from *New Hampshire*.

We would have softball games on the lawn in front of the hollow with our cousins. We spent time in the fields breaking off pieces of sugar cane to chew on. We would tell ghost stories!

The area was full of stories of men killed or wounded during the Civil War. This includes the story of our Great-Great Grandfather, Captain David J. Hoyt. His death was a result of the Civil War.

Captain Hoyt's job was training the recruits for the Confederate Army. At the *Battle of Pleasant Hill*, March 21, 1864, the Sixteenth Regiment of Indiana Mounted Infantry captured him, and later they released him, because he was so ill he was slowing them down.

When they realized they had someone who was important and they had released him, the Union Soldiers recaptured Captain Hoyt and marched off toward *New Orleans*, where he was to be incarcerated.

He died in route when they stopped to rest. He was last seen lying propped against a tree, leaving his widow with five living children and 150 acres of land. When his wife went to *New Orleans* to claim his body, they couldn't find it. So where is the body of Captain Hoyt? His ghost is present among the sugar cane, on a hot day when one feels a sudden chill. It means that someone has walked across his grave. Where's the grave?

My grandpa, Sam, became the man of the family from the time that he was twelve-years-old. His mom, Mary Jane lost her husband Joe and raised seven children on her own. The story is told, that Joe's doctor advised him that his heart was weak and he needed to work at night and stay out of the sun. Joseph L. Hoyt died at the young age of 36, swinging an ax. If you listen closely at night, you can hear the rhythm of the ax hitting the wooden stump. Thump! Thump! Thump!

Then, she told her sister that the ghost of her husband came to her in a dream. He told her that the baby was to come with him to heaven. The baby died just two months later.

She was crushed by the loss of her baby. Mary Jane managed to take in an orphan girl named Cordie Herring to help with the children. She gave her the same love and attention that she gave to her own children, with all of the discipline and education that she possibly could. Mary Jane only lived another seven years, and she died leaving the children to fend for them-selves, with Sam being the eldest.

There were no government handouts in 1901. With my Grandpa, Sam, as the head of the household, the children kept the family together.

They sold cows to pay the doctor and funeral bills, then went to work planting mustard seeds and growing their own food.

A woman called "Grandma Shoebrooks" (no real relation) helped to raise 37 children orphaned after the Civil War. Mary Jane had been one of those children and now the family would look after her in her old age and bury her in the cemetery near the home, on Hoyt, Road.

These are only a few of the ghost stories told over the years. If the cemetery on Hoyt, Road could talk, I'm sure there are hundreds of stories to add to our nights of terror.

We cousins especially loved the ghost stories in the midst of a thunderstorm when the lights would go out in the house. ...The electricity in the house was a bit primitive, and running the vacuum and the dishwasher at the same time could blow a fuse.

The first time I can remember visiting *Cheneyville*, I was five-years-old. That was in 1962. There were ten children in the family at the time. Patsy was the baby. We borrowed my Uncle Bob's vehicle for the trip. It was a Green Briar Van. The luggage was tied to the top of the van and the family of twelve was driving with the windows down.

We had the radio blasting for a while. Soon it became impossible to find a channel we could pick up a reception on that wasn't fuzzy. Daddy had it figured out, organized noise was better than chaos. We loved to sing songs when we were on the road.

We sang every song that we knew, some of them more than once. This was a good way to keep the driver awake and Daddy was getting tired. The drive from *Oklahoma* to *Louisiana* was probably 12 hours back then. (I-49 had not yet been completed from *Shreveport* to *Alexandria* and wouldn't be for probably another fifteen years.) We were driving on old Hwy 71. Daddy stopped in for some coffee while he gassed up the van. A truck driver had been driving beside us commented to my daddy on how much he was enjoying listening to the children singing.

We were back on the road again. I saw the truck behind us with its lights shining in the rear window. There was a loud pop. One of our tires blew while we were going full speed on the highway at a curve in the road.

Kitty screamed! "Daddy what are you doing?"

It all happened so fast, it's difficult to know exactly what happened. Daddy fought the wheel as the car tried to pull him into oncoming traffic on this two-lane road. We pulled right instead and hit a deep ditch on the side of the road. It caused the top-heavy van to roll, once, twice and nearly a third time!

The truck driving behind us saw the whole thing, and he called for the emergency vehicles. He kept his lights shining so that Momma and Daddy could see as they checked on each of the children. A woman who lived near Hwy 71 opened her home to us. They cleaned and wrapped our wounds in clean white towels.

My momma found me. Face wounds can be deceiving, and they can be terrifying because they bleed a lot. Momma thought at first that I had lost the left side of my face. She carried me to the woman's home, where two ambulances would come and take Bo, Bryan, Sarah and me to the hospital. Uncle Possum came and took several of the other less critical family members to the hospital as well.

Bo was bleeding badly. Without Daddy's knowledge as a medic, we probably would not have Bo with us today. His cuts were on his legs and one had cut especially deep. Bo lost a lot of blood. They had smelling salts and kept Bo and I awake throughout our trip to the hospital.

The truck driver who had been behind us all of that time said; "it must have been a miracle. The vehicle rolled twice and threw everyone out of the van. Had it rolled the third time, it would have smashed them, but as though angels picked it up, the van tipped, and then it rolled back on all four tires!"

Patsy, the baby, flew out the window and landed on a pillow. There wasn't a scratch on her. She had been sleeping on the floorboard, on that same pillow.

At the hospital, they cleaned and stitched our wounds. Several of the family members would need stitches here and there. Bryan needed stitches over his eye. He had been sitting in the front seat, between Momma and Daddy. Sarah needed stitches on the front of her lower leg. Momma needed stitches on her arm. Bo had a triple layer of stitches between his legs.

I had 54 stitches across the left side of my face. Dr. Brown was a plastic surgeon and did a fine job of making my scar look like a smile line. I didn't realize how scared the family was when they saw the wounds on my face. Bryan said that they were most worried about me.

Yet, from the perspective of a child, the most traumatic thing that happened to me was that I had to wear boys' underwear. This was a difficult thing for a five-year-old girl to take. Some friends of the family went shopping for clothes for us to wear when we left the hospital. The underwear came in packages of three and Bo needed underwear.

Kitty and Billy had concussions. They were watched closely at the hospital until the doctors were sure that they were going to be all right. Kitty would relive the terror every time she was in a car and it took a turn or came to a sharp curve for weeks.

Kitty asked Momma, "Why did God let this happen?"

Her reply, "It's easy to love God when everything is going perfect in your life. Can you say that you love him when things are going wrong?"

It wasn't the answer Kitty was looking for. Still, the answer stayed with her. Kitty would remind herself often to say; "I love you", even in the most difficult circumstances.

Kitty and her husband Russell would share some very difficult situations together over the years. I can honestly say, without a doubt, "Kitty loved God, even when things were going wrong". She never looked at it as a test. I think she sees her suffering as a badge of honor. If she suffered, perhaps someone else would not suffer. She was following Christ's example, bearing the suffering for the world.

That year of the car accident, we still made it to *Louisiana* for the 4th of July and I stayed at Grandma and Grandpa's house.

I'm an early riser. I watched my Grandma run the hairbrush through her long blond hair. She told me she brushes it one hundred strokes! She brushed it every night and every morning. It came all the way down to her waist.

"Grandma, I didn't even know you had long hair. It's pretty. I've never seen it when it wasn't pinned up." I said.

Grandma Katie changed the dressing on my face and packed ointment into the deepest wounds and I followed her as she went about the chores on the farm. People in the country move slower and they talk slower than people from the city do. I tried to imitate my grandma's saunter as she and I went outside to feed the two cows, Heart and Seven.

When you wake early in *Cheneyville* and head out the door, there's heavy dew on the grass. One can smell the bayou, freshly cut grass and the pollen in the air. You can see your footprints in the lawn as you make your way to the fence to feed the cows. The humidity is always high when you're that far south down in *Louisiana*. Then, the nose detects when you are coming nearer to the cows. That scent was stronger than the pollen and you didn't want to stand around there too long!

The next chore was collecting eggs. If the cows didn't offend the nose enough, the chickens were going to make your nose run. Once I got used to the smell, I enjoyed helping Grandma collect eggs in the hen house. We would put them in a basket. The basket had a dishtowel in it and we would separate the eggs with the towel. Then, we would take them in the house and have eggs and oatmeal for breakfast. I remember Grandma putting a peppermint in my oatmeal.

"Grandma that is something I have never eaten before. It's good"!

My grandma said; "It helps to cut the taste of the well water".

I understood that! The well water was kind of, sweet, but it tasted funny. I didn't like it.

That trip we would complete by taking a train ride back to *Tulsa*. I had never been on a train. It was a little noisy, but we forgot about the noise after awhile. The motion of the train nearly rocked you to sleep. Everyone was somewhat traumatized, yet feeling blessed to be alive. My scar became, yet another story to tell and a badge of courage to wear proudly.

After that trip, we always took more than one vehicle. When we would leave, to drive back to *Tulsa*, it was never empty-handed. We would have boxes of pecans and vegetables from the garden. Aint Jenny Sue would send us with jars of homemade jelly and preserves. There would be a crowd to see us off, waving until we were gone.

They were probably wiping their brow when we got out of sight! We were a hand full. Daddy would never stay more than a few days. He used to say; "You want them to be happy to see you coming and sad to see you go.

Yesterplaces, By: Wm H. O'Brien (Billy)
(Published 1999 THE HOYTS-A *Louisiana*/Canada Connection)

Fish and chips
Lemonade in a barrel
A long distance Christmas Carol
      Personalized jellies
      Biscuits from scratch
      An old cedar stump
      A door that won't latch
A weathered pump house
Two gravel drives
Huge pecan trees
Razor sharp knives
      A fish-cleaning machine
      Jumping jacks
      The Bayou Boeuf
      The railroad tracks
'Maters and beans
'Taters and rice
An ice cream bucket full of ice
      A bountiful garden
      Limbs, heavy with figs
      Minnow traps
      Assorted jigs
A riding mower
A demitasse
Magnolia blossoms
Spanish moss
      A snake in the kitchen
      A soothsayer's grave
      Chili sauce
      A receipt for a slave
An armadillo
Folding chairs
The dinner bell
Brick stairs

White-haired uncles
Bald-headed nieces
A dining room caucus
A lamp, "broken to pieces"
Misty eyes
Long embraces
Memories of " Yesterplaces"

CHAPTER FIVE

SHARE EVERYTHING

♫

In a large family, you recognize the troubled teen. He was once your brother. You know the tired man who is ready to meet the maker, because he was your grandfather. You have witnessed what it's like to succeed and to fail. You recognize where you need to step up to fill a spot when someone else is in need. We know what it's like to share someone's joy, their sorrow, their pride, their embarrassment. We know jealousy, anger, empathy, sympathy, and most of all we know and understand love. We're not afraid of hard work; a positive attitude is very much a part of our make up. We know how to give hope.

You learn to share everything. In my younger years, it was clothing and shoes. There were times when we shared our friends. You had to share your toys. You shared a room. You shared beds. You often shared your bathwater!

Before 1960, this was before Patsy and Punkin were born, we lived at a house on the north side of *Tulsa*. It was a small house; I call it a Cracker Jack box. It was one of many homes that went up in the mid 1940's to house the booming population after the war. There were lots of newlyweds and young families after WWII. All of the houses looked the same. I have only sketchy memories in that house on Vandalia, but my siblings have shared many happy memories with the rest of us.

Momma and Daddy had nine children in that tiny home. The house on Vandalia had three bedrooms and a living area. There was a dining area connected to the kitchen, plus one bath.

There were double bunk beds in both bedrooms and barely enough room for a dresser, barely enough room to move. Bryan, Danny, Ray,

Billy and Bo shared one room. Christy, Kitty, Sarah and I shared a bedroom. Momma and Daddy had the master bedroom, but there was another baby on the way.

We were not getting any smaller in numbers, and we were growing in age and size at the same time. They felt it was definitely time to move on; time to look for something bigger. Remember, there was only one bathroom to share between the eleven of us! That's sharing!

We shared everything, not just tangible objects. We were fortunate enough, to share the same parents. That does not mean there was no one to sing you to sleep or to read you a book. Christy would read books and four or five of us would listen.

By the time Patsy and Punkin, the two youngest, came along they had several of us lined up to read books. You have to share your parents. That doesn't mean you don't have anyone at the ball game to cheer you on. Between the family and extended family, there may have been as many as fifteen there to cheer for you.

My memories of my childhood are embedded deep within me, at the home located at 1307 South Newport. We would live in that home from the time I was three-years-old, to the time I became a sophomore in high school, at the age of fifteen. Patsy and Punkin were born during the time when we lived on Newport. I remember Sarah's First Communion, Bo's First Communion and my own First Communion. Bryan, Danny, Christy, Ray and Kitty graduated from high school during that time, and eventually they moved away from home. There is a timetable in my mind of what happened when we lived in which house.

I would have my first kiss on the old front porch, with half of the family peering through the windows and out the door. Jim Clark was my boyfriend. His momma was sitting in the car in front of the house. We were in a no win situation.

Jim and I would spend hours talking on the phone at night. I would hide in the closet upstairs, where the phone cord would reach and I could close the door. If someone knew I was on the phone, the timer was turned over and I had three minutes to talk. We didn't have call waiting in those days. Sometimes, people had a difficult time getting through on the line, and they complained to Daddy. Occasionally, the operator would break in and tell us that someone was checking the line.

When Bryan graduated from *Bishop Kelley High School*, the family stood in front of the house on Newport trying to get a family picture for what seemed to me to be hours. It wasn't always easy to get all thirteen O'Brien's together at once for a picture. Then, there's trying to get us to hold still and look at the camera. The Fetters next door owned a camera and organized us for this photo. It's one of the few photographs of the thirteen of us together.

Our dining room table was a gift from my Aunt Bea and Uncle Bob. It easily sat twelve people with two wooden slats that fit in the middle to make the table large enough for all of us to fit around it. The dining room table had a wooden trim that was indented all of the way around. We used to pretend that the indentions were piano keys. We would sit and play the piano and sing songs.

The dining room table was the focal point of the entire household. We spent many nights around that beautiful wooden table, talking and playing cards. We shared many special meals at that table. I don't know if my Aunt Bea and Uncle Bob have any idea what a great gift it was to our family.

Momma always said; "The dining room table and the front porch should get the most use of anything in any household." She was not talking about eating!

There was other activity happening in the dining room as well. Christy would put on the **Beatles** or **Beach Boys**, and she would iron for hours in the dining room. The little kids would do their homework at the dining room table. Momma cut out patterns for clothes that she made us and made repairs to our hand me downs. She kept her Singer sewing machine in the dining room too. That's where the boys sat to count their collecting money, from the newspapers they threw. Then, we would help roll the coins.

This is where we would sit and lick the green stamps to fill the books for Momma. When the books were full, she would save them until she had enough to purchase something special for the house, like a six-slice toaster or a mixer.

We didn't have air conditioning in those days. We had a water cooler downstairs, which blew across the dining room table, and we had a water cooler in Kitty and Christy's room, upstairs. Many warm nights I remember sleeping with my pillow in the windowsill, hoping to feel a breeze across my face.

Nothing cooled things off much in the *Oklahoma* summer heat. Sometimes the sidewalks were hot enough to fry an egg on them, and that is no exaggeration. The boys had a box fan in their room, and they set it in the window. There were some uncomfortable nights. In the daytime, you spent all of your time outdoors and came in for a drink of water occasionally. You waited your turn to stand in front of the water cooler, lift up your shirt, and "Ahhhh!"

Walking home from school, there was an air-conditioned doctor's office with a drinking fountain in it. We would stop in for a cool drink of water. Not once do I remember anyone complaining about us popping in for a drink. We were greeted with a smile and a wave. *Tulsa* was a friendly place to grow up.

How many gallons of milk does a family of eleven children go through in a week? Our family went through 15 gallons a week. We had a milk dispenser in the utility room, like the ones they have in restaurants. It was always fresh and came out ice cold. It held 20 gallons at a time.

Momma bought oranges in ten-pound bags. She made corn bread and muffins for our snack in our lunches, sometimes, but most often, she would go to the day old bread store and buy Honey Buns.

Friday night, *Bishop Kelley* football games were a family requirement. In the early years, everyone who was anyone went to the football games on the weekend. I was not allowed to date much my freshman year, but I was able to go to all of the football games and out with friends for pizza at *Clancy's*, as long as my older brother, Billy, went with me.

I could go to anything as long as it revolved around *Bishop Kelley High School*, school dances, bon fires, etc…, again, as long as Billy went with me!

"It isn't good for a girl to be seen without an escort." Momma would tell me.

Clancy's was a pizza place, owned by Mr. and Mrs. Clancy. Mr. Clancy was once a Championship Wrestler on TV. He was as nice as he could be. All of the *Bishop Kelley* students went to *Clancy's* after the game. It had the red and white table clothes and looked Italian, but the windows would have "Go Comets!" written on them in the BKHS red and white. All of the cars in the parking lot were decorated with red and white crape paper and streamers. Football was a big thing back then.

Later in the Seventies, when Mr. Clancy's place was no longer the only hang out. We would go to *Shakey's* pizza and sing along with the live entertainment there. Billy and his friends went to *Shakey's*, so that's where I went.

We shared pizza and coke, and we had many good times together. Billy's friends, became my friends. I missed them when they graduated two years before me.

We didn't have a football field of our own in the 1960's and 1970's. *Bishop Kelley High School* home games were played at *Cascia Hall*, several miles away. The *Bishop Kelley* parents would need to go pick up their football players after the game. They greeted the school bus at the top of the "U" shaped driveway at *Bishop Kelley*, and they cheered the students as they went to the locker room, win or lose.

The parents would then have a *Bishop Kelley Athletic Association* meeting in the cafeteria, while they waited for the boys to shower. This was usually a large gathering. They had wine and beer with some snacks. It was about visiting over the game, more than it was about anything else. Then, the boys finished their showers and joined their parents for the rest of the evening, or held out their hand for pizza money and the car keys.

Our entire family was full of school spirit. Our lives revolved around *Pop Warner Football, Marquette School, Henthorne Recreation Center* for wrestling, and *Bishop Kelley High School*.

The pep club would make signs, sell ribbons and hold a pep rally each week. I loved going to the football games and being a part of the pep club. We would play with our friends under the stands when we were very young. Then, as we began to understand the sport better, we found our seat with the rest of the family, under the score box on the fifty-yard line. Everyone but Daddy! He would be pacing the sideline, always with his cigar!

Wrestling was my favorite sport to watch. It was easy to understand and you only had to watch one match at a time. There wasn't too much going on at once. We made wrestling a family affair as well as football. All five of the brothers were wrestlers. Nearly all of the matches were my brothers or their friends participating. This made it interesting for us to watch. You began to know and respect the competition as well.

The transportation was much easier for Momma. The boys were in a car pool, so she only had to drive when it was her turn, and then the other parents took their turn to drive the boys. The brothers, even Bo, were all going to the same place for practices and matches. Wrestling tournaments would go by weight class and not age. Momma would actually have a chance to sit and watch all of them participate in one activity, without having to run all over *Tulsa*.

The first *Bishop Kelley Wrestling Homecoming Dance* was in our living room in the 1960's. We moved all of the furniture out of the living room and dining room. I know my older brothers and sisters worked hard cleaning, buffing, and polishing the wooden floors to get the house ready for homecoming.

Our TV room also became a trophy room. The boys built a cabinet for their wrestling metals, ribbons, and for their various trophies'. I looked forward to the day that I could add a trophy to the cabinet.

The Gilpin boys were wrestlers too. Mike, Frank, Mark, and Luke were the ones I knew well. They would share the car pool to and from school, and to and from practice. Our families were very close friends. They had several children and lived nearby. Mr. "G" worked with Daddy at *Oklahoma Steel*. He helped Daddy coach at *Marquette,* and they would come and play cards at the house a lot.

Becky Gilpin was close to my age, and she was my friend. Becky and I would play together at the *Pop Warner* football games, with Juanita Smith, Jill McCarthy, Camille Quinn and other girls our age who had brothers playing football. Sometimes we would pretend to be cheerleaders. Then, we would spend the time together at the *Marquette* games either playing with friends and cousins under the stands, or cheering on the sidelines.

Becky became a cheerleader at *Bishop Kelley,* when we made it to high school. I think she was the best cheerleader they had. She was an all around good athlete.

When my brothers were playing baseball, my momma said she spent the entire time driving from one field to the other field dropping off, and then, from field to field picking up. She never had time to watch them participate. She was grateful the boys enjoyed wrestling more than baseball.

Daddy had a rule, two sports or activities per year, tops! There were so many of us, Momma and Daddy had to keep our time under control. He had to keep the cost under control too. My interests were basketball and softball, but I squeezed in track and student council, and I never heard a complaint; I think, perhaps the reason was that track and student council didn't require a ride. I could walk to and from *Marquette*.

My sister, Christy, is the one that I remember pushing my swing at the park. She shared her time with the little kids often. I think she was keeping us out of Momma's hair, but I also believe it was by choice. She was a perfect big sister. She loved holding babies and rocking them. She would swing us around in circles. She would dance with us around the living room to *The King and I* (1956), *Oklahoma* (1955), *Bye, Bye Birdie* (1963), *Mary Poppins*, (1964) and *The Sound of Music* (1965). We all knew the words to the songs.

Christy, and her best friend, Kathie Sullivan, volunteered as basketball coaches when I was in 4th and fifth grade. Christy made a huge impact on all of our lives, because she was willing to share so much of her time. When she was older, she led the fight with Daddy that gave O'Brien women the right to go to work outside of the home.

It was not an easy battle. Mrs. Sposato was a teacher for the St. Johns Hospital Nursing Program; she came over and helped Christy in her quest for freedom. Christy went to nursing school and, she became a Licensed Practical Nurse. We were all very proud of her accomplishment. She worked long difficult hours.

You would have never known Daddy fought with her about her right to work. He was prouder than anyone was when she began to work at her chosen profession. Aint Jo was a nurse, Daddy had been a medic during WWII, and I think he had great respect for nurses.

Daddy also would remind Christy that when she became a mother, a woman's place was in the home. That was a fight for another day. Christy could handle it. She is as tough as nails.

Waking Nurse Christy in the morning was nearly impossible. On Easter morning, she would let the little kids have her Easter basket full of candy, if they would just leave her alone and allow her to get some sleep. I doubt that Christy worked any harder as a nurse than she did helping take care of all of us. I never once heard her complain. She loved us and had such pride in all of us.

Prior to Christy going to work, if she were not babysitting at home, Christy would be babysitting across the street. The Powell's lived at 1308. Norma Jean and Don had four children, Kim, Barry, Kelli, and Kandi. Kim and I were the same age. She was my first best friend. We met when we were just five-years-old. Barry was my little sister, Sarah's age, Kelli was my little sister, Patsy's age and Kandi was closest to, Punkin, the baby's age.

I loved playing with Kim, but they had a lot more rules than we did. They had to wear shoes every day. Their parents wouldn't let them play ball in the street. They had to be in before dusk. When the Powell children were in trouble, their mom, Norma Jean, would make them go and get a switch off the tree. That had to hurt!

I wasn't afraid of Norma Jean, even when she was holding the switch because she was always very kind to us. When we played at their house, it was usually in the backyard or basement. I liked it when she cleaned house because she would hum and sing. She had a voice like an angel.

Mr. Powell, Don, had a deep voice when he spoke, but he was usually very quiet. He wore dark sunglasses all of the time. When I was young, I was scared of him. Then, as I got older, I found out he was nice. He wore dark glasses because he was diabetic and needed to protect his eyes from the sun.

Kim Powell and I made many mud cookies together on my back patio. We would decorate them with leaves, which we pulled off Mrs. Garrett's mimosa tree next door. We had tea parties and played hopscotch and foursquare.

One day when Kim and I were out on the driveway playing foursquare, and I began to tell her the story of Christ. I had always gone to Catholic school and it never occurred to me that everyone wasn't familiar with his story. She was familiar with the story of his birth, but she was unaware of how he died. It made such an impression on her; when I reached the part of his crucifixion, Kim cried.

Norma Jean and Don allowed their children to pick their own religion. They didn't want to force it upon them. It would be several years later when the entire Powell family would be baptized. Rather than have one-person stand as God Parent, our family stood as Godparents to their family. The celebration was very uplifting. I felt honored to be a part of it.

The time came when Christy moved out and got an apartment just a few blocks from the house. Again, she was a pioneer. Imagine, a girl living out of her home unmarried. She had two roommates. They were girls who she had gone to high school with.

Christy was more fun than anyone else I knew in my life at that time. She would have Charade parties and Jeopardy parties at her apartment, and even the little kids were invited. She was never one to exclude anyone. The more the merrier was always the rule. She was still willing to share her time with us. How many children can say that about an older sibling? She was never too cool to have her brothers and sisters around, even on a Friday or Saturday night.

There was a time in my youth when I was trying on different personalities. Trying to find myself would have been the psychological jargon of the day. I tried hard to be like Christy. I felt she was a good role model, though some of the words that came from her mouth I could not repeat at school. I remember one of my teachers, Kathie Sullivan, yes, the same Kathie, pulling me aside.

She said, "Christy's my best friend and you know I like her. I like you too. You need to stop trying to be your sister and be yourself."

It was hard not to want to act like Christy. She was popular. I liked her friends, especially Kathie. She had a dry wit and a quick sense of humor. Kathie Sullivan is still like family today.

Her father, Tom Sullivan, was one of the first inductees into the *Bishop Kelley High School, Hall of Fame.* He was selfless in his love for our community and showed it on a daily basis. Once he retired, he became a full time unpaid employee at the school and a man of all hats. Whatever they needed he would step up to the plate. Kathie would later follow in her fathers footsteps and be inducted in to the *Bishop Kelley Hall of Fame.* This was a huge honor, especially in our circle of friends.

I would remember the speech, which Kathie gave me, for several decades. I tried on many personalities before I finally found the one that fit. I feel pretty good in my skin now. I'm grateful to Kathie for giving me permission to be myself.

Once we were at Christy's apartment having a Jeopardy party. We heard a large explosion nearby. It shook the entire apartment. We looked outside and saw nothing but other people opening their doors and peering through their windows. Next thing you know, our brother, Ray and his best friend, Joe, came running in, laughing so hard they almost fell on the floor! They knew we were all upstairs playing, so they lit fireworks downstairs and nearly scared us to death. They had been working at the fireworks display-selling fireworks over the summer. The next morning there was an article in the newspaper about the explosion.

When we played games at Christy's apartment, several of their high school friends joined us; Tom Burton, Kathie Sullivan, Linda Hellinghausen, Chris Saunders, Russell Otterstrom and Dink Jones are the names that would resonate through the years. Not just for games and play, they would become family, or like family.

The Catholic schools, kindergarten through eighth grade, would have a wrestling tournament of their own each year. The various grade schools would have boys from the high school go and teach them enough about wrestling that they could compete in just the one tournament. My brothers volunteered their time for this tournament. Kitty would help by running the clock at one of the mats.

Kitty taught me all of the cheers for pep club before I even started at *Bishop Kelley*. She was proud of the pep club and the cheerleading squad. Nearly three quarters of the girls at school were in the pep club. During the years that Kitty was involved at *Bishop Kelley*, the pep club was highly disciplined.

The pep club wore their school uniforms, including the red school blazer to the football games, basketball games and wrestling matches, and they sat together. The girls in the pep club were not allowed to wander around the stadium or gym at will, they had to stay in their places. Then, once a year they would have a huge bonfire on the school grounds. It was truly something to be proud of, because of their restraint and order and because of their school spirit.

Kitty was usually the one who helped Momma in the kitchen. She took home economics at school. I'm not so sure sometimes she wasn't in the way, right under Momma's feet. Rather than helping, she would be cooking something that wasn't on the menu, like coconut cream pie, lemon pie, or German chocolate cake. Her heart was always in the right place, but the help Momma was looking for was probably not in the dessert category.

Her specialty was fried chicken. She made great fried chicken, she would double dip the chicken in the milk mixture and then into the flour. It gave it a good crust. Kitty's fried chicken was Ray's favorite. He would sneak into the kitchen and start eating it before dinner was ready and she would be slapping his hands. When Kitty made fried chicken, she really was helpful to Momma. It would be one night each week when Momma didn't have to cook dinner.

At school, we learned about the Ten Commandments and stories of the Old Testament. Then, we learned about how Jesus lived and died in the New Testament. Living the Gospel is what we are called to do. We learned to practice it at home. We were not perfect, but we were working on it.

We had examples in the selflessness of the Benedictine Sisters and Lasallian Christian Brothers who were so much a part of our daily lives. They took a vow of poverty when they joined their order. This is something that priests are not required to do, but some do anyway. This commitment to God was lived out through example and I was awestruck. I remember buying gifts for nuns, only to have them ask if it would be ok if they gave it to someone else, because they could not keep it for themselves. Everything they did was selfless, and they worked very hard.

Brother Bernadine would mow several acres at the school with the help of volunteers like Tom Sullivan and Mr. Heckenkemper. They would care for the football field and the practice fields, giving them the proper markings.

High School students drove the school bus every morning and afternoon. How scary is that? Brother "B" trained them. The steering wheel was bigger than Krissy Hershel. She stood about five foot four and couldn't have weighed 100 lbs. We would have volunteers drive the busses to football games, basketball games, wrestling matches and track meets.

Then, there were the examples in our family, through the Knights of Columbus, coaching, time spent reading to the kids or helping in the kitchen. Doing for others, service orientated jobs like teaching, nursing and military service, are honorable things to do.

With eleven children at home, I can remember my mother making the time to be the block walker for the March of Dimes! She felt blessed to have eleven healthy children. She wanted to give something back to God.

Many books I read today talk about doing things for myself. Quit smoking, lose weight, do it for yourself, you can't do it for others. BUNK!

I can honestly say I find it easier to do things for others. Quit smoking for your children. How many women can quit smoking during pregnancy, only to start back after the baby is born? I contend, that if you quit for your children during pregnancy, you can stay quit for your children, because the odds of them smoking as adults is much greater if you smoke.

You need to lose weight today so you can be around to see your grandchildren tomorrow. You should eat healthy and exercise so you can remain healthy and not cause your family undue stress and anxiety. Get a college education for your family, not for yourself. Your children will learn through your example. You will be rewarded in return. Anyway, it feels good to do things for other people.

In our society, people don't think of themselves before running into a burning building to save a child. You don't think of how it's going to affect your life before you give CPR to a stranger. We work better when we are working for others.

What's best for the family? What's best for the community? What's best for the whole? Have you noticed that it's about time and talent, not money? Sometimes money represents your talent and it's good to share it as well.

I think, "Your time will make a much larger impact in the lives of others than your money. Money is easily flushed down the toilet." In one of the **Steven Covey** books, he speaks of the "circle of influence", which we have. The basic idea is we have more influence around those closest to us if we spend time with them. The more pulled apart we get by spreading ourselves too thin, the less influence we really have, even over those in our immediate family.

Sharing time and talent is what the community I was raised in did best. We were not perfect people. We made mistakes, but our hearts were always in the right place. Our hearts are with the family and the extended family trying to do for others in any way that we can. If someone were ill, the *Christ the King Women's Club* at the church would fix meals and bring them over until you were healthy enough to cook. If there were a death in a family, the women's club would provide food and help in the kitchen.

If someone were dying after a long illness, people in the parish pitch in and help families by visiting the ill, delivering communion or helping with the children.

Each year, for lent, we would give something up. It's a practice in self discipline that co-insides with prayer and fasting, as Christ did. As you got older and had a better understanding of giving up something and practicing self-discipline, you would find creative ways to share your time and talent with others, as a sacrifice and a way to put on Christ during lent.

Kitty was in eighth grade when PJ Keeley, an eighth grade boy, picked on another kid with a broken arm, playing ball in a field next to *Swan Lake*. Kitty had PJ sitting on the ground and his face in the dirt before he knew what hit him. That's taking up for your neighbor. Ok, sometimes we are misguided, especially, since Kitty had a crush on PJ later that year and he didn't want to have anything to do with her.

I picked a fight with an eighth grader, when I was only in the fifth grade, because he accused my baby brother, Bo, of trying to steal his bicycle. We brothers and sisters can pick on each other, but it doesn't mean anyone else has the right.

Picking a fight is not always the right decision! Thank goodness that Mr. Heckenkemper came along and broke it up. The kid had already hit me in the face and stomach, and I didn't get a swing in yet!

I don't remember where I heard the sermon, which preceded this analogy, but it stayed with me. When God created the world, He said, "This is good!" Ok, so far it's the Bible so it's not plagiarism.

What did he see? If you look at each individual leaf on every tree, you will see a spot or some imperfection. If you look at every tree in the forest, you will see some sign of disease, but if you look from the sky on a fall afternoon at the forest and beyond, with all of its beautiful colors, you would have to say, "This is good"!

I think; God knows we're not perfect. Whoever, or whatever God is, we work together to make a whole, for the common good. Absent of perfection, the whole is still good.

Would you rather do the wrong thing for the right reason, or the right thing for the wrong reason?

Actually, I prefer to do the right thing for the right reason, but that can only happen part of the time. (wordiness) We're not perfect! Now, if that doesn't give you food for thought, nothing will.

CHAPTER SIX

O'BRIEN CULTURE

Kitty was the moral compass in our family. She made sure the girls did not wear too much make-up or wear fishnet hose. She nixed the pierced ears and halter-tops. She flipped out when I shaved my legs for the first time. I was much too young.

I never understood why kids in my class fought with their parents. Still, "man, did we siblings have some fights". I'm talking, pull the hair out and drag 'em to the ground kind of fights. However, no kicking! "Kicking is against the rules!"

As I got older, I talked to Christy and Kitty when I had questions about boys. It was Christy and Kitty I called when I had problems with babies. All of my siblings, I called when I had problems with teenagers!

Daddy put Momma in charge of finances. She kept the books and knew how much money was coming in and how much money was going out. Daddy had one requirement. There would always be meat on the table and at least two vegetables for dinner each night. The rest was up to her.

I see now how she sacrificed and bought little for herself. Our teeth were looked after, but you never saw Momma going to the dentist. She did look after herself throughout each pregnancy and took her prenatal vitamins. She had beautiful hair and nails as a result. She dyed her own hair. Her hair was beautiful and blackest black, with a naturally curly wave. She wore eyebrow pencil and used it for eyeliner too. Momma wore red lipstick and sometimes used her lipstick for blush.

Momma said the most difficult time in her life was when she had four children. She was chasing Ray around the table, trying to hit him with a shoe, "Ray, I'm going to box your ears!" Bryan, Danny and Christy were hiding under the kitchen table pointing and laughing at her.

That was the breaking point for Momma. Somehow, she saw herself through their eyes. She relaxed and began to let us raise each other. If the coats were buttoned crooked, it was acceptable. If our shoes were on the wrong feet, it was not a problem. The world was not going to end. The older children pitched in with the younger children and it became much easier for Momma.

Momma rarely ever had to discipline us. Either she said, "Just wait until your father gets home", or she used good old-fashioned guilt. We knew, when, "Mamma said", then, it was the rule. You didn't question Momma!

I tried a couple of times and had several of my siblings all over me. Momma tried to be fair all of the time, she missed a couple of times, but she was wise and wonderful. We knew she had our best interest at heart, always! Therefore, I guess you could say we lived in a monarchy and Daddy was the enforcer. That's O'Brien culture!

Daddy put Momma on a pedestal. In all of the years I lived at home, I never once heard my daddy raise his voice at my momma. I never heard my parents fight, ever! Daddy would speak of Momma as though she was a queen. She would never allow us to badmouth Daddy either. I knew she didn't always agree, but she wouldn't challenge him in front of us. I asked her one day, why she would not challenge him?

My momma said, "One day you children will be gone and on your own. My relationship with your father is forever. I choose my fights carefully. If we disagree, we will talk about it when we are alone."

Momma and Daddy had a unique relationship. Momma said she tried hard to be the person Daddy thought she was. He made her feel special. She said after wrestling the children all day, she would be hot and tired, at wits end. Daddy would come home and tell her how beautiful she was.

Momma also chose to overlook Daddy's little imperfections.

She said, "Dwelling on the negative only brings out negative." If I dwelled instead on the things I love about him, then those traits become dominant."

She understood Daddy. She loved football and baseball on TV as much as Daddy did. Momma was never a nag, not to us and not to Daddy. She would rather do something herself rather than nag someone else to get it done. Whining wasn't part of her style either.

Momma was from a family of ten children, and so was Daddy. Eleven children was not a result of lack of birth control because we were Catholic. It was a choice Momma and Daddy made before they got married, to have a dozen. They loved coming from a big family and wanted the same for us.

Unlike so much of *Europe,* where they are landlocked and overpopulation is a worry, there was plenty of land in *Oklahoma.* My parents thought it was pleasing to God if they had many children.

My biology teacher made a comment to me once, that having a large family was selfish. I told my Momma and she cried. I guess it wasn't the first time that she had heard this remark.

Momma was raised Methodist, but she converted to Catholicism before she and Daddy got married. She told me she loved the Roman Catholic Church because of their respect for life and the way Catholics handle death and mourning. A funeral is a celebration from death to life with Christ in heaven. We talk to the dead as though they are still with us; not out loud, but in our minds. We ask them to pray for us when we feel we are in need of prayer, which is almost all of the time.

My folks shared with us, their love of the community of *Tulsa,* and they shared their faith. They gave us an education in both and they gave us unconditional love.

Let me ask you, "What else could one ask for?"

What my husband, Paul, and I want to share with our children, are the same morals and values. You belong to a community and belonging matters. You receive love and a sense of belonging, but you also must give back. Living the faith and not just spouting it, whatever that faith might be, is what makes someone honorable.

I've tried to help my children understand, I don't care what community they belong to or what religion they are. Whatever they decide to be a part of, I want them to be involved and live by their convictions. "Live by the rules that you set down for yourself and hold yourself accountable. Never be judgmental! Others must seek their own disciplines and live by those."

Father Dorney, from *St. Pius X,* had a sermon, which he would give to the eighth graders each year at their graduation. He would offer this advice: "Choose your friends wisely," he would say. The idea is to surround yourself with people you respect.

My faith is a large part of who I am and not what I am. I always try to do the will of God, but sometimes over the years, I tried to make my will, His will. I'm still trying to discern.

"How much are we allowed to manipulate in our own little world?" I wonder.

Every family has its' rules. Our family was no exception. Our social order was brought about through regulations, which were understood by all parties. We functioned well most of the time. Here are some of the rules without detail, but I'll give examples to clarify.

1.   *Respect your elders!*
2.   *What Momma says goes!*
3.   *Punish the tattle tail!*
4.   *You must be in before dark.*
5.   *Ask! Don't tell!*
6.   *Don't ask in front of your friends!*
7.   *Don't kick!*
8.   *Don't bite!*
9.   *Don't pull hair!*
10.   *Never kick a man when he's down!*
11.   *A man's only as good as his word.*
12.   *Don't cheat at cards. Ever!*

Then, the Ten Commandments applied as well. In a Catholic family, that's implied. I'm sure my siblings will be able to add a few more of the rules to this list.

Number one; respect your elders. An elder was anyone older than you were. Granny and Grandpa, teachers, neighbors, parents of friends, most importantly, whomever our momma and daddy left in charge when they were gone! That was your elders! The price for not treating them with respect was a boot in the ass!

Number two; what Momma says goes! That means; you asked Momma once and when she said no, and not maybe, you questioned it. Bad idea! One of your siblings called you on it and the result is a boot in the ass!

Number three; punish the tattle tail. I hated that one! I was in about third grade the first time I remember this one coming to bite me. We were all watching a program on TV and it was bedtime. The older kids came up with a plan. We would all go upstairs except Danny. He would hide downstairs in the TV room and finish watching the program so he could tell us how it ended.

I was the tattle tail. I was in trouble with my daddy and my older brothers and sisters. Daddy was actually willing to turn his head and pretend he didn't see Danny. Perhaps he helped hatch the plan. It was a school night and Daddy was trying to get the little ones to bed.

When I was teaching, many years later for the second grade, all things had to be fair and everyone was a tattle tail, I understood! (Important stuff, where someone's life might be in danger, telling was O.K.)

Number four; be in before dark. That was just common sense. If you didn't get home before dark, dinner was gone and there would be no leftovers. "First come, first serve!" Momma made large quantities of everything, but there was never a sure count of how many would be eating on any given night.

Number five, ask don't tell. That meant if you were going to the library, the park, out for ice cream, whatever, you didn't tell Momma you were going. You asked Momma if you could go, and you waited for her reply.

Ask, don't tell applied to money too. Even if it was money you earned on your own, the same rule applied. "You ask before you act!" This was a good rule and I should have held to it with my own children when they were growing up. Money in your pocket makes you very popular, and not always popular with the right crowd.

Number six; don't ask in front of your friend. I found this one to be very difficult. Here is an example. You are playing with your best friend at 8:00 p.m. on a Friday night.

Your friend whispers in your ear, "Ask your momma and daddy if I can spend the night."Then they're looking over your shoulder, to see if you ask.

The penalty for breaking this rule is. You guessed it, a kick in the ass! It would put Momma and Daddy in an awkward position.

Number seven; don't kick. That applied to children only, because how else were you going to get the boot in the ass? It was from Daddy, usually on your way up the stairs, where you were going to have some time to think about which of the rules you just broke!

Number eight; don't bite. I didn't realize the importance of this rule until I bit Patsy and hurt her pretty bad. She had to wear a sling on her arm and it swelled.

I found out years later, that Momma put Patsy's arm in a sling to make me feel guilty and then gave Patsy tons of attention. We both got what we needed. Patsy was in need of the attention, and I was in need of the lesson. Nothing worked better than guilt. Momma could win a prize at putting on the guilt.

Number nine; don't pull hair. That was a good rule because the boys didn't have any hair they wore a burr haircut and we girls did have hair. Anyway, "only girls pull hair and boys would never fight like a girl." (What…?)

Number ten; never kick a man when he's down. That goes along with no kicking as far as we were concerned. If he's down, it was time to pile on and smear his face in the dirt. *(I'm just kidding.)* Really, it just meant; when the fight is over, it is over. Leave the guy with enough dignity he can walk away a loser! (Then you don't look like the bad guy.)

Number eleven, a man is only as good as his word. If you said you were going to do something, you did it. It took too many years for me to understand the importance of this. I am guilty of covering my butt a time or two and am not proud of my misgivings.

Telling the truth in all situations is probably the most important thing I could teach my children. Earning trust after being dishonest is extremely difficult. Living with guilt over a lie can plague you for life. The greatest gift a man can give himself is the respect earned through honest behavior.

Faking sick from work, clocking in on time when you're late and cheating your company is unacceptable. If you're employer cheated you on your paycheck, you would not tolerate it. There should be no double standard here. You owe your employer an honest day's work.

Volunteer work is taken seriously as well. If you say you are going to be there, then be there. People should be able to trust that you will do what you say you are going to do.

Number twelve, never cheat at cards! No one in our family would consider cheating at cards unless it was a joke. That rule covered a great deal at the card table. "No talking across the table," "No putting your hand on your chest if you wanted your partner to bid hearts," "He who takes the trick, he leads", and the list goes on and on. We would put a blanket over the mirror in the dining room when we played cards to prevent anyone from accidentally letting their eyes roam.

In jest, we once caught big brother, Bryan, stroking his thick black hair, while passing the ace of spades under the table between his big toes. I remember another time, while his opponent was in the restroom; he switched card hands with him. His opponent had no trouble figuring it out, because the cards were already in order by suit, accompanied by the "s---- eating grin on Bryans face."

We had lessons on how to give a firm handshake, and look someone in the eye. That we practiced frequently.

Daddy said; "You can't trust someone who has a limp handshake or can't look you in the eye. " Then he explained; you say, "Yes ma'am" and "no ma'am", "yes sir", and "no sir".

Ray learned in the service, you didn't say them with a smile unless you wanted to see the bunt of a gun in your face!

These are another set of rules, I learned on my own while growing up on Newport.

13. *Don't run away from home unless you tell someone first.*
14. *Don't lose your ball in Mr. Dent's front yard.*
15. *Dogs are territorial and they will bite.*
16. *Don't hide it from yourself if you hide something.*
17. *Don't borrow Sarah's shorts without asking!*
18. *Money doesn't grow on trees.*

Number thirteen, this is pitiful. If you were going to run away from home, you had to tell someone first. Otherwise, no one would miss you. Bo and I ran away once with our clothes tied up in a scarf and on a stick, like the hobo's would do on cartoons. We were probably eight and ten-years-old. We made it all the way to *Arnie's Bar*, on 15th, Street. That's about a mile from the house. The Gilpin kids saw us.

"Hey, it's OB's" They shouted, pointing. We ducked down behind a parked car and tried to sneak our way back home before we were missed. We did!

Billy, when he ran away from home, it was a little more serious. He told me through a note he left for me on the car window, at school. He ran away from home in the winter the year Danny died. It was cold out. Sometimes, *Oklahoma* can get cold in the winter. Billy had jumped a train and was headed to God knows where. He got so cold; he hopped off the train to light a campfire. He couldn't light a match to start a fire because his hands were frozen stiff and he kept dropping the match. He recognized the veteran's hospital our brother, Danny, had visited from time to time, in *Muskogee, Oklahoma*. Billy phoned home from there. Ray and Kitty went with Daddy to go and pick him up. I think he was surprised when he wasn't in trouble after they picked him up. We were all just glad to see Billy was ok.

Number fourteen; don't lose your ball in Mr. Dent's front yard. The Dent's had a beautiful garden, but they had no gate in their front yard. When we played ball in the street, it often went into the Dent's yard. Mr. Dent would sit on his porch for hours and watch us play. If it went into his yard, he would overlook it.

He never took the ball until his wife came out. Then, it became important for him to take the ball, and he would not give it back. He would just walk inside the house with it. I think his wife must have nagged him to be mean to us. I can imagine this pile in his living room; three square yards of balls of all kinds, from floor to ceiling.

Number fifteen; dogs are territorial, they will bite. In the first grade, I was walking to school with my big brothers and sisters. We were already a couple of blocks from the house when I realized I left my homework. I ran home, but stopped to pet the neighbor's bird dog. It was the same dog, which my brothers had teased not 15 minutes before.

His name was Champ. Champ wasn't a bad dog normally, but he was protective of his home when he was on a leash in his front yard. Champ didn't want me to pet him and he made his point quite clear.

One of his teeth got a hold of my nose and I ran home screaming! The nose required six stitches at the hospital. It wasn't as if I didn't already have enough scars on my face. I must have spent the majority of my first grade year with a patch.

There is another dog story. I didn't learn my lesson the first time. I had to test the theory one more time. I was introduced by a friend, to a short cut on the way to school. It could have worked beautifully. We climb over a chain link fence from the back, skirt the yard and scurry over the fence in the front. This way one could skip going around the block. You could cut a couple of minutes off your walk to school. One of my friends had shown me this short cut. I forgot the warning that came with the directions. "If the dog's out, don't do it!"

I had Patsy with me. She wasn't a very fast runner; she was only in the first grade. She did distract the dog long enough to get me over the fence, for which I am grateful. Unfortunately, she had to show her bottom to the principal! Momma had to pick her up at school because the bite broke the skin.

Number sixteen; if you hide something, don't hide it from yourself. In my lifetime, it has happened more than once, but the time that made the largest impact was when I was about eleven-years-old.

Jenny Hawkins and I wanted badly to go to the **Monkees** concert with Kitty and Mary, Jenny's big sister. We only had about a month to save $5.00 each, which was a lot of money back in the 1960's. I wasn't old enough to baby-sit for compensation yet. We had to be creative in how we were going to earn our money.

There was a woman who would pay me a quarter to play with her young son, while she practiced the violin for the orchestra. Then, Jenny and I would go around the neighborhood and ask people if we could pull their weeds in the garden for 25 cents. It was getting very close to concert time. I hid my money away in a very safe place. It was so safe I couldn't find it. Years later, when I was cleaning out the kitchen cabinets, I ran across a sugar bowl. Inside, I found five dollars in quarters, wrapped neatly in an envelope marked, **Monkees!**

Number seventeen; don't borrow Sarah's shorts without asking. Shy, quiet little Sarah wasn't as timid as she looked. I found this out when I borrowed her shorts without asking, to wear under my school uniform. She told me to take them off, and I said, "Make me"!

She did! I learned a new respect for Sarah on that day and I didn't challenge her again. She's strong when she's mad. Unlike the dog challenge, once was enough!

Number eighteen, money doesn't grow on trees. We purchased my first new coat when I was in the fifth grade. Up to then, it was always hand me downs. I felt bad when we went shopping for my new coat. I remember we couldn't buy the coat I really wanted. It had a matching dress and was beautiful. We couldn't afford it, and I made my momma cry.

That didn't happen often, so I'm sure that's why I remember it so vividly. We found something I liked which was more "practical", was the word Momma used.

There you have it. Those are the rules that we lived by in my youth and some of the lessons that I learned in the earliest years of my life. These are the rules we understood, right or wrong.

CHAPTER SEVEN

FALL IN OKLAHOMA
AT 1307 SOUTH NEWPORT

*

Each year, when the leaves would begin to change and the fall winds would blow, it rained my favorite colors of reds and browns. This would take me back to my childhood. It was a time when the whole world seemed to revolve around me. I spent little time thinking about how my world would affect anyone else. It was a carefree time in my life.

In the fall, we would spend entire weeks collecting leaves. A mound of leaves, which looked more like a mountain, was our goal. We kids would jump and wrestle around in them, scattering them across the lawn. Then, we would stack them up again, only to repeat the same little rough and tumble.

One year we took the leaves from the entire neighborhood. We were competing with the Sposato family of twelve kids who were trying to build a larger mountain than ours. They lived about three city blocks from us.

Mrs. Sposato taught nursing at *St. John's Hospital*, and she volunteered for the March of Dimes, and Mr. Sposato ran for Street Commissioner of *Tulsa* several times. Once I remember he lost by less than one-percent of the vote. I know he was fighting urban renewal, but that meant nothing to me as a child. I understood there was an expressway, which was coming through our neighborhood. The Broken Arrow Expressway was going to connect from Harvard to downtown and cloverleaf right near our house. One day we would all be relocated.

I went to *Marquette School* with several of the Sposato children. Stephanie was in my class. She was cool and very popular. She had pierced ears and she wore the latest fashion on dress up Friday. One Friday, every month, we could go to school without wearing our uniforms. For a while, I wanted to be like Stephanie.

I honestly don't remember which group won the leaf-collecting contest. We took the leaves and put them under the tire swing in the largest pile I had ever seen. Then, we would swing from the roof and drop into the pile of leaves. By the end of the evening, our hair was full of leaves, eyes felt like sand paper and the nose would be running. If you blew your nose, well you can imagine the mud.

This lasted a few weeks, until the neighbors complained because our leaves were blowing into their yards. They were also beginning to break down and smell a little. We had to put an end to the fun and load the leaves up into garbage bags. There would always be next year!

One of my favorite memories of my daddy was in the fall. If Daddy was preparing dinner, you can bet he was barbequing, and on this particular evening, his choice of meat was chicken. The grill was set up under the oak tree in the backyard, on the patio and Daddy was puffing on his cigar. I loved the smell of Daddy's cigar combined with the scent of the lighter fluid, starting the burning of a charcoal fire. I was taking in the scene, which surrounded me, the colors of fall and the birds flying overhead.

I was pumping on a swing, with the wind sweeping through my hair, forward and back and the blood filling my head. The higher I would go the better the chance of getting that sinking feeling in my stomach when I was coming down. Then, I coasted back to a near stop and lay back so I could observe the bright blue sky. I remember watching the birds flying south for the winter, in huge flocks that seemed unending. If you have ever seen **Alfred Hitchcock's**, *The Birds* (1963), you know exactly what I'm talking about, black clouds of birds.

These birds were so noisy that you could not hear anything else. It was as though all of my senses were heightened. They were teased by this beautiful fall afternoon, just preceding dusk.

That's the memory. Nothing had to be said. We were enjoying the perfect day together. Often, my favorite times were spent doing nothing. It's enough to be there, together, experiencing perfection.

My daddy was a jolly Irishman, with a big open mouth smile. You could hear his laugh from across the room. He laughed a lot. Daddy's bright blue eyes would twinkle when he smiled. When he was a young man, he had a head full of blonde hair, but it thinned early, and most of the years that I remember him; he had a shiny bald spot on the top of his head, where he would try to do a comb over with a long piece on one side.

Daddy was not a small person. He stood about six foot tall. He wasn't a thin man, but he didn't appear to be overweight, other than a bit of a beer belly. He loved to laugh, he loved to sing, he loved to eat, and he loved sports, he loved our friends, he loved family, and he loved Momma.

DADDY LOVED LIFE!

One fall evening we were all gathered around watching **Alfred Hitchcock's**, *The Birds* (1963). During one of the most intense moments of the movie, a commercial came on. Daddy thought it would be funny to pull the fuse and make the lights go out on us. He did! Yeah, we screamed! We got a chuckle out of it.

We screamed even more, when the fuse wouldn't work when he put it back in! Someone had to run to the *One Stop*, (a small grocery store) down the street, for a new fuse! As a result, we missed part of the movie.

In *Oklahoma*, fall starts on September evenings with sweater weather. As the sun goes down, the sweaters come out. Then, the winds kick up and the next thing you know, you are sitting in the bleachers at the football game sipping on some hot chocolate. A wonderful thing about fall in *Oklahoma* is the smell of the leaves and the cool crisp weather.

Now, we call it "football weather". It's just cold enough to see your breath when you breathe out on a cool misty overcast day. My husband, Paul and I agree; fall is our favorite time of year. When we were dating in high school, we would drive in Paul's blue convertible with the top down and listen to **John Denver, Seals and Crofts** or **Neil Diamond**, as loud as we could play it on his eight-track player.

I enjoyed climbing under the stands and playing chase with my cousins under the stadium seats when I was young. Once I started school, I would find my school friends, Becky Gilpin, Jill McCarthy,

Alice O'Brien, Juanita Smith, Camille Quinn, and others, and we would toss a football around and play keep away, or we would strike up a little game of our own.

Before the *Cascia Hall* stadium lights would come on, bats would chase the ball. You could throw the football up in the air, and three or four bats would fly after it. Once the lights came on, the bats would go after insects attracted to the lights.

The Pop Warner ballgames were for the young boys who played football. Those games were early on Saturday morning. Again, we would spend our time playing with friends, not really paying attention to the game. I began to understand the game a little better as I got older and Becky Gilpin, Jill McCarthy, Juanita Smith and I would pretend we were cheerleaders and we would lead the crowd and visit the cheerleaders on the other side of the field.

By mid afternoon, we would be at *Cascia Hall*, watching the seventh and eighth graders. I found those games to be a lot more interesting because I knew most of the players.

By the time I was in the eighth grade, I really was a cheerleader for *Marquette*. *Marquette Meteors* had a great pep club and a good crowd at most of the games. Our pep clubs were as competitive as the football teams.

The best pep club, I hate to admit, was *St. Pius X*. They were organized long before the rest of the schools were. They always had the most school spirit. Mrs. Fairley was the pep club sponsor, and a teacher at *St. Pius X*. Her son, Jim, was very dedicated to his mother and assisted her weekly. She was in a wheelchair the entire time that I knew her, but it never slowed her down. Jim Fairley was my age, he was a thoughtful son, and he and his best friend, John, were always at his mothers' side.

The fact that it was football season was the best part of fall. One year, during the Super Bowl, my uncle Pete would call our phone, (long distance) each time his team, *Kansas City*, would score, and then hang up before anyone would answer. He was living in *Kansas City* at the time. Daddy decided to make sure that Uncle Pete had to pay for his prank. The next time his team scored, my daddy grabbed the phone just as it began to ring and caught him. Daddy's family was always playing games like that.

We stayed up late playing cards one evening with several of the aunts and uncles. At 6:00 a.m., Daddy called Aunt Dodie and said, "Pee call, time to get up and pee." Then he hung up real fast. That silliness went on, often. They were like kids who never grew up. Aunt Dodie didn't think it was funny, but we did.

Halloween was exciting for us when we were little! This was another big happening in the fall. All for the love of candy! You had to keep up with the big kids though, and sometimes you would trip and have candy spilled all over someone's lawn.

Truth is sweets didn't usually last long at our house. If Momma did the big grocery shopping on Saturday, the candy or cookies would be gone by Sunday. Pre-sweetened cereal at our house wouldn't last more than a day or two. We would go through our ten pounds of oranges in a week.

Halloween, my brothers would decorate the house and hang ghosts in the trees. They would dress up in scary costumes and try to scare kids that came to the house. We would trick or treat until we could not walk anymore. Then, we would all sit in a circle and trade things we didn't like, for things that we did.

"I will give you my Snickers Bar for two Smarties!" That was the kind of trading. Then, I would eat all of my candy in a couple of days and make myself sick to my stomach.

Sarah would save her candy and eat just a little each day. It was always so hard to watch her. She would have to find new hiding places for her candy to keep the rest of us out of it. She would do the same thing with her Easter candy. It was torture!

Sarah was quiet and reserved, very shy. She and Patsy looked like twins. They both had blonde hair and were thin, but their personalities were the difference between night and day.

Patsy had a temper and could growl like a lion. If she didn't want to hear what you had to say, she would cover her ears and make noise. She had the emotional strength of a lion as well. She persevered through college and became a Respiratory Therapist, and then went back to school to become Anesthetists.

Patsy was the cutest baby I had ever seen. She had brown eyes the size of nickels and a little Pug nose. When she was little, Patsy could not pronounce her L's. Her favorite book we called, "Look, Look the

Clown Book". Pronounced, "Wook, Wook the Cwown Book". Our favorite page was the L's, "Wittle Wions Wike WoWipop's".

We thought she was going to be the last baby. We had five girls and five boys. Momma had problems giving birth to her and we all thought Momma was done making babies.

That was not the case. In November of 1964, our mother went into labor early with child number eleven! You can't imagine the excitement! The possibility of having another baby in the family had us all abuzz. With the household divided with five girls and five boys, the girls were pulling for a girl and the boys were pulling for a boy. Naturally, we didn't want to give a majority to the opposite sex. The baby was also the tiebreaker on the number of blue and brown-eyed children in the family. Her eyes were brown. I had brown eyes, my oldest brother, Bryan, had brown eyes, Danny had brown eyes, and the youngest three girls had brown eyes. Her real name was Donna Kay, but since she was born between Halloween and Thanksgiving, we called her Punkin.

I was too young to understand the danger that Momma's life was in when she delivered the "preemie".

I was also too young to appreciate the fact; we almost lost little Punkin, weighing in at four pounds and five ounces. She lost weight at first. We wouldn't get to bring Punkin home until she reached five pounds.

The hospital had a rule back then; unless you were twelve-years-old or older, you couldn't go to see the new babies at the hospital. Daddy arranged with one of the sisters at the hospital to bring us up the back staircase so we could see the new baby at a time when the hospital wasn't too busy. When they held little Punkin up in the window you couldn't imagine the excitement for us. Then, a closer look revealed the tears welled up in Daddy's eyes. He was so proud! He was proud of every one of us!

While Momma was in the hospital, we kids sat around the dining room table, with crayons making get well cards for her. There were cards with pictures drawn of dirty dishes piled to the ceiling and "hurry home" written on them. There were cards with dirty diapers drawn in piles to the ceiling saying, "Hurry home". Looking back, I'm not so sure that this was good incentive.

It was when we children were sitting around the dining room table making the cards, that Punkin got her nickname. She is really named after my aunt Donna, Uncle Les's wife. Aunt Donna was Momma's ride to the hospital. Punkin's middle name was Kay. She was born on my cousin, Kay's birthday. Christy wrote a card asking when Momma was bringing the Pumpkin home. Some of the other children followed Christy's lead, and how the spelling changed, I'm not so sure. The name Punkin stuck!

Our momma decorated the house for every season. Fall was no exception. She had fake flowers, mostly mums and leaves which she would bring out and put on the mantel and in strategic places around the house. She would put Halloween decorations on the windows and we had an Advent wreath and a turkey centerpiece that came out after Halloween.

I felt something electric in the air the first time I would come downstairs in the fall, and all of the decorations would be out. There were enough of them to give the room a different feel. The fall colors would give me a warm sensation. To see the seasonal changes could bring a lump to my throat and a tear to my eyes. Momma was always good at setting the mood for the next holiday.

She would set us down at the table with paper and crayons and have us draw pictures to decorate the refrigerator and picture window, Halloween pumpkins and witches, turkeys drawn with five fingers spread across the paper. Then, Christmas cards hand drawn that showed the house all decorated or a beautiful Christmas tree adorn with multi colored lights. They were projects to keep us busy so she could get some things done and to give us practice in art.

Momma's sister, Sue, was a very good artist. Momma thought that eventually one of us might just take that road as well. She once told me that she thought I was going to be the one. I scored well in school at art, music and creative writing. Everything else was a struggle. We didn't have any music in high school, but we put on a musical each year and I participated in those.

The artistic side of my brain definitely worked the best. There's always someone better, but there's always someone that's worse. In math, I doubt there was anyone who was worse. Creativity was always my strength!

One Halloween, when Punkin was about four, she had a great time and felt that she had the trick or treat thing down to an art form. Punkin took herself trick or treating for a week after Halloween, dressed in her beautiful costume. The neighbors thought it was so cute they would give her something each time, reinforcing the behavior. Finally, one of the neighbors told my momma what was going on. Momma was so embarrassed she wanted to crawl into a hole. We all got a good laugh out of it.

Thanksgiving was interesting with a family our size. I remember one year when we tried to pull all of our family including the extended family, Granny and Grandpa, aunts, uncles, and cousins, together at one place. We rented a room at *Henthorne Recreation Center*. The women cooked while the men watched the ballgames on several TV's, which they brought in. We kids had fun, but it was far too much work on the women.

I liked our traditional Thanksgiving, when we would watch the parades in the morning and help my momma make the cornbread stuffing. She would put the cornbread into grocery sacks and we would knead the bread into tiny crumbs. When we were done, we would take our sacks into the kitchen, to Momma.

Then the football games came on and we would all watch the games together in our little TV room on Newport. By the end of the evening, Momma would be so tired she couldn't keep her head up. She tried to watch TV. She would fall asleep and her head would jerk when she would wake herself up. We called it the "Hoyt thing". When we would visit Momma's family, Grandma, Uncle Possum, and Aint Jo, they all did the same thing.

We would laugh, "Look at Momma! She's got that Hoyt thing going on!"

The new school year always started in late August or early September. I would be excited for school to start. I couldn't wait to see who was going to be in my class and who my new teacher would be. You would have to check the list on the door to see if your name was on it before you entered the classroom. They were good at keeping the information quiet so the results would be a surprise.

Each year started out easy, because we would be reviewing last year's work. I was never in the smart class. I struggled with reading, and I struggled with math. By the time I was entering the fifth grade, I was tested in the public school system for classes I would be taking the following summer.

There was always someone to help me with my homework. We used flash cards and played a game called, giant step to math problems. The rules were; you could take a giant step if you were the first one to get the answer correct when Daddy would hold up the flash card. I would get beat by my little brother, Bo, every time. Humiliating! Bo's a professional engineer now, so I don't feel as bad as I did back then.

I especially struggled with reading. My teachers were concerned because in middle school, the amount of reading doubled and I might not be able to keep up with my class. I had my eyes tested to be sure I didn't need glasses. I had to go to the public school to be tested for learning disabilities. Then, the year between the fifth grade and the sixth grade, I had to go to summer school.

The idea of going to summer school was degrading to me. I would have to go to a public school. Public school was an unknown entity and the thought of it caused me a great deal of anxiety. I would not know anyone. I would have to walk from the public school to Granny and Grandpa's house and wait for my daddy to get off work before I could go back home. I was expecting this to be the worst summer of my life.

This did not turn out to be the torment I had prepared myself for, at all. It was the best summer of my life. I went back to school with a mischievous streak, but I had found a piece of myself. I was an individual for the first time in all of my eleven years of life, I felt special.

Summer school lasted only half of the day and it seemed easy to me. I was finally going to school with children who were further behind than I was, or were at least at my level. It gave me confidence. By lunchtime, I was headed to Granny and Grandpa's house. It was only a few blocks from the large red brick school to their home. I would carefully cross the busy street, Lewis where *Perry's* food market was located. I would walk one block and turn left on North Lewis Place. That's where Granny and Grandpa's one story, white house with the big front porch was located. It was only a two-bedroom house, but the yard was big, and they had a clubhouse in the back.

Granny prepared a hot lunch and we would sit at the table and eat lunch together, usually just the three of us. I especially loved when Granny would cook homemade sourdough bread. Their whole house would smell like bread when I arrived. It was Daddy's favorite, so Granny would make a loaf and send it home with me, for Daddy.

Granny explained to me, that when she made bread, she used a starter. A starter was what she called the yeast that she would split and share with my Aunt Norma. Then, Aunt Norma would make bread, split the starter and send half back to Granny. The yeast would die if it sat too long, so they had to keep it going.

One time, I remember Christy and Kitty came to pick me up because Daddy was unavailable. Granny had made an extra loaf of homemade sourdough bread for Daddy. We took it with us in the car, but it smelled so good, we couldn't resist.

We started out, just eating a little. Fear of being caught made us rethink. Hmmm!

We might have a problem if we come home and Daddy's loaf of bread is not whole. Maybe if we eat the whole loaf Daddy will never know.

Granny called to see how Daddy liked his bread.

Ooooops!

At lunchtime, on any given day, my uncle Dick, uncle Les, or my uncle Bill would drop by for lunch at Granny and Grandpa's. Sometimes, I would get to see my cousins too. The best days though, were when it was just my grandparents and me. I had them all to myself.

I did however enjoy when my cousin Kay came and stayed one time to keep me company. Kay was the sweetest and most generous person I knew. If you gave her a dime, she would spend it on you. That's just the way she was. She went to *Marquette* and was a grade under me. Kay had long black hair and she was very tan. I was a little jealous of her, because she was much prettier than I was, but I loved her because she was my cousin, and she was so nice. She always included everyone when we would play. Granny made us mashed potatoes and groovy gravy for lunch that day. Groovy was the big word at the time. We ate roast beef and peas. This was my favorite meal. Then, we helped with the kitchen and followed our granny out to the garden. There I could show Kay what an expert I was at watering and deadheading the flowers.

Grandpa and I would sit on the porch swing and watch the birds splashing in the birdbath or eating seeds from the feeders in the yard. Grandpa knew I didn't like the blue jays because they were mean to the other birds, but I thought they were pretty. He would tease me and tell me he was going to send all of the blue jays to 1307 South Newport, where I lived! Grandpa had a bird book. We would look at it from time to time to help identify birds, which we were not familiar with by their beaks or tails.

He was funny and always made me feel like I was his favorite. If you were sitting on his lap, he would tell you that you were his favorite. Come to find out, he said that to all of us. That's O.K., even knowing this was the case we still appreciated the attention.

Granny liked to work in the garden, and I liked working in the garden with her. I would help her water and plant. She taught me the difference between annuals and perennials. Granny showed me how to propagate begonias and wandering Jew. In her backyard, she had an old tire. Inside the tire, we planted wandering Jew. The beautiful purple vine crawled over the sides of the tire and the tire kept the weeds from getting in with the vine.

Along the fence, she had planted daylilies that bloomed orange flowers all spring. They spread across the entire north side of the fence. Granny and I had to divide them to keep the blooms coming the next year, and we planted the ones we divided on the north side of the clubhouse.

In her pots, she planted begonias. She said that she never had to buy new ones because she would start new plants from the old. She showed me how to snap the cuttings at the node of the plant and put them in a glass of water. The roots of the cutting began to pop out within days.

Granny gave me leaves from her African violets to grow a plant from one leaf. I thought it was remarkable. She showed me what kind of food they required to grow and to bloom. I filled the kitchen window at home with all of my beautiful new plants. I would win a ribbon at the school science fair with my plants the following year.

The time I spent, one on one, with my grandparents proved to be some of the most precious days of my childhood. My grandparents were very special to me. They still have great influence on the person I am today. Now, when I work in the garden, I feel my grandmother beside me. I take her with me wherever I go. Granny treated me special and helped me feel I was someone special to her. I think she prays for me even now.

Summer school had other benefits as well. I took a speed-reading class and other reading classes, which helped me get caught up with my class. I wasn't alone. James McCullough and Jim Leonard were in my class at *Marquette*, and they had to go to summer school too. We became good friends.

The following fall, at the beginning of the new school year, I was much more self-assured. In summer school, I was mostly with public school kids, some who were further behind than I was. It helped me to feel like I was not stupid. There was hope for me yet.

The public school children were not as well behaved as the children I went to private school with. They taught me it is sometimes O.K. to talk out. I could be playful with the teacher especially if I was the one sitting in the front row next to the teacher's desk. That's where I made the choice to sit for the next three years of school. I loved being close to the teacher because I became more involved in the conversation that way and paid attention much better.

Another benefit to spending time at Granny and Grandpa's was getting to know my Aunt Dodie better. She and my uncle Larry lived in the house across the street from Granny and Grandpa and had three children at the time, Pete, Billy and Paul. TJ and Robyn would come along a little later.

Aunt Dodie and Uncle Larry drove a Red 1964 Mustang, with bucket seats. I thought it was the coolest car I had ever seen. She was up on the latest fashion and music. She was just cool!

Aunt Dodie was the youngest in Daddy's family and was closer to the ages of Bryan and Danny. She became my mentor. She took me under her wing and gave me guidance in my teenage years. I think every teenager needs an adult, who's not one of his or her parents, to help give guidance in these difficult and impressionable years. She was easy to talk to and she listened well. She could give advice without sounding preachy.

I became the babysitter for Aunt Dodie once I hit my 13th birthday. She trusted me and had confidence in me and she worked hard on helping me with my self-esteem. I would spend the night at her house and then she would buy jelly-filled doughnuts for breakfast in the morning before she would take me home. Sometimes we would go shopping or out for a burger. It was sad for all of us when Uncle Larry was transferred and they had to leave *Tulsa*.

Life is unpredictable. You could feel it in the air; much like the changes in the colors of the leaves, change was coming to our lives. There was a new season upon us.

CHAPTER EIGHT

INAPPROPRIATE LAUGHTER

♫

"What is inappropriate laughter?" asked Lori, my brother Bill's wife, when she saw the chapter I was writing in this book. Billy said, "I bet she's writing about laughter in church, or passing gas in the TV room full of people."

That is a fact! That would be inappropriate laughter. We have been guilty on both counts; but this chapter is on subject matter of a more serious nature. For whatever reason, we have never learned to take life seriously. In this chapter, you will learn, inappropriate laughter is a curse on the O'Brien family.

My oldest brother, Bryan's, first Christmas, Momma and Daddy asked him what he wanted Santa Clause to bring him. All he wanted was a Christmas tree. Bryan's love for Christmas decorating didn't stop with his first Christmas.

Putting up the Christmas lights on the house became his responsibility. The lights would go up after Thanksgiving. All of the windows and the eaves of the house he outlined with multi colored lights. Our Christmas tree was located in a prime spot, centered in the picture window. It had the steady lights, but then the tree also had lights that would twinkle.

Bryan took great pride in his work. One year, he made a large tin foil star, and he outlined it with lights and put it in the center of the house above the first story. Our house was the prettiest on the block and it was visible from 13th, Street by all of the passers by.

Each baby, over the years would bring the Christmas tree down at one point or another. Baby would crawl up to see the pretty lights or ornaments and grab a limb to pull up, bringing the tree tumbling down. We would have to keep the plastic ornaments within the grasp of the crawlers and not the breakies. Patsy, I believe gets the prize for sacking it the most. She was an active crawler and kept her guardian angel very busy.

When Patsy was a baby, she would climb to the top of the stairs and cry for someone to come and get her. She didn't know how to make her way back down the stairs. She knew one direction only, which was up! We responded as quickly as we could when we would hear her wailing at the top of her voice, but she tumbled down a time or two.

When Bryan went off to college, we failed to put the lights up right after Thanksgiving. I was experiencing a little anxiety. It was time for the lights to go up and it didn't seem to be getting done.

I asked; "Momma who was going to put up the Christmas lights, now that Bryan is gone?"

She handed me a hammer. Sometimes that's how Momma spoke. That would be my new job. Momma was probably waiting to see who would speak up about it first. I got a hammer in my stocking that year for Christmas. It was Momma's way of letting me know that she was passing the hat.

Our Uncle Possum, from *Louisiana*, would always send each of us $5.00 for Christmas. He did this every year for as long as I can remember, until we all had children of our own. Momma appreciated it as much as we did. She knew it would give her hours with no kids in the house.

We didn't keep the money to spend on ourselves. We would walk down 13th, Street, and Elgin, Ave., to *Ziggler's Catholic Book Store*. They also sold medals, crosses, rosaries and pictures of our patron saints. We bought presents for each other.

Christmas was never about presents with us. It was about being together as one big happy family. There was a Spirit, it lived within us and we could share it with our neighbors, friends and family. We celebrated the birth of Christ by spreading love and cheer.

Then, we would all file into church. We were never early enough to get a seat. The church is always full on Christmas Day. We were standing in the back trying not to laugh at Punkin as she entertained us. Daddy was holding her and she couldn't stop making cute little sounds. Daddy took his hand and placed it over her mouth, and she kissed his hand.

Punkin was getting away with things clear up into high school by using that technique. It's hard to be mad at someone who is happy and smiles all of the time. Ray had this mastered as well!

The Christmas music would come out right after Thanksgiving. We listened to **Johnny Mathis, Nat King Cole, Bing Crosby** and **Frank Sinatra, Perry Como,** among others. Then, we would make and decorate cookies, fudge, peanut brittle, divinity and more. We would fill the house with the scents of the season. Momma would bring out the winter clothes from the basement and we would go through the hand me downs to see what size was going to fit this year.

Each year, as far back as I can remember, we would spend time practicing Christmas carols. We would go caroling several times throughout the season. Momma would buy special clothes and shoes for us to dress up in for our tour. We would begin on the twenty-second or twenty-third and carol friends and neighbors one day. Then, on Christmas Eve, we would go to Granny and Grandpas and sing for them. As the family grew, we had to take several cars from house to house. We would practice singing our songs on the way. If the roads were icy, it could be difficult. I don't remember a year when we didn't make the effort.

Daddy figured out when we kids were very young, if you were going to have several children in the car at the same time, you needed to have organized noise. Otherwise, it would be nothing but fighting and chaos. That would not be a pleasant experience for anyone!

Any time we were going to be in the car for any length of time, the repertoire of songs came out. The family began learning songs when Christy went to kindergarten, and she would come home and teach the songs to us. Our list of songs began there and never stopped.

From the time I was quite small, I remember loving to sing. Momma would play records from movie musicals and theater. We would dance and sing the songs. I loved when Daddy or Danny would pretend to be **Dean Martin**. "Everybody Loves Somebody Sometimes!"

I remember Daddy teaching us how to dance an Irish jig in the kitchen on Newport. He actually showed us a few ballroom dance steps as well, just for fun. Daddy was a good dancer and had a great voice!

It's amazing that in a family of thirteen, we could all keep pitch. As we got older, we learned two and three-part harmony, each of us teaching the other what we were learning at school.

We thought we were going to be the next **King Family**. If you were raised in the Sixties, that would mean something to you. They were a family our size who had their own musical variety show on PBS. Their musically inclined family ranged from little children to senior citizens.

One year, the boys thought it was no longer cool to sing Christmas carols anymore. They joked around and were not being very serious. We were all laughing and carrying on. This is inappropriate laughter! Momma and Daddy did not appreciate the hilarity of the situation.

Ray had a New Year horn. When we sang our song, "Little Drummer Boy" and it was time to sing, "Purr-um-pa-pum-pum", Ray would blow the horn and we would all laugh and giggle.

Daddy got so mad I thought his big blue eyes were going to pop right out of his head. You could see the veins in his forehead bulging out. His face was as red as a beet. Daddy took the horn and he stomped on it, breaking it into a million little pieces.

We showed up at Uncle Pete and Aunt Kathie's house. There were two packed carloads of us. We tried to be real quiet. We snuck up to the door. We lined the youngest children up at the front, closest to the door, so they could be seen. "Shhhh"

All dressed up in our Sunday best. We knew all of the words to the songs and sang full voice. We had practiced "Little Drummer Boy", because that was Uncle Pete's favorite Christmas carol. Then, when everyone was ready, Daddy gave the signal to ring the doorbell.

"Come they told me, Toot Toot Toot Toot Toot!" Man was that the wrong thing to do! Ray had a second horn in his pocket, and he pulled it out at just the right moment! We laughed in the middle of the song and Daddy was as mad as I had ever seen him.

We had to laugh! Ray was the jokester. Uncle Pete and Aunt Kathy were laughing! I think Daddy being so mad is what made them laugh the most!

The folks did make it clear, the show would go on, and the boys best take part and do it right, or else. They got past their embarrassment and negativity and we never had the problem again.

Another year, I remember Momma cried. Ray was going off to the Marines and she knew in her heart, times were changing. We would never be together, all thirteen of us again in one place singing our songs. Momma wasn't far off. Little did she know, when Ray came home, it would be for Danny's funeral.

Winter can get cold in *Oklahoma*. A few of the freezes would require you to leave the water dripping and to take special precautions not to let the pipes freeze. Many cars would have a difficult time starting when the weather was too cold.

Some years we would get snow, and it would stay on the roads for a week or so. The roads were slick and cars would have a difficult time getting out of downtown *Tulsa*.

We would go to the bottom of 14th, Street and push motorists, east, up the hill to keep the traffic moving. We had cardboard, boards and bricks to put under the tires if they got stuck. It was fun for us to do things for other people, they were always very appreciative; but in reality, mostly, it was amusing for us. It was dangerous too, but we were kids, and we didn't recognize danger when we saw it.

Ronnie Hunt got a sled for Christmas one year. He was good to share it with us. We had fun taking it to the top of the hill at 14th, Street and sliding north down Newport, toward 13th, Street. 13th, Street didn't have a lot of traffic in the afternoons. It was a one-way street and headed west, toward downtown. 14th, Street was one way headed east, out of downtown *Tulsa*.

The boys always had to make things a little more dangerous than they had to be. They would ride the sled on their bellies until the last minute and just before they were going to hit the car parked at the curb in front of our house, they would roll off the sled and let it go under the car. They would save themselves, like a **James Bond** movie, just in the nick of time.

Ronnie raised his head up a little too late. He smashed into the car and bloodied his nose. He took his sled back across the street to his home. The sad thing about it is that we probably laughed. We laugh when someone gets hurt. I don't understand why. It's like watching "Americas Funniest Home Videos", thirty years before its creation. Some would call this inappropriate laughter!

One afternoon, Billy jumped from the roof to a limb on the old elm tree in the front yard. The idea was to swing the legs up and shimmy down the tree. Billy was dangling from the tree by a limb, about roof high. Ray was down below, visiting with Edith Penix, holding Sammy the black cat, as usual.

Ray said; "Billy, you are going to fall!"

Billy swung his legs to grab the limb.

Ray shouted, "You're going to fall you dummy!" The limb snapped; he fell out of the tree and hit the brick ledge below.

Ray laughed, "Billy, do it again!"

Billy scraped the bone on his shin on the cinder ledge. You can imagine how painful it was. Ray picked him up, and he took him inside so that Momma could nurse his wound. Billy's leg became infected to the bone, and he almost lost his leg.

Ray is not alone in his laughter toward accidents, which are actually not funny. To this day, I still have to fight the urge to laugh when someone gets hurt. Inappropriate laughter is a curse. I have however been on the receiving end of the laughter. I can still have a sense of humor about it.

There was a young man, probably in his thirties, who lived in the corner house of 14th and Owasso. We would walk by everyday on our way to and from school. He always had a pencil and a pad of paper, and he would stand in the front yard. If we said hello, he never responded, but he kept going about his business.

We would often guess at what he was doing.

"I think he writes down the license plate numbers of people who are speeding". I guessed.

"No, I think he's an artist, and he's making sketches". Jenny would say.

Who knows what other speculations we made about him? He was very quiet. His facial expressions never changed. Perhaps he was deaf. It was kind of creepy.

I was in about sixth grade, walking east, along 14th, Street, toward Peoria, Ave. on my way to school. I was reading a book; holding it about waist high, and I was not paying attention to where I was walking. I bumped my head into a pole supporting a no parking sign. The sound was either a Ping or a Thud!

My instant reaction was to raise my head and to straighten up. "Ooofff!" I crammed the book into my stomach, and it knocked the breath out of me.

This caused me to bend, grab my stomach, and again, bang my head into the same poll. "Thud!"

Creepy was laughing so hard I thought he was going to fall to the ground. From that day forward, he always smiled when I walked by, and he gave a little wave. I call that, "inappropriate laughter."

My teacher, Mrs. Smerker, would have called it "Rude, crude and socially unacceptable." She said that a lot. Every school has one teacher who all of the children are terrified of. Ours was no exception. Mrs. Smerker wanted the classroom so quiet, "that you can hear a pencil drop!"

She's my favorite teacher to this day. Make sense of that! She pushed us; she was strict, but she also believed in us, and she encouraged us to be leaders. She talked me into running for President of the Student Council, encouraged me to sing in the school talent show, and she helped me with my science fair project. I began to succeed at some things. While some people are self motivated I was one who needed a push from behind, for fear of failing. She held the cattle prod.

Fear is no longer a problem; I've worn so many hats I can't remember what all I've done. It's why I needed to write Hopes n Hats. So that I won't forget my successes, failures, and the lessons I've learned along the way. …The memory is beginning to fade.

We've all had our embarrassing moments. We can laugh those off. Actually, if you're an O'Brien, you can laugh at almost anything. It's probably our way of not having to face the reality of a situation or the negative feelings, which may have ensued.

One day, I remember, Bryan, with his handsome and youthful face, he practicing how to throw a shot putt, in the house. He would let it go and catch it all in one move. It was a great trick, until he missed, and he hit the mirror.

That was funny!

Christy threw a dart from the top of the roof when we were visiting at Granny and Grandpa's house. Bryan was the target, at ground level, and the dart stuck into his leg. I'm sure it was funny for some of us, but it was not funny for Bryan. "Ouch"! You can bet our momma and daddy didn't think it was very funny.

You didn't want to do anything bad in front of Granny and Grandpa, because Momma and Daddy would give it to you twice as bad, once on the spot and again on the way home.

Danny fell asleep on his paper route while riding his bike. They found him sleeping in the bushes. I'm sure it was funny to those who found him. Another time, he put hot dogs in the oven to cook and fell asleep on the couch. They burned so badly that the kitchen was covered in ash, all the way up to the ceiling. Daddy made the girls clean it up. (In hindsight, I wonder if this may have been an early symptom from Danny's illness.)

Kitty did a cheerleading kick in the living room, in front of the mirror. She was wearing her blue and white gingham, tight dress, and she pulled her other leg right out from under her. She landed on her tail. That was funny!

We gave Bo a nickname for a while, "The Bull". He charged at someone, and his target moved. He put his head through a window, and he broke the glass. It's amazing how we could have survived our childhood.

Inappropriate laughter is our greatest flaw, and yet, that laughter is what gets us through the toughest times. Other people look at us and are bewildered by our ability to deal with crisis and pain. Laughter makes it tolerable, but we still have to deal.

In the early 1970's, the neighborhood began to change. In the night, you would hear big trucks. If you looked out of the window from upstairs, you would see flashing lights, and a house on the back of a truck. It would be driving slowly toward the west, escorted by police motorcycles. Slowly, the houses around us were being vacated. Any morning you could wake to another empty lot on the block.

Christy, she had a special place in the front yard, up in one of the old elm trees. This is where she would take a pillow and a book, and she would hide away to relax, like a bird in a nest. It was a great place to go to observe what was going on around the house, without actually having to participate. There, Christy could read, and she wasn't bothered by any of us kids. Furthermore, Daddy would not see her sitting and find some work for her to do. Out of sight, out of mind!

There must have been another place for her to hide in the winter. Without leaves on the trees, I doubt she was hidden well enough, we would have found her with a snowball or two.

In the midst of a huge thunderstorm, the walls of Christ the King Church protected us. As Student Council President, I gave the graduation speech to my eighth grade class. "We are unique, made up of every person, every event which we have been exposed to…"

My whole family came to the graduation. When we returned home, the storm had taken down a huge limb from the tree in the backyard right where Danny always parked his car. If he had not decided at the last minute to join us for the graduation Mass, he would have been without transportation.

I graduated from *Marquette* in May of 1971. Kitty graduated from *Bishop Kelley* the same year. There would be a lot of stress and change in our lives over the next few years. It was in October shortly after the start of my freshman year when we lost Danny. We moved from the house on Newport the following summer.

Christ the King Church protected us from life's storm as well. The words of my graduation speech took on new meaning. We had all taken a piece of Danny with us, and the exposure to his courageous exit from this life would help to form the unique character in each of us today.

CHAPTER NINE

OUR LIFE ON JOPLIN
MORE INAPPROPRIATE LAUGHTER!

☺ ☺ ☺

There is a timeline in my mind. It helps me keep track of the years of my life and the happenings around me. I divide it, not by decades or years, so much, as by where we were living at the time that an event occurred.

Momma and Daddy seemed happy with the offer that they received from the City of *Tulsa*. It wasn't easy leaving our home at 1307 South Newport, especially knowing our home was being destroyed. We knew the day would come. Still, most all of my childhood memories were in that house. Playing in the leaves, climbing the trees, jumping from the roof, sunbathing in the backyard, making mud pies with Kim Powell and telling scary stories, all are memories now.

One evening, I drove to 1307. The house was gone. I found a piece of a puke green brick, and I picked it up. It was all that was left of my home. I looked to see if among the debris I would find the doll that my brothers threw down the chimney or the necklace that I got for my birthday. It fell behind the mantle piece above the fireplace. I looked for something, anything that would take me back to a simpler time.

The trees were still there. I stuffed the green brick in my jacket, and I climbed the tree. There I sat in Christy's nest, and I cried. A good cry always had a way of making me feel better.

I wondered, what's going to happen to our neighbors, the Powell's, Fetters, Garrets, Hunts, the Scotts? What about Jenny, my best friend in the whole world, what about Danny, he's frozen in time as a 23 year old. Would we be able to carry the memories with us or would we allow our pain to cause us to leave him buried in the rubble of 1307?

I took the ugly green brick with me. It's a reminder of who I am and where I came from. Today, I use it for a paperweight. One of my most treasured possessions.

Our home on Joplin had a circular driveway and a two car garage; it had plenty of room for the number of cars that we were accumulating with all of the kids who were now of driving age. The house was Spanish. It had bay windows and a wrought iron entry with outdoor lighting. It was a single story dwelling, built in an L shape.

When Danny passed away, he had the American flag draped over his casket. The Marines presented it to Momma in a ceremony at the cemetery. For Christmas, the year before we moved into the house on Joplin, Billy surprised us with a 50ft flag poll, so we could fly the flag proudly at our new home.

The pole was in three sections. Each screwed in to the next section. We had to have the fire department come out and put the last section on for us, with their tall ladder. They did it gladly. We flew the flag proudly for all of the years we lived on Joplin. It was right in the middle of the yard surrounded only by the circular driveway.

Inside, there was a terra cotta entryway, which opened to a formal living room. The view from the front entry was straight out to the backyard through a sliding glass door, which was in the formal living room. Momma purchased new furniture, two light blue velvet chairs and a yellow and blue velvet floral print couch that coordinated. On the wall, behind the couch, was a black velvet seascape painting Danny's girlfriend Judy brought back with her from *Mexico*, as a gift to Momma.

The house had a formal dining room, tucked away, between the formal living room and den. Behind the table was a picture of the Last Supper. We didn't use the dining room table on Joplin the way we did when we lived on Newport. The kitchen had a small dining area. That table got the most wear.

We had TV cable boxes, and we were one of the first neighborhoods to get cable TV in *Tulsa*. One was in Momma and Daddy's bedroom and the other was in the den. I missed Daddy when he got a TV for the back of the house. I liked it best when we were all watching together in the small TV room on Newport.

There was a sliding glass door in the den, which led to the back patio, and across from it, was the sliding glass door to Momma and Daddy's bedroom. It was a nice layout.

By the time Sarah made it to middle school, she had learned to hold her own. She was no longer shy, she certainly was not afraid of Patsy; I can remember her having me on the floor in a headlock a time or two. She didn't scamper after sandwiches for Bo, or any body else.

Sarah and I would share a room at the new house on Joplin. We had a king size bed with matching side tables and a triple dresser. Momma purchased them new and they actually matched! The set was Mediterranean, which was a popular style at the time. The entire house was air-conditioned, and it had white carpet throughout.

Bo's room would be near the kitchen and garage door. He had a bathroom right outside of his bedroom door. No longer would Bo have to fight for his right to eliminate!

All of the other bedrooms were on the other end of the house. The girls would share a bathroom. It was plenty big enough for our curlers and curling irons. Momma and Daddy had their own bathroom in the master suite. We felt we were living like royalty. Our neighborhood had a swimming pool, and it was just a couple of blocks from our house.

Most importantly, we were only a mile from *Bishop Kelley High School,* and I was going to be a sophomore. The Bullock family of nine children lived just a couple of blocks away. Jenny Bullock and Sarah became best friends, and Sarah even had the opportunity to go on vacation with the Bullocks over the summer to visit their relatives in *Mobile, Alabama.*

I babysat on most weekends, and I had an occasional date. I met my first love, Rodney Rounds, my sophomore year, and I lost him my junior year. Rodney's feelings for me were not the same as the feelings I had for him. It ended up being a blessing, because through Rodney, I met Paul. Paul is my heart and soul.

Our lives were far from normal on Joplin. Things were happening fast after Danny died. In this family, life always follows death. We had a population explosion!

In August, Bryan and Debbie had a baby girl. They named her Stacy. She had dark hair and brown eyes, like Bryan and me. She looked more like me than she did her own mother.

Christy and Dink had a baby boy before Christmas. Todd was a strong healthy baby. He was holding your fingers, and he was standing with support, a week after he came home from the hospital.

Dina got pregnant, and Billy and Dina got married in the dining room of our house. It was an informal ceremony with just family. They had a baby girl, born one day after Danny's birthday in July. Billy and Dina named their little girl, Diane. Billy graduated from high school, joined the Marines, and they left *Tulsa*.

One morning, I woke to get ready for school. I went in the bathroom to plug in my curlers; there was a note on the mirror, which I saved. I still have it in a file today. Ray had been promoted to Sergeant, and De was pregnant! She would give birth to a boy, and they proudly named him Ed, after Daddy. I can't tell you how happy this made Daddy.

Little Ed was born in June of 1973 and his sister, Sheena followed just ten and a half months behind him, on Bryan's Birthday, April 21st.

Life for the next few years was babies, babies and more babies. Less than two years later, here came Shelly, Jess, and Little Billy. Christmas was wonderful!

The family got so large that it was not possible to keep our traditional Christmas caroling going in its original form. There were too many of us. Daddy, in all of his wisdom, started a new tradition. We had a huge Christmas caroling party; invited all of our neighbors, friends and relatives, present and past on the 23rd of December, leaving the 24th and 25th for individual families to do their own thing.

The Powells, the Wrights, the Fetters all of the old neighbors came. Everyone brought cookies, fudge, or something to contribute to the party. We sang every Christmas carol we knew, some of them more than once. Then, we sang the songs from our childhood, like *"Oklahoma."*

We're on the fourth generation now. Many of our neighbors, friends and family have passed on. They are brought back to us in our memories on the 23rd of December, a day that will be planted in our minds, as familiar as the 25th.

One time, some of the cousins were at the Christmas party and were not taking the singing seriously enough. With Momma and Daddy now long gone, I made it clear that the show would go on. Take part, do it right, or else. They probably laughed at me, the way Uncle Pete and Aunt Kathy laughed at Daddy.

To this day, the caroling is the highlight of our Christmas. My children will tell you, the Christmas music comes out after Halloween, and music doesn't stop until after the Epiphany.

Paul and I began dating in October 1973. I fell in love with Paul easily, because he listened! He validated my feelings, and he explained things to me if I didn't understand them. He didn't laugh and make me feel stupid. Paul was a master communicator. He still is!

Until I met Paul, life was always about the guy. Most guys love to talk about themselves. Not Paul, he was different. He was uncomfortable if I bragged on his accomplishments in front of people. He downplayed himself, where most guys make themselves sound better than they really were.

If we were going to a movie, Paul would ask what I wanted to see. If we were going to dinner, Paul would ask where I wanted to go. He made a real effort to be considerate of my feelings. He treated me as if I was someone whose opinion mattered!

I got up at 4:00 a.m. to catch a bus for a wrestling tournament in *Miami, Oklahoma*. It was winter and very cold. We had an ice storm the night before. I went out to my car, and Paul had scraped the ice off the windows and mirrors. Paul got up, came to my house, and he had my car ready to go. That's the kind of thoughtful person he was and is.

If I lacked self-confidence, Paul would build me up. He believed in me. He truly knew me. He knew my interests, my talents, my positive attributes, but he also knew my annoying habits as well. He didn't mind trying to help me mend them, but always in a thought out way that was respectful of my feelings.

My mother fell in love with Paul, because he was the first person in my life who knew how to handle my excessive personality. I could be a real pain.

One night we were watching TV, and I kept teasing Paul, as if I was going to pour coke on his head.

He said, "Don't do it!" "I don't get even, I get ahead!"

"I had to test him!" I thought. "That was like a dare."

We had chili for dinner that night. The pan was in the sink soaking with a little soap in the water. Paul dunked my head in that nasty greasy water.

Well, there were several other tests along the way, and I found that Paul meant what he said. It's one of the many "Huberisms" of today. (Huberisms are a list of things that Paul says often.)

"Paul doesn't get even, he gets ahead"! Anyone who knows him knows it's the rule.

Paul say's what he means, and he means what he says. He expects the same from you. If you make a promise, he'll hold you to it. That also means being places on time!

One night Paul and I were visiting in the front yard. We noticed the neighbor across the street had just returned from a date, and she was giving a goodnight kiss to her boyfriend. There was someone passing by on a bicycle who was so interested in the couple kissing, he hit a parked car going full speed. You can imagine his embarrassment when he realized we saw the whole thing.

His wheel was bent he would walk his bicycle home, limping away sheepishly.

We spent a lot of time visiting in the front yard. It was less hectic than inside the house with TV's, the stereo, telephones and my younger sisters. They were at the age where they were always trying to show off for Paul, and they could be a little obnoxious.

June 8, 1974, is a day recorded in the history books if you're from *Tulsa, Oklahoma*. If you were living in *Tulsa* at the time, you know where you were on June 8, between 4:20 p.m. and 5:50 p.m.

School was out for summer break. Paul stopped by after work. We were standing on the front driveway, watching the storm clouds. There were thunderstorms all around us, but where we were standing, it was dry. The state of *Oklahoma*, known for its exciting weather, was especially electrifying that spring. On this day, there was a lot of wind, and you could feel the pressure dropping. The dark clouds had a tint of green to them.

Daddy drove up, and he was commenting on the fact that the storm was approaching from a different direction than normal. He pointed out funnel clouds and various phenomenon's', which were beyond my knowledge. I wasn't sure he knew what he was talking about, because I thought that maybe he was teasing me. I was trying to talk Paul into staying until the storm blew over.

Daddy said in a rather excited voice, "See the cloud dipping down? It looks like a woman's breast with a nipple, and the nipple is dipping down? Oh, it just hit the ground! It turned black, that's debris!"

I'm laughing, thinking he's just trying to scare me. Right, we're standing out here watching a tornado. The tornado sirens went off! That was at 4:20 p.m.

I ran into the house and the TV was already on a channel with the weatherman pointing to the various storms surrounding the city. That day several tornado hit *Tulsa,* one F2, one F3 and two F4 tornado's from 4:20 p.m. to 5:40 p.m. The worse storm related event in *Tulsa*'s history.

Daddy did know what he was talking about, because several severe storms were hammering *Tulsa.*

Another stormy day, in May, approximately one year later I came very close to breaking up with Paul. It was my senior year and I had senioritis. I was spreading my wings a bit and felt Paul was too controlling. I told my momma I almost broke up with Paul.

Her reply surprised me, because it was so unlike her to say anything that would encourage or discourage a relationship. She looked me straight in the eye; got very serious and said, "That would be the stupidest thing you ever did in your life". She knew Paul brought out the very best in me.

It was no secret. Everyone knew Paul was good for me. Mrs. Short, my Art and Creative Writing teacher told me we were the subject at a teachers meeting. My grades went way up after I started dating Paul. Paul was born with a gift of motivating people.

I was a senior in high school when Daddy announced there was going to be a curfew of 9:00 p.m. weekdays, and 10:00 p.m. on weekends. In my world, if Daddy laid down the rule, you didn't question it.

Paul thought this was unjust and wanted to know why Daddy was putting a curfew on us. We didn't do anything to deserve it. What was his reasoning?

I tried to explain to Paul, that you don't ask why, you just obey! That's just the way it is at my house. Paul wanted to call a meeting with my parents.

"What! Are you crazy? You don't negotiate with my folks. You do what they ask and you don't question!"

Next thing I know, we're in the living room with Momma and Daddy having a Po wow!

I have an even better understanding now, than I did then. Still, the talk really opened my eyes to what my daddy was going through at the time. Decisions he had to make, which I know must have been difficult. Perhaps, they were decisions as difficult as pulling the plug on Danny!

Daddy was having many sleepless nights. He needed the family to be in early, with less for him to worry about. Perhaps he could catch a little sleep here and there. He had some decisions to make, which were going to affect all of us.

Paul and I negotiated for later hours on the weekend and 10:00 p.m. on the weekdays. I was stunned. Whoever thought you could negotiate with Momma and Daddy?

The communication opened up a new understanding, an adult relationship with my parents!

In addition, Momma and Daddy treated Paul and I to dinner at a fine restaurant one evening and explain the decision they made.

They were selling *Oklahoma Steel Castings Company*, and Uncle Les and Uncle Jerry wanted my daddy to buy it with them. Daddy had to do what he thought was best for the family considering that we still had so many mouths to feed at home. He decided the best thing was to accept an offer for a job he had received from a company in *Jacksonville, Florida*. They were leaving *Tulsa*!

I'm glad that my uncles bought the company. It was so much a part of the past for our family. Daddy had 35 years in at *Oklahoma Steel*. The decision must have been tearing him up inside.

Having an adult relationship with Daddy was so different. I didn't have that childish fear any more. It was like seeing him as a person for the first time. Daddy showed a softer side that I wanted to learn to know better.

Paul and I had our first prom together. It was Paul's Senior Prom, in 1974. I was one class behind him and graduated in 1975. Paul wore a red velvet tuxedo with a black velvet collar. We had a great time with several of our friends that night and ate at a fancy restaurant. Until I dated Paul, I had never been to anything nicer than *Sizzling Sirloin*.

After the dance, we all went out to *Keystone Lake* for a romantic evening under the stars. *Keystone Lake* was about a forty-minute drive from *Tulsa*. We had permission to break curfew for the special occasion.

The following year, Paul was a college student. "College students are poor. They have no money."

I would say these words hundreds of times to myself and to my children in the coming years.

Paul was committed to paying for as much of his college education as he could. His parents were willing to supplement anything he could not pay for. He spent one summer roofing an apartment complex, another summer he would work construction. One year, he worked at *Flo Bend*, doing foundry work.

When he came home for Christmas or holidays, he always had work lined up. I remember him working 12-hour shifts and sleeping on many of our dates. We played a lot of cards, because it was free entertainment. Christy and Dink were our card partners most often.

The first year that Paul and I dated, he drove a beautiful blue **Buick Electra** convertible. This was his parent's car, and when he went to college, the convertible went to his brother, John.

Paul purchased a car from a friend, Tim Hogan, for $80.00. The transmission didn't work, and it needed a new carburetor. The floorboard was eaten through, rusted out. The gold, **1964 Ford Falcon** station wagon was missing the rear window, and the window on the driver side would not roll up. Paul would have it all in working condition before he went to college the following year.

Paul and I were both good at not spending money. Daddy understood that. He had an appreciation for what we were going through.

For my senior prom, there was no tuxedo. Paul wore a suit. We still made it special, but not without the help of my daddy. Daddy cooked our dinner. He sat a formal table in the dining room, with a white tablecloth and candlelight. He cooked us a steak dinner and served us a five coarse meal, as though he were our waiter. I can't say how much that means to me, today.

Though I can't remember if we took him up on the offer, he offered his car. No one got to drive the company car. This was special.

One weekend in the winter, snow was falling. Paul was headed back from *Norman* on the turnpike. He had to roll the window down to pay the toll, and the window would not roll back up. Paul would have to make the two hour drive with the window rolled down. When he arrived at my house, he was freezing. The moisture on his eyelashes was frozen.

Our romance was not the only one blooming at the time. Sarah was dating a young man, Stan Hoffmann who was a year behind me. He also was a student at *Bishop Kelley*. Stan played football and baseball. He ended up with a scholarship to *Tulsa University* in baseball. They would carry on a long distance relationship for several years.

I can remember when Stan flew down to *Jacksonville, Florida* for Sarah's homecoming. He flew down for her prom. He made a great deal of effort to keep the relationship together. Sarah dated other guys, but always made sure that whomever she went out with knew that she had a guy she was committed to in *Tulsa, Oklahoma*. When she graduated from high school, she moved back to *Tulsa* and got a job.

Kitty decided to move in with Granny and Grandpa for a while because Grandpa could no longer drive. Granny never learned to drive and didn't have a license. They didn't have a washer and dryer, and they would have to go to the laundry mat. They also would need someone to take them to the grocery store and to Mass on Sunday. If Kitty saw a need, she was one to fill the slot.

Kitty would date a lot of fellows in that time, but Granny was scrutinizing each and every one of them. She quizzed them on the phone and in some instance's she told them Kitty wasn't home, even if she was. If Granny didn't like them, they didn't have a chance.

Then, Kitty was asked out by a really great guy who we all knew very well, Russell Otterstrom. Russell was Danny's best friend in high school. He had always been a close friend of the family. He was often present at the card table, Charade parties and Jeopardy parties at Christy's apartment. He was older than Kitty by several years and came from a family of nine children.

Russell was a quiet guy. He was often a spectator. When we lived on Newport, he would come into the living room and sit. Then, he would just observe the coming and going.

Russell would go over to Granny and Grandpa's house, and they would play cards together. Russell has a great laugh. He gets pretty tickled with Kitty especially when Grandpa was around because Grandpa would tease her and play tricks on her. He would hide things from her in plain sight or move something just to see how long it would take her to notice.

While Russell was courting Kitty, she was still accepting dates from other guys. Granny didn't mind telling Kitty she thought she was crazy.

"Russell is the one! Why are you wasting your time with these other Bozos?

One night, while Kitty was getting ready for a date with Russell, Granny was lying across the bed visiting with her. "Do you want me to ask Russell what his intentions are?"

"No way!" Kitty said.

Later that night Kitty told Russell what Granny said, and they both got a laugh out of it.

It wasn't long before Kitty had a ring on her finger. (Who knows, maybe the nudge from Granny helped.)

Momma was trying to keep the house clean so she could sell it. She was sewing and making the dresses for the Brides-maids for Kitty and Russell's wedding. She was stressed, probably as bad as I had ever seen her.

Debbie, Bryan's wife, had left her contacts in overnight, and her eyes were burned, so Momma was babysitting Stacy and Shelly. Daddy was already living in *Florida* and praying Momma would sell the house and join him soon. He was really missing Momma and the family.

This was a really difficult time for Momma. She would be packing the house and moving to *Jacksonville*, by the end of May. She would be saying goodbye to her children and grandchildren, moving to a place she had never been before.

I was employed at *Metropolitan Life Insurance Company.* Mr. Don Lyons was my boss. He was a decent man and treated me fair. We would become good friends.

Daddy was living in *Florida* at the time, but he was home on a visit, and I would receive a call at work. Daddy was asking me to come home. He wanted to talk to me before he went back to *Florida*.

I explained; Daddy, I can't leave work. It's against the rules to leave unless you are sick or dying!

A few minutes later, Mr. Lyons came to my desk. He had tears in his eyes. He told me that Daddy had called; I had special permission to go home for as long as my conversation with my daddy would take.

Daddy said it hit him; they had not focused on how this move was going to affect me. Daddy offered to let me move to *Florida* with them. It must have been tough for Momma and Daddy. I suspect they went through each child one at a time, beating them selves up for breaking up the family.

It was nice that Momma and Daddy offered. It had not even crossed my mind. I was focused on a life one day with Paul.

CHAPTER TEN

SOME HAVE MORE, SOME HAVE LESS,
IT'S A FACT OF LIFE!

≤ ≥

It was May of 1975, when I graduated from high school. By the following May, the family had moved on to *Florida*, and I was self-supporting. I never had to borrow money from the folks the entire time I lived on my own. I'm grateful for that, but I bet they were even more grateful.

I was living in a one-bedroom apartment. I didn't own much. I owned a couch that folded in to a bed. I purchased the used red and green floral couch for 300 dollars from Momma and Daddy. Paul, my brothers and brother-in-laws will tell you; it was very heavy! Their backs had to lug the awkward couch up two flights of stairs. I also had a black and white TV, which picked up two channels, given to me by Russell. The windows of my apartment were lined with my African violets and Boston ivy.

Paul and I were concentrating on a future together somewhere down the road. He was going to school in *Norman*, two hundred miles away. I would be proving my independence while waiting until I could one day be with him.

My job at *Metropolitan Life Insurance Company* was secure. It was steady pay. I had medical benefits and life insurance. That was enough. Anything else was icing on the cake.

My first automobile was a 1967 Buick Le Saber. I paid 300 hundred dollars for it. It looked more like a big silver tank. It was safe! It was paid for. Who could ask for more?

I would wake at 5:00 a.m. each day. In the winter, my car needed a dipstick heater left in it overnight, to keep the oil warm; otherwise, I couldn't get the car to start in the morning. The extension cord ran under the front door, out to the parking lot. Then, I had to unscrew the wing nut on the air filter. It covered the carburetor. I would lift the air filter, spray ether into the carburetor and start the car. Sometimes it took more than one try.

On days when the weather was below 0 degrees, it could be rough, because my hands would be cold. It was hard to work the wing nut with gloves on.

While the car was then warming up, I put the air filter back on, wrapped up the extension cord and locked up the apartment. Then, if it was icy, or snowy, I removed the ice from the windows, mirrors and windshield and, I still managed to get to work by 6:00 a.m.

Paul taught me how to take care of my car. It had a bad oil leak and I needed to add oil on a weekly basis. He also taught me how to change a tire, which I would have to do twice that winter. One time, it was in the snow, after work and in the dark! "Burrrrrrr!"

On the very weekend that Momma and Daddy loaded the car and drove to *Florida*, *Tulsa* was flooded! It was the worse flood in 500 years! Thank God, the folks got out of town before things got really bad!

Someone had parked in my parking spot in the raised parking lot. I had to park on the street. As a result, my Buick got flooded! Water got in the transmission, and I had to purchase a used transmission to get it running again. Paul helped me find someone who would get me used parts, and the guy did the labor for me for free. The smell of the mildew in the car was enough to make you nauseous.

"I really don't feel sorry for myself," is what I thought, "There is always someone who has more, and there is always someone who has less! It's a fact of life!" I will take that lesson to my grave.

In this case, it was Christy and Dink who caught the worst of the 500-year flood. Christy and Dink's house at 4th and Mingo got flooded! A boat came to rescue Christy and the boys from their front porch. Once the water receded, there had been several feet of water in the house. Their insurance would only cover the dwelling. They lost everything!

Billy and Dina had just moved back to *Tulsa*, living in the *Mingo Apartments* near Christy and Dinks house. They lost their brand new car in the flood! Dina was visiting with Christy while their children played together. They watched from the living room window as Dina's car floated down *Mingo Creek!*

I had used all of the money I had saved over the last year moving into my apartment; spending it ondeposits on utilities, the first months rent, and on the red and green couch, which I purchased from the folks.

I still had 200 dollars in my account for an emergency. I just didn't realize the emergency would be a transmission on the first day my momma and daddy left. I was feeling a bit anxious.

When I went to the laundry mat to do my laundry, I broke down, and I cried when I realized I didn't have enough money left to put fifty cents into the dryer! A stranger came along and gave me some change. Fifty cents and I'll remember that stranger for the rest of my life!

Here I was, living alone for the first time. I was very proud of what I had accomplished so far. I was getting a lot of overtime, working from 6:00 a.m. until 6:00 p.m., and I would save as much as I could, for a rainy day. I purchased gas and groceries. I allowed myself ten dollars a week for lunch and breaks at work.

The only thing that was still unsettling was eating alone. In a short period, I had gone from eating with a family of thirteen, to eating in a quiet little apartment, all by myself.

I made chili, or gumbo, and I froze them in one serving Tupperware containers. I made spaghetti sauce and sloppy Joe, and froze them in Tupperware containers. I got three different meals from boiling a chicken. I skipped lunch and ate ½ grapefruit and oatmeal for breakfast.

My friend Donna Jones would feed me on weekends when Paul didn't come home. We would play cards at her house with her husband Lloyd and his friend Fuzz. Many times, I would spend the night with Donna and Lloyd, so I didn't have to warm up my car or spend gas money driving across town. I would have been driving back to Donna's the next day anyway, to play another round of cards. Donna and Lloyd's children, Tommy and Tammy were kind enough to let me bunk in one of their rooms.

My favorite night of the week was Monday night. I would go to Granny and Grandpa's for dinner. Then, we watched my favorite TV show, <u>Little House on the Prairie</u> (1974). Granny gave me a little brandy for a nightcap after dinner. Then, she shared with me, stories of the past, and filled me in on family gossip.

Granny taught me how to cook. She was a very good cook and made healthy, well-balanced meals. Granny used to be a cook at *St. John's Hospital* so she really knew what she was doing. She was very health conscious and tried to see to it that Grandpa ate well too.

Granny would tell stories of their days in *Kansas*. She and Grandpa survived the Great Depression and the dust bowl. The old homestead is still there in *Kansas*. Many of my daddy's cousins are still living in *Great Bend*.

Granny gave a vivid description of what it was like to live in *Kansas* during the eight-year drought. They would push towels under the door to try and keep the dust from coming in the house. Still, she would have an inch of dust accumulated overnight. There was lightning in the sky, even though it wasn't raining. After a long struggle, the family lost the farm and moved to *Oklahoma* looking for work. It's hard to imagine 500,000 American's homeless. Their story of survival is an inspiration to me.

CHAPTER ELEVEN

TRUE LOVE!

♥

Divorce is not for Sissies. Our family would have to endure three divorces, within a few years after the folks moved to *Florida*. Momma said that moving to *Florida* would make it or break it. She was right!

Bryan and Debbie had three children, Stacy, Shelly and Danny. They would split, and Debbie had custody of the children.

Christy and Dink split; they had three children, Todd, Jess and Clint. Christy had custody of the boys.

Billy and Dina split. They had three children, Diane, Billy and James. Dina had custody of the kids.

I'm not going to dwell on the negative in divorce. Everyone had their own pain to work through and lessons they would learn along the way. I can say every marriage and divorce has an effect on many more than two.

The positive, was there were three fabulous children from each of the three marriages. All of the children have both a mother and a father who love them very much. They also have involvement and advice from their aunts and uncles on both sides of the family whether they want it or not, but it was given with love.

Ray had to go to *Japan* for a six-month term. This is a reality of military life, sometimes families are separated for long periods of time. De, Ed, and Sheena came and stayed in *Tulsa* so they could be around family. I got to know De better during that time. With all of the divorce and heartache going on, I suspect she wished they had stayed in *California*.

We didn't see each other real often. I was working too many hours. When we did visit, De impressed me with her worldly knowledge. She was always learning, reading, and she was improving herself. It was from De that I first heard the analogy of life being like water.

When water is moving over rocks and hills, it is clean and fresh, supporting life. If water doesn't move, it gets stagnant. Stagnant water gets diseased and smells. I like that analogy. I agree it is important to keep feeding the mind and to keep growing as a person spiritually, into the best that we can be. If we refuse to think, grow or change, especially in mind and spirit, we will whither away.

This will be the most difficult chapter to write. Paul is a very private person. He doesn't like me sharing old love letters with the kids, or exposing his inner most feelings. Out of respect for him, I won't go there.

I will however, expose the things I love and respect the most about him in the stories and experiences I share in this book. We are as different as night and day when it comes to left versus right brain. Spiritually, we are on the same path, trying to bring out the best in each other.

My senior year, we wrote each other everyday. I'm sure it was a security thing. The next year, we wrote when we had something new or interesting to say. The more secure the relationship felt, the less we needed the daily communication. The third and fourth year, we rarely wrote each other at all.

Paul phoned me on the weekend if he was not coming home. He usually came home every other week, unless there were finals coming up. Then, school came first, always!

We share the same values, our faith, family, community and country. We both value education, though how much took convincing. Some of the smartest people I know never got a college education.

I have since learned that education gets your foot in the door. Then, you have a better chance of proving yourself.

We enjoy each other's company, but respect each other's independence as well. My strengths are Paul's weaknesses, and his strengths are my weaknesses. Together we make a pretty good team.

Paul and I took a summer vacation and drove first to *Houston*, to see his sister, Kathy, who had settled there; then, we drove to *Florida*.

It was the first time I had been out of *Oklahoma* other than to go to *Kansas, Texas,* or *Louisiana.* It was a long drive. We stopped in *New Orleans* along the way and visited the *French Quarter.*

When I clicked my heels and saluted a police officer as we were walking toward our car, Paul convinced me that I had had enough to drink. We headed back on the road again the next day.

The drive through the panhandle of *Florida* was the toughest part of the trip. The trees all look the same, the road has no bends or curves, and the ground is just flat. I don't know how Paul stayed awake. He had to get out of the car and walk around to stretch his legs and wake up a little, several times. The road has a way of hypnotizing you. Rolling down the windows helped some.

I was getting anxious to see the folks. When we turned up the street toward their house, I wasn't sure what to expect. There was Daddy, waiting for us in the front yard with that big Irish grin on his face, and his baby blue eye's twinkling. As I got out of the car, he plucked a magnolia blossom off of the tree, and he handed it to me. It smelled so good.

I walked inside, and immediately I felt like I was home. "Home is where your Momma is", I said.

It was so comfortable. The school Bo, Sarah and Patsy were going to was *Bishop Kenney High School,* the same red and white BK, and Punkin was going to a Catholic grade school, *Assumption.* They had new friends; a new support group but they went to Mass on Sunday and had their new routine. Bo was wrestling, Patsy was cheerleading, and Sarah was knitting. (She was always the domestic one.)

Punkin wanted to be called Donna, the name she was now being called at school. Nope, she's still Punkin to us. She had given up the Barbie dolls, and she was beginning to show interest in boys.

Daddy declared; "An O'Brien Holiday" in our honor. Punkin, Patsy and Sarah went with us to *Disney World.* Bo had finals that week and chose to go to school. I saw the ocean for the first time. Daddy took us to *Mayport.* We saw ships and aircraft carriers, and we collected seashells to take home with us.

The backyard at Momma and Daddy's new home in *Jacksonville* had a patio with a swimming pool. It had a diving board and a slide. They had a eucalyptus tree, bottlebrush and several pine trees. They must have been two hundred feet tall. Momma and Daddy had come along way from the little house on Vandalia.

I taught the dog, Butkus, to swim and ride around on the rubber raft in the pool. This was something that Momma wished I hadn't done. She said that after I left, they were forever trying to keep the dog out of the pool. The filter kept getting clogged with dog hair.

Butkus would play hide and seek with us. She knew everyone's names well enough that we could hide; we would tell her who to go and find and she would find the correct person. I guess she was using her nose and following the scent. I wasn't raised around dogs, so this was remarkable to me.

This was my first trip to see the ocean. It was magical. We took some bread from the day old bread store so that I could feed the seagulls. Seagulls were special to Paul and me because we had recently read the book, purchased the **Neil Diamond** album and seen the movie, *Jonathan Livingston Seagull* (1973), which expressed a freedom to strive for perfection.

I have pictures of us playing on the beach, feeding the seagulls and collecting shells. I have pictures from our first trip to *Disney World* and all of the magic that goes along with that. Still, the thing about the trip that I recall most vividly is the picture in my mind, of Daddy's wide smile and the magnolia blossom.

Paul and I dated 5 years before we got married. We went through counseling with Father Tom Hildebrand and Pre-Canna classes through the church to prepare us for marriage. I was impatiently waiting for him to finish school and still working at *Metropolitan Life Insurance Company*; we called it "Mamma Met."

For a year or so, I worked two jobs. Sandy Bardsley, a friend of the family helped me get started. I sold *Mary Kay Cosmetics* on the side. I made enough money that it helped me put away what was needed to pay off the business loan to purchase the cosmetics, and it helped to pay for my church wedding.

The last year before we married, I moved in with a roommate, Shavian Brennan. She was a friend of ours, from the group, which we ran with at *Bishop Kelley*. Sharing expenses also helped me to put some money away. We had some really great times together. Sometimes it was stressful, as with any roommate situation. Still, we shared so many of the same friends over the years; it was fun to see who was going to show up at the door on any given weekend.

Spring break was great. One evening we stayed up learning how to do the "hustle" and the "bus stop," (popular dances of the late 1970's), while listening to Shavian's **Boz Scaggs** album. I was ready to listen to anything but **Fleetwood Mac**, and Shavian was ready to listen to anything but **Barbara Streisand** or **John Denver.** We usually took turns putting our music on the stereo because our taste was so different.

Another evening was spent driving out to *Keystone Lake*. All of the old high school friends were in town for spring break. Our apartment was large enough it became the place where everyone would meet.

Donna Jones and Kitty each had wedding showers for me. We registered our china, but that is all most people registered back then. Then, we received about four Presto Hamburger Cookers and enough towels to last us ten years. It was better than Christmas, opening all of the wedding presents and the girls made a hat for me out of the ribbons and bows.

At last, the day finally arrived. Paul's mom and dad, Rita and AJ had the rehearsal dinner for us at the *Candlewood Club*. We had a lovely dinner, and then the rest of the evening was spent on the dance floor. They invited the entire family to the dinner, rather than just a chosen few.

It was important to me that Paul and I have a big wedding. Big back then was nothing compared to big today. We had a wedding cake and punch with mints and nuts on the table. There was wine and beer. No open bar or catered food like you would get at a big wedding by today's standards.

Instead of having flowers at the altar, we borrowed two large ferns from a woman in the parish and placed them on each side of the altar. My wedding colors were peach and green. The Bridesmaids, dresses were floral, rather than the typical one color. The style looked like something out of the 1920's, long and flowing with a ruffle at the bottom and they tied around the waist. The Bridesmaids, Donna Jones, and my sisters, Sarah and Patsy, carried single roses, and my bouquet served as my going away corsage. The Paul and his groomsmen, Jeff Dalton, Tim Mackin and Paul's brother, John, wore tuxedos that looked almost black, but were actually dark green, to offset the green in the girl's dresses. They wore carnations in their lapels.

Momma and Daddy made sure I understood that if they were going to have to drive or fly all the way from *Florida*, that I would have to pay for the wedding myself. It was smart; there is no better way to keep the costs down. I borrowed my wedding dress from a friend.

Gerald Bullock played the guitar and sang **John Denver** songs at the wedding, with *Annie's Song*, which we considered to be, "our song" as the highlight. The organist was late, so he had to play them more than once. I am sure it was a nightmare for him. I was so happy; I could have cared less whether things were going to plan. Liz Dodd, (angel voice), sang the *Ave Maria* and I was finally a "Sadie". *"Sadie, Sadie, married lady"*, a quote from a song in *Funny Girl* (1968). I was practically dancing on the altar when Father Tom pronounced Paul and me as man and wife.

Momma looked beautiful when she arrived for our wedding. You could tell she was tired when they left *Tulsa* for *Florida*, just a couple of years before. She had a beautiful tan and she had lost weight. Momma said they had joined a gym, and she was working out.

Momma wore a long baby blue gown with a matching cape in the wedding. The cape covered a broken arm. Momma, hurrying down the hall with her stocking feet, slipped and broke her arm. It wasn't the first broken arm she's ever had. I think this was the third. Looking back, maybe she was a klutz. Not really, just kidding, she had osteoporosis from having so many children.

In *Tulsa*, Momma was a member of a bowling league, back in the 1960's. She got a trophy for most improved player when she began using her right arm, after a cast came off. That arm she broke when she fell off of a ladder in the basement on Newport, while organizing our hand me down clothes.

Momma and Daddy surprised me and pitched in on our wedding reception. It was much appreciated! One detail that I forgot to take care of was a clean up crew. After the wedding, Paul and I had to come back to the reception hall in our wedding clothes to clean up and sweep. Billy took over, and he sent us on our way.

Our first stop was at *Lepley's* for a car wash. Paul wasn't one to let shoe polish sit on the car and perhaps ruin the paint. Then, we headed off to find something to eat.

We forgot to make reservations for dinner, and we couldn't find a place without a long waiting list. We went to *Mondo's Italian Restaurant.* It was appropriate. That was our favorite restaurant, and it was affordable. *Mondo's* was a restaurant, dealing mostly in pizza. They had an informal salad bar with the best balsamic and vinaigrette dressing in town, if you like that kind of thing. It wasn't a big place. They had one area set up where they would show silent films on a large screen, usually the old **Laurel and Hardy** clips, or the **Three Stooges**.

When we showed up in our wedding attire, they asked if we were "just married".

We told them, "yes" and, they laughed.

"You're our second couple tonight."The waiter pointed across the room to another couple that was a little overdressed for the red and white plastic table clothes. That night I was served the largest dish of lasagna I had ever seen.

Paul's sister, Karen, was able to get us a room at the prestigious *Camelot Hotel,* in *Tulsa.* She was working there, with her degree in hotel and restaurant management. The suite was lovely. I hid in the bathroom in my beautiful white nightgown, waiting for room service to hurry and bring up the corkscrew. I didn't want to ruin Paul's surprise. It was a long wait!

The next day, we drove to *Grand Lake* and a cabin on *Monkey Island.* The cabin belonged to someone who Paul's mother often worked with at her office. After a few days, Paul's family joined us, and we went boating and swimming.

Then, it was back to reality!

Grandpa's health was declining. He had emphysema; he could barely make it to the mailbox on the porch and back to his chair in the living room. He stayed in his chair; watched TV until dinner and, then he would saunter back to his chair.

I don't think he could hear very well, but he wouldn't admit it. Granny thought it was selective hearing. It drove her crazy. Granny and Grandpa would argue over every little thing, but it was funny to listen to them. I think they argued just to fill the time and keep from being bored. Sometimes, it made me uncomfortable, since I had never heard my own parents argue about anything.

It wasn't fast. Grandpa's health was on a downhill slide over the next year. I learned a great deal in that period of time. Often people would look for the perfect gift to bring when they came to visit. Someone bought a lambs-wool blanket so he wouldn't get sore sitting in the same place for a long period of time. That was a great idea. He got beautiful sweaters to keep him warm. He had poor circulation and would often get cold. Then, there were coffee table books with beautiful pictures. There were many good ideas, but if you didn't have something special in mind, there was nothing more valuable than your time.

When you have accumulated possessions for eighty years, there is only so much that one can fit in a house. It took some thought to come up with something that he didn't already have. If he needed it, he already had it.

I can't take credit for the idea that sprung between Kitty and me. The aunts said it was wonderful and made the day really special. Grandpa's birthday was coming up. We wanted to get something that would improve the quality of the day. Even if it was only one day! We found a girl who dressed in Traditional Irish clothing; to go to the house, sing a couple of Irish songs and deliver a happy birthday bouquet. The girl delivering the bouquet touched by the situation when she got there, she stayed and sang every Irish song that she knew.

My aunts were all gathered around to help Granny take care of Grandpa. He was bed bound in those long days that preceded his death. I tried to keep a little distance, knowing that his children were there, and he needed rest. Everyone did get a chance to go and say goodbye!

I was touched when Paul's mom and daddy, Rita and AJ, came to Grandpa's funeral.

Our presence during the difficult times is as important as our presence during life's happy moments. Perhaps it is even more important, I thought.

I received so much from my grandparents, in the stories and lessons that they shared with me over the years. Mostly, I learned to enjoy the company of elderly people who were much wiser than I was!

I thought, "Even with so very many off spring they had enough love to go around!"

Two weeks before school started, I went to Main, Street in *Norman, Oklahoma*. I found a job at the first place that I applied, *Red Carpet Real Estate*. It was right next door to the unemployment office.

Our first year together was priceless! Paul would have dinner ready when I got home from work. There was one evening that he had night classes. Other than that, we spent the evenings together, usually relaxing and watching the TV by candlelight.

We were a little fanatical about OU Football. We still are! **Thomas Lott** was the quarter back for OU, he was known for wearing a bandanna in the ballgames. I would drive around with a bandanna and a magic marker in my glove box, just in case I ran into him on campus. Then, I could ask for an autograph.

I did find myself complaining halfway through the season. Game day was Saturday, Pro games on Sunday. Then, there was Monday Night Football. We would watch the replays of the OU game and the Barry Switzer Show. There were interviews with **Kenny King** and **Billy Sims** on the Today Show. The straw that broke the camels back, was the Thursday Night Addition to Monday Night Football!

"Ahhhh!" "Momma, how much is too much!" I was complaining over the phone.

Momma made a comment that I have never forgotten and appreciate to this day. "Can you imagine a life without football? What if he wasn't interested?"

Football had been a part of my life for as long as I could remember. "I would hate being married to someone who didn't want to watch sports."Once again, Momma was right!

I don't complain anymore! I'm addicted to football, basketball, golf, even baseball if it's playoff season! Thank God, I married someone who enjoys the things that I enjoy!

Still, there are some things in life that I enjoy, and Paul does not. He gives me the freedom to get involved and never complains if I'm not home. This has given me the opportunity to wear a different hat with every move we have made. Paul makes enough money; I haven't needed to work for the past fourteen years. It has afforded me a chance to try my hand at just about everything that interested me.

I'm trying to learn to keep the arm down long enough to let someone else have a chance to volunteer. I go into meetings with my hand stuck under my buttocks now! Still, I do have the opportunity to be as creative as I want to be.

Paul's rule has always been that I could do anything I wanted as long as I didn't volunteer him as well. I tried a couple of times. It didn't work.

After our first year in *Norman*, Paul graduated from *Oklahoma University* with a degree in Civil Engineering. He had several interviews with engineering companies and oil companies, mostly in *Texas*. Paul accepted a job in *Tulsa* for *Dresser Engineering*. His daddy, AJ, saw an ad in the paper and sent them Paul's resume. It was something close to home. The company had about fifty employees.

Paul worked as a civil engineer. He worked from eight to five, five days a week and sometimes we would meet for lunch with friends at a place across from the *Tulsa University Campus.*

Paul's sister, Ann and her husband Terry live in the original farmhouse in the *Pecan Grove Subdivision*, in *Tulsa*. Their home dates back to about 1900. It's built of native stone, and it's very quaint. Ann has it decorated in a country style, with several antiques and lots of stained glass. Her house looks like it belongs in <u>Country Living Magazine</u>.

In the living room, there is a large fireplace, and the living room has a pitched ceiling with wooden beams that look like they are built to support the ceiling. Then, the living area leads into a dining area and a study, both open. It's a fabulous floor plan for entertaining.

Terry, an attorney, is now retired. When Paul and I were first dating, Ann and Terry were newlyweds. They had a baby boy, a junior; we called "Little Terry".

Ann is the oldest of Paul's siblings. All of the girls look a great deal like their Mother, but none of them looks more like Rita, than Ann. She has blonde hair that she wears short. It's thin, and generally needs a bit of teasing.

Ann nearly always dresses professionally, or a little artsy, whimsical. She teaches at *Tulsa Community College,* and I'm certain that her students help her stay young. Ann has a doctorate, in Liberal Arts.

I used to call on Ann for advice. She and Terry helped us find our home. Then, I called on her to help me decorate. I loved living close to family. When their son, Sean, was born, I couldn't wait to get my hands on him. I love babies!

Ann called us in *Norman*, before we ever moved back to *Tulsa*, to tell us about a house that was for sale across the street from her friend Connie Sullivan in *Pecan Grove Subdivision*. The same subdivision Ann and Terry were living in, how great is that. She knew we were going to be looking for something.

This was a red brick, three-bedroom, one story home on Rockford, Place. The house was on a quiet street, near *Heller Park* on Utica. *Heller Park* was full of beautiful pecan trees that were hundreds of -years-old. It had tennis courts and playground equipment for the kids. There was a creek, which ran through the park, and the park was big enough we could play football or softball with no interference.

Paul and I would live in that house for eight years. It's the longest we've lived anywhere to present. Once Paul and I got settled in our new home, I went back to work at *Metropolitan,* and we were living our dream! We had a fabulous backyard. Paul had a vegetable garden where he grew okra, tomatoes, carrots, lettuce, pumpkins and gourds, and we even tried watermelons.

In 1980, John, Paul's younger brother, and his wife Kathy, moved to the pecan grove. We had progressive Christmas parties where we would travel from one house to the other singing carols and drinking eggnog. Ann always put on the largest part of the feast.

One year, Paul's sister, Karen, brought sets of reindeer antlers and dinosaur faces for the Christmas party. They were hilarious. It had been an unbelievably stressful year for everyone, and the atmosphere was perfect for silly antics. By the time the progressive party made it to our house, everyone was relaxed and giggly.

Ann and Terry still have a Christmas party for the Huber family each year. Paul's folks have six kids.

They've been multiplying nearly as fast as the O'Brien's. The youngest members of the Huber gang put on a Christmas pageant and light an Advent wreath at Ann and Terry's house.

After my folks moved to *Florida*, we continued the O'Brien Christmas caroling parties.

Kitty and Russell hosted them for several years. We added some families to the group.

Sarah's sister-in-law Chari, and her husband Alan. Chari went to school at *Bishop Kelley* and was in Kitty's class. They were involved in all of the same things that we were and became like family. Rose's family joined us, and some members of Russell's family joined us too. The group was getting so big we even tried renting a hall one year, but it didn't feel personal enough.

Bryan and Rose began hosting our Christmas parties because they had the larger house and our families were growing! Now it feels like home again.

Once Momma and Daddy moved to *Florida,* their portion of the family began hosting a party on December 23rd with their neighbors there. We started making long distance telephone calls from our caroling party to theirs. (Wouldn't this make a great AT&T commercial?) Phone calls on the voice box to *Florida, Louisiana, Kentucky* and *Georgia* to sing with family members who couldn't make the trip to *Oklahoma* for the holidays. Sometimes, I'm pretty sure I hear **Dean Martin** in the background.

Every year, we have a difficult time remembering the words to the song, or order of the *Twelve Days of Christmas.* It became such a joke, that Norma Jean Powell and family presented us with a gift, which had the *Twelve Days of Christmas* in order.

In later years, I taught music at *St. Pius X,* and we learned actions to go along with the song. We taught them to all who were present. Now, several family members act out the parts. The largest laughs usually come from *"six geese a-laying",* (something rather difficult to act out), or at Uncle Les, when he stands and creates the hand movement for the *"five golden rings"* with great emotion!

Our Thanksgiving tradition revolves around the Huber gang. We all meet at *Heller Park* for the annual Turkey Bowl, rain or shine. Some of the group will watch while the younger members of the family participate in a friendly, non-competitive game of football.

Paul's parents, Rita and AJ hold the family tradition of Thanksgiving dinner at their house. We always take time to give thanks to God in prayer, lead by AJ, as the head of the family. Then, we go around the table to say what we are thankful for that year. Terry will say that he's thankful that the "turkey is moist" and he always remembers to thank Rita for preparing the dinner. Each year, a great deal of thought goes into this prayer. Energy is spent months in advance by each of the family members, thinking of what they are going to say and how best to express it.

St. Valentines Day is not forgotten either. AJ, with the help of Rita, buys special gifts for each of the girls in the family and delivers them on Valentines Day.

Mother's Day we would go to church with Rita and AJ at *St. Mary's Church* and then go out to breakfast. The church would take up a special donation for the *Madonna House*, which was a special home for unwed mothers supported by the Catholic community in *Tulsa*.

Mother's Day was sometimes difficult for me because I was so far from my momma, but I would call her and have a visit over coffee. AJ and Rita would have everyone over for burgers on the grill and soon I would forget that Momma was thousands of miles away.

Our children didn't come right away. I had a difficult time getting pregnant. For that reason also, Mothers Day was difficult. All of my friends were having no problem procreating but nothing was happening for me. Dr. Zanovich, my OBGYN put me on clomid. That was the fertility drug of the day. I began taking natural family planning classes at the hospital. While most people took the class to keep from getting pregnant, I took the class to help me get pregnant.

The next step, I was keeping a calendar and taking my temperature every morning and evening. By charting my temperature, we would be able to tell when ovulation would occur. It wasn't an exact science, but it beat standing on my head after sex. You can believe me I tried that too!

I loved being married. It was well worth the five-year wait. Paul was my best friend. Now, I just wanted to be a mommy. Then, I was going to retire. A career was not in my game plan.

I began taking classes after we returned to *Tulsa*, at *Tulsa Junior College*. I wasn't looking for a degree I was taking insurance classes and business classes. These were classes to help with my career development, until I did get pregnant.

Paul's mother, Rita was very supportive. She gave me valuable advice that I share now with my children. Rita said, "Take one class each semester, that's just for fun."

I decided to take voice lessons. The class had about twelve students in it. Each time the class would meet, the group would get smaller as students would drop out. I'll never forget how scared I was the first time I had to sing something all by myself.

We were all sitting in a circle in the classroom. When it was your turn, you would stand and sing a song that you had practiced all week. When it came to my turn, I stood and belted out *"Edelweiss"*, from the *Sound of Music* (1965).

I was shaking so bad you could see me shake. I told myself, you could do this Cheryl, no pressure! I felt like I was going to pass out or throw up, but I didn't.

The teacher made me sing it again, only higher. Then, she made me sing it again, and again, in this stupid opera type voice. I'm thinking; my siblings would laugh at me if I sang like that!

The teacher told me that my homework was to go home and practice singing in that voice. It was uncomfortable, but it got easier. I began to get used to what my voice sounded like. I didn't have to belt every song as if I was Barbara Streisand. There was a soft voice with a vibrato, which needed to be trained, and the vibrato needed to be controlled.

Voice II, was even more magical, as I began to learn to control the vibrato and, when and where I might be able to belt it. At the end of the semester, we would have a recital and invite family and friends to come and hear us sing a couple of songs. I invited Paul, Kitty and Paul's folks Rita and AJ.

Kitty was impressed with where I was going with this newfound talent. She decided to join me in Voice II, the second time that I took it. We would take the class over, and over because it was cheaper than private lessons, and the class size for Voice II was very small.

When Kitty and I took our first class together, I chose to learn *"Danny Boy"*, because it was my daddy's favorite old Irish song. I wanted to record our recital and send it to *Florida* for Fathers Day. We needed two songs for the recital. The other song was *"Look to the Rainbow"*, another Irish song. This one was from *Finian's Rainbow.* (1968)

The lyrics were all too fitting.

On the day I was born,
Said my father, said he.
I've an an elegant legacy
Waitin' for ye,

137

'Tis a rhyme for your lips
And a song for your heart,
To sing it whenever
The world falls apart.

Look, look
Look to the rainbow.
Follow it over the hill
And the stream.
Look, look
Look to the rainbow.
Follow the fellow
Who follows a dream.
Follow the fellow,
Follow the fellow,
Follow the fellow
Who follows a dream.

'Twas a sumptuous
To bequeath to a child.
Oh the lure of that song
Kept her feet funnin' wild.
For you never grow old
And you never stand still,
With whippoorwills singin'
Beyond the next hill.
Look, look
Look to the rainbow.
Follow it over the hill
And the stream.
Look, look
Look to the rainbow.
Follow the fellow
Who follows a dream.
Follow the fellow,
Follow the fellow,
Follow the fellow
Who follows a dream.

As fate would have it, Kitty and I had invited Granny to the recital at the end of the semester. Granny would bring with her, a surprise for us! Just by coincidence, Daddy was in town, just passing through on business, and he stopped in to see his mom.

"Hmmm. What are the odds?" I thought. "Sometimes things are just too coincidental."

Paul's mom was my cheerleader. She would encourage me each Sunday in Mass; "sing louder!"

I would listen to the cantor in church and think to myself. You could do that! Was I hearing my own thoughts or Rita's words? Finally, I was convinced that I should volunteer to cantor.

I was a nervous wreck, but I was learning so much. I became good friends with the organist and the choir director. I cantered two Masses on Sunday and, I loved singing in the choir. Music became my life.

I took private voice lessons from a good friend, Mark Watkins, and I began taking piano classes at *Tulsa Junior College*. I was enjoying my life more than ever.

Bryan, still youthful and with his dark hair and eyes, fell in love with a girl who had graduated with Ray's class at *Bishop Kelley* in the class of 1969. Rose Kline was younger than Bryan was by several years. She was a teacher, living on her own and self-supporting.

It took awhile for us to get to know Rose. She was very shy and quiet. I think being around our family makes a lot of people seem shy and quiet, because we are all the opposite. It would be hard to get a word in if you weren't a little bold. Rose was not. Therefore, she sat quietly.

Rose was beautiful. She looked a lot like **Crystal Gale**, a country music singer from the 1970's. She had long thick black hair that would almost reach her knees. Her eyes were green and her skin fair. She was soft-spoken and very polite.

Over the years, Rose would prove just what a perfect wife she was for Bryan. Rose was also a much-needed presence for the children. Debbie had legal custody of the children, but Bryan was raising them.

Rose and Bryan became the stability that the children needed, and Rose brought out the very best in Bryan. She was a disciplinarian when she needed to be. She changed the course of their lives.

Rose and Bryan adopted a little red haired girl named Shannon. Shannon looked more Irish than the O'Brien's did.

If all that is necessary to raise a child were love, Shannon would be the perfect child. No child could have been loved more. She didn't have just one Mom; Shannon had her sisters who mothered her, cousins and aunts with valuable advice. She would never lack someone to talk to about anything. Still, no one gets more credit than Rose does. She poured her life into their child.

What is true love, if not that?

CHAPTER TWELVE

MEET ALVA!

♥

Paul was awarded *Tulsa's* "Young Engineer of the Year" by the Oklahoma Society of Professional Engineers in 1980. He was the Master of Ceremonies at the Engineers Week Banquet and, he sat at the head table with the Mayor of *Tulsa*. The same day, he sent me flowers at my work. How considerate that he was thinking of me. I was so proud of him.

Things were going well for me at work. I was making decent money, and the benefits were good. I was still getting education from *Tulsa Junior College*. For the very first time in my life, I made the dean's list, "B" honor roll. I wasn't even thinking about the fact that I would be getting a report card. I was just taking classes for fun at this point.

"Are we always better at things we enjoy, or do we enjoy things we are better at?" I pondered. I still don't know the answer.

Sarah and Stan got married at *Christ the King Church* and the folks came to *Tulsa* for the wedding. We would have a family picture taken out in front of *Fletcher Hall*, our parish hall, across the street from the church.

As beautiful, as everything seemed to be going for Paul, and me, I shed many tears in those days. We were four years married still no babies. Kitty and Russell had two now, and one was on the way. Kitty's first born, Katie, was one of my Godchildren. I was using Kitty's children to fill my need for parenting whenever I could. I would call Kitty every day to find out what the kids had said or done that was cute or funny, and I was probably driving her crazy.

"Kitty, the baby book says this. The baby book says that". I was coaching Kitty the best I could without having children of my own. Kitty was going to have natural childbirth with her next child.

"I'm terrified of the aspect of such a thing. Not me, I'm not letting Paul in and I want drugs, lots and lots of drugs."

Well I can tell you, with me on clomid and Kitty pregnant, this argument was going nowhere. The hormones got the best of us. I almost ended up without a ride home from school that night. I was walking in downtown *Tulsa*, and Kitty was driving beside me, "get in the car", screaming at me out the car window, obscenities flying in both directions!

Paul was working at a job sight in *Maysville, Oklahoma*. It was a few hours from home and he wouldn't be back in *Tulsa* until the job was finished. Between the job and classes, it was enough to keep me busy, but this was not going to help in the baby-making department.

In January of 1982, I got a call from Momma. Daddy had a heart attack, and he was in the hospital in *Jacksonville*. The younger kids were with Momma, and she saw no reason for us all to come down.

"Daddy's going to be alright, the doctors are just running some tests." She said.

For a week, I would talk to Momma everyday. She always made things sound positive in her tone of voice, yet the words she used were not positive. I sensed there was something more.

It was a difficult time not to have someone to lean on. When Paul and I would talk, it was on the company dollar, so our conversations were generally short and to the point. Paul's never been good at talking on the phone, regardless. He hates talking on the phone.

I learned something about myself during that time. I can't focus when I'm under stress. I couldn't concentrate at work. All I could think about is what the family was going through in *Florida*. I should have taken some time off of work. I remember trying to type a letter on the company letterhead, and I kept making mistake after mistake. Instead of correcting the mistake, I'd tear them out and start again. I think I was a bit bonkers.

On the fifth day after Dad's heart attack, I called the hospital waiting room to check on Dad. Momma told me, "Daddy said the holes in the oxygen mask were just the right size for his cigar to fit in." He was still in good humor, despite the seriousness of the situation.

Everyday when I would check in, I would get an optimistic view, but the words and the attitude didn't seem to go together. Finally, it was like pulling teeth!

"Momma is it serious?" I asked.

She said, "Well... 'Em Yes."

I said, "Momma is it critical?"

She answered, "Well... 'Em Yes."

"Momma, let me talk to Patsy!" I said.

It took a week to get the real story. I knew it! Momma was being so optimistic; she wasn't telling us the whole truth! Maybe she thought it was too much to expect us to try to come all of the way to *Florida*.

Patsy told me, "Cheryl, if you want to say goodbye, you needed to be on the next flight to *Florida.*" I knew that Patsy would be direct.

I phoned my siblings, and we were all on the next plane to *Jacksonville*. Two of my daddy's brothers, Uncle Pete and Uncle Les, were on the flight just behind us. Ray was on that same flight. I'm grateful that Uncle Pete and Uncle Les came, and I'm glad that Ray didn't have to fly the last hours alone this time. We needed them there, especially for Momma. There is strength in numbers.

Daddy motioned for a pen and paper from Momma. On the paper he scratched, "I love my friends, I love my family, and I love you, Al!"

We did all have the opportunity to give our final farewell to Daddy. Momma gave our daddy the option to go on a respirator, and she informed him; all of the kids were on the way to say goodbye. He chose the respirator, so he could hang on long enough for us to get there. Daddy was only 55-years-old.

I took my turn to go in and tell Daddy that I loved him, but I didn't feel comfortable getting too close because of all of the things hooked to him. I saw Christy go in after me and ignore all of the wires. She gave Daddy a big bear hug, just like the ones he always gave us!

The only reason that Daddy was still living was to get those hugs! Screw the wires! How I wished I could have do overs. I will never miss an opportunity like that again.

It was odd from my perspective, I was happy to see Daddy because I could see how happy he was to see us. Yet, from Christy's point of view, she wished she had not seen Daddy like that, because of the fear she could see in his eyes. Isn't it interesting how two people can be exposed to the same situation walk away with a totally different experience? Perhaps Daddy let Christy see his fear because she was a nurse and he thought she could handle it.

We had split into shifts. Some of the kids had gone to Momma and Daddy's house there in *Jacksonville*. The others stayed at the hospital. Those of us who had gone to the house received a call to go back to the hospital the moment we walked in the door.

We arrived in the hallway, outside of the ICCU waiting room, and out came the doctor and one of the nurses, who had obviously been crying. She was holding a box of kleenex for us.

I will never forget how Momma handled the situation. She reached out her hands, like the wings of a dove, and she said, "Doctor, this is our family!"

You could see the look on the doctor's face; this is no ordinary family! More like this is no ordinary woman! Momma was remarkably strong.

We made our way back to the house. Each one of us was making an effort to process what we had just experienced. Momma pulled out the piece of paper.

She said, "These were Daddy's last words, and we have them in writing."

"I love my friends, I love my family, and I love you, Al".

I've purposely quoted the note twice. It's what his life was all about right up until the end. I wonder if he thought a long time before he wrote his own epitaph! Was it so ingrained in him that it came out naturally?

We were representing *"Big Ed"*, as we all greeted the guests when they entered the church. Many of us had never met Daddy's friends there in *Florida*. We would introduce ourselves by number and name.

"Hi, I'm Cheryl, Ed's #7." They usually laughed a bit, but they appreciated the introduction just as well. People anticipated such great sorrow under the circumstances, and they were relieved when we were approachable.

All of the readings were chosen and read by family members and, we led the songs, also chosen by family members, rather than have a cantor. There was a Spirit alive in the church, which I can't describe in words. I tell you, I felt like Daddy was with us, and he was proud of the way we were handling the situation.

We made the final preparations to take our daddy from *Jacksonville*, back to *Tulsa* and have his funeral there, with the rest of the family. On the way out the door, we grabbed our coats from the coat closet. The temperature was to reach 8 below zero in *Tulsa* the day of the funeral. One of the slats from the dining room table was stored in the coat closet. It dropped onto Momma's toe. I felt awful because I was standing next to her, yet there was nothing I could do. She broke her toe, so she couldn't wear a shoe. We all traveled together and Dad's family, along with Kitty, greeted us at the *Tulsa International Airport*.

Uncle Dick started laughing when Momma stepped off the plane. We couldn't figure out what he was laughing at. "Alva, what are you doing limping? Last time I saw you, you had a broken arm! I think you're just looking for attention." He said.

We all laughed. Daddy's sisters laughed through their tears as they watched us file into the airport. Uncle Dick had succeeded in lightening up a very tense moment, which we all feared, knowing we would be vulnerable to our emotions upon seeing each other through red and swollen eyes.

Kitty was the only one of the children who did not have the opportunity to come to *Florida* for the services there. She was pregnant and due any minute, and her doctor advised her not to travel. Kitty would go into labor during Daddy's funeral. How perfect, the cycle of life happening before our very eyes.

We tried to recreate the same Spirit that we felt at the services we had in *Jacksonville*, for the family members in *Tulsa*. You can't recreate something like that. It was never our creation to begin with. Credit belonged to the Higher Power. Still, we did see Daddy off the best we knew how. There were several priests and the Bishop at the funeral, and the church was full.

That night, after the funeral, we all went to Kitty's house and played cards around her dining room table and, we had a third game going in her living room. She was still in labor, but she didn't want to miss time with the family. This is typical of Kitty. She never wanted to miss anything. She waited until the last minute. We barely had time to park the car and get to the nursery to see the nurse hold up Kitty and Russell's new son. He was named Michael Edward.

The truly amazing thing though, was Kitty. She came down to the window to see the baby with us. She had the baby without drugs and looked wonderful. Her long blonde hair was clean and draping down her back, and she had that wide O'Brien smile.

To Father, With Love
By: Wm. H. O'Brien (Billy)

Oh, Lord, I praise Your holy name.
I know my soul is Yours to claim.
Each day I grow to love You more.
Please help me now as You have before.

I was weak and You made me strong.
In my moment of sorrow, you filled me with song.
When I saw death in my fathers face
You fed my spirit. You gave me Grace.

You helped me to face the tasks ahead
And accept the fact that Dad was dead,
When you wiped away my tears
With memories of happier years.

You told me what to do for Mother
And how to comfort each sister and brother.
Our love for Dad was never stronger
And we needn't mourn a moment longer.

The man had never really died.
He just took his place by Your side.
Now, from his vantage point above,
He could watch us with undying love.

On this earth, he was spread to thin.
Now, by Your Grace, He can help all men.
It's what he had always tried to do.
He just needed a little help from you.

Oh, Lord, to me You are so dear.
Help me to make my message clear.
I want everyone that hears my voice
To realize they have a choice.

They can call on Dad and in awhile
They'll feel the presence of his smile.
He will help in any way he can.
He always was that kind of man.

Thank You, Lord, for all Your time
And the ability to make this rhyme.
Just one more line before I run;
I sure am proud to be Ed's son.

Paul was still at the job sight in *Maysville, Oklahoma* when I called him with the news about Daddy. He would have to meet me in *Tulsa* for the funeral, and two days later, he headed back to the job sight.

I look at it as a miracle. Others may look at it as a coincidence. I got pregnant during Paul's short trip back to *Tulsa* for my daddy's funeral. In our family, you need to look for a population explosion after a death! Remember! It happens every time!

Daddy's death, without a doubt, has been the most difficult situation in my life to deal with. He was young and so happy. Life was going extremely well for all of the family in *Florida*, especially my momma and daddy. There were still children at home! It would be difficult to get past. Daddy didn't deserve to die this young.

For the first time in my life, crying did not relieve the pain. No matter how many tears I shed, I didn't feel any better. I would have a headache, full sinuses and feel sick to my stomach but I felt no release of anxiety, just a broken heart.

One other realization for me, perhaps another miracle, was; if Daddy had not coincidentally been in *Tulsa* for our voice recital just a few weeks before, I would have never been able to share the Irish songs, which I had prepared especially for him.

He didn't live to Father's Day.

Momma was going to be lonely without Daddy. They were so much a part of each other. Momma was going to have to find herself. She was no longer, Momma, or Ed's wife. She was Alva.

I tried to talk Momma into moving back to *Tulsa*, so she could be around family. My momma was happy in *Florida*. She wasn't going to rock the boat. She had a group of neighborhood women with whom she had become good friends. The kids were happy and settled in school. She would remain in *Florida* throughout the rest of her life.

Years later, I asked her what it was like, trying to go on without Daddy. She said he was with her. That she understood how Daddy thought, because they had been married for so long. If she had a decision to make, she knew how he would weigh in. It was as though he was on a business trip, and he was coming home soon. She missed him when he traveled, but she always knew he would be coming back to her.

It was more difficult than she let on. Once, we were together for a family reunion in *Edmond, Oklahoma*. I had a CD in my car from *Sleepless in Seattle* (1993). The song "*Stardust*", by **Nat 'King' Cole** came on. Momma sighed, *"Oh that was our song."* She was caught a bit off guard. Then, the tears began to stream down her face. Once again, it was music that always had a way of touching Momma's soul!

Stardust, Nat King Cole

And now the purple dusk of twilight time
Steals across the meadows of my heart
High up in the sky the little stars climb
Always reminding me that we're apart
You wander down the lane and far away
Leaving me a song that will not die
Love is now the stardust of yesterday
The music of the years gone by

Sometimes I wonder why I spend
The lonely night dreaming of a song
The melody haunts my reverie

And I am once again with you
When our love was new
And each kiss an inspiration
But that was long ago
Now my consolation
Is in the stardust of a song
Beside a garden wall

When stars are bright
You are in my arms
The nightingale tells his fairy tale
Of paradise where roses bloom
Though I dream in vain
In my heart it will remain
My stardust melody
The memory of love's refrain.

The first Father's Day, after my daddy passed away, I asked AJ if he would be my father. There's never a replacement for the real thing, but I appreciated having a representative. My daddy was there for Ronnie and Jenny in the past, and AJ has always been there for me, through the good times and the tough times. He is ready to step up when called upon.

It was in preparation of the Thanksgiving prayer, when I was 45-years-old; I realized that AJ had been my father for the same number of years as my real daddy. I was 23-years-old when Daddy passed away. I still miss him and carry him with me wherever I go.

CHAPTER THIRTEEN

POPULATION EXPLOSION

☺ ☺ ☺

I felt like this was the longest nine months of my life. I was so excited! I couldn't wait for the baby to come. Paul and I took classes together so I could try to have the baby natural. Yes, Kitty convinced me to pass on the drugs and let Paul into the room. She made it look so easy with Michael Edward.

I remember when I went into labor with my little girl. My water broke about 10:30 p.m., just after Paul and I went to bed.

I told him, "Paul, my water just broke!"

He didn't believe me. I think he was wishing I would wait until morning, but the baby had another plan.

"Are you sure you didn't just wet the bed?"

We went to the hospital, and the entire time I'm putting on my makeup in the car, my water is leaking. Paul had me sitting on a stack of towels to protect the seat of his car. We knew from our classes if the water broke, we needed to get to the hospital quickly; otherwise, there was a risk of infection.

They put me in a room and got things ready, then let Paul in. He tried to help me with the breathing, as we learned in class.

I threatened to kill him; he decided to just sit quietly instead. ... Good Plan!

There was a time my heartbeat was too rapid, and they put the baby and me on a monitor. I had to spend the majority of the time I was in labor, on my left side. The monitor was hooked to the top of Kelly's head. Kelly was showing signs of stress and they worried that the cord might be wrapped around her neck. They gave me an epidural for the pain, known to slow labor, but I was exhausted from the long hours of pain. I had been in labor for just under twelve hours, and the pains were not strong enough to bring the little girl out of my body. The epidural had the opposite effect and the labor became more intense. Just as the doctor was about to give up and prepare me for the C-section, the tide turned, and a star was born!

Kelly had maconium in the water, usually a sign of stress, and she was a little jaundiced. We kept Kelly under a special light in the hospital, and we put her in the window when we brought her home.

I was a bit over protective with Kelly at first. I made everyone wear a mask and wash their hands when they came in. The kids in ball uniforms had to put towels on their laps before they could hold the baby. They could only hold the baby if they were sitting down.

Paul was a natural from day one. He looked really comfortable holding little Kelly. The first thing Paul did when he walked in the door after work was to give me a kiss, and he asked how my day was as he was headed to the bassinette to get his little girl before I had time to respond. He would hold her all night long. If I wanted a turn to hold the baby he would say, "You get to hold her all day, now it's my turn."

She was Daddy's angel. I don't think there was anything she could have done that he would not have thought it was cute. That little girl had her dad's heart from the start.

I adopted a policy from Kitty. Dad couldn't change dirty diapers. Only wet ones. I stayed with it pretty well with the first baby. Once the other two came along, it was a little more difficult to stay with the plan. Some things demand immediate attention.

Kelly loved music day and night. She would listen to *Wee Sing* from the time she was whisked from my womb. She was tapping her foot from the day she was born. At six months, she would dance to **Michael Jackson's**, *"Beat it"*. It was hilarious to see her. If I put Kelly in the baby swing, with the music playing, she was fine. If the music stopped, the crying started.

It was the Eighties, everyone was on a health kick, and exercise was at an all time high. Most of the women I knew were taking aerobics. I would watch **Regis Philbin's Health Styles** when I was nursing the baby at 1:00 a.m. and 3:00 a.m.

Cable TV also had aerobic programs that you could follow along with, several times a day. By the time Kelly was old enough, she had little pink leg warmers and tennis shoes, so that she could join me in aerobic exercise and stretches on the floor.

Kelly and I did water babies together and she learned to swim under water at three months. She loved the water and had no fear of it. She could kick her way to the top, flip over and float on her back.

I would baby-sit for Ann and Terry's kids, Little Terry and Sean Malloy in the summer. Terry and Sean were the first-born nephews on the Huber side of the family. Ann and Terry were good to us and didn't mind giving their opinion. I was always asking for advice on something.

Sean and Terry treated Kelly as if she was their little sister. They shared their old children's books and enjoyed reading them to her. They would play with her and push her on her tricycle, as she got older. Terry would put Kelly on his shoulders and run around with her. She would squeal in a high-pitched voice. Terry would dress her in his football shoulder pads and helmet, and she would charge at him.

Terry and Sean called her "Monster Baby". *Then,* she would growl. When **Michael Jackson's**, *"Thriller"* would come on the **Music Television Video**, they would all run in and try to imitate the dancing.

They were cute together, Kelly and her cousins. She did have a temper, and if they made her mad she would give them what for, and Kelly would wag her finger in their face.

Sarah got pregnant just one month behind me; Little Bo was taken by C-section one month from the day that Kelly was born. He was a little blonde baby; his hair was very light, so he looked bald. He was tall and lanky, and he was as strong as an ox.

He looked like a cross between Yoda and **Winston Churchill**. Paul thinks all babies look like **Winston Churchill**. Bo was all boy!

Kelly and Little Bo grew up together the first few years of their lives. They did everything together, mostly because my sisters and I did everything together.

Our husbands were all members of the Knights of Columbus. They formed a softball team and named it *"The Family"*, because the majority of the team members were family. Billy's best friend Willie was the only non-family member. He'd been around since grade school.

Our families would come together on Sunday to watch the games, played at *Saints Peter and Paul.* The team stayed together for a period of about seven years. I used to bring my homework and study on the sidelines in the earlier years. Then, I began doing counted cross-stitch during pregnancies. Sarah would bring her knitting needles and work on various projects on the sidelines. As the number of children began to multiply, our hobbies went to the wayside. We would supervise the children while cheering the guys on. The kids would be running back and forth between *Arby's* next door to the ball field and the ball field itself. These were truly good times!

Paul and I, along with Sarah and Stan, decided to go to *Florida* for vacation. We wanted Momma to meet our newborn babies. We had not been on the road for twenty minutes before we had to stop to go to the bathroom.

"Damn, we're not even out of *Tulsa*", Paul barked.

"Can you hold it?"

We all laughed. Sarah and I were both pregnant with child number two at the time. Again, I used fertility drugs in order to get pregnant, and success came a little easier the second time around.

We asked the guard at the turnpike gate if we could use the restroom there, and he obliged us.

Our stops were frequent, and the guys thought we were never going to reach our destination. When we did finally reach Momma's home in *Jacksonville*, we unloaded our luggage, playpens, walkers, high chairs, and God knows what else.

Kelly and Bo both had walkers, with wheels so they could scoot around in the kitchen. Bo kept playing bumper cars with the walkers, but poor Kelly wasn't as thrilled about the aggressive play as Bo was. I don't think I thought it was as funny as Sarah did, maybe because it was my kid screaming and her kid laughing.

We put the babies on the floor so they could watch *"Grandma Cookie"* (the name given to Momma by the grandkids) feed the squirrels on the back patio. The squirrels would come and beg at the kitchen window. When they would see Momma get the birdseed and peanuts, they would meet her at the sliding glass door.

Bo crawled over Kelly as if she wasn't even there. He had the army crawl down to a fine art. He was a bit of climber too. He broke his collarbone climbing on the doghouse before his third birthday.

No one who thinks boys and girls are born the same has been a parent of both a boy and a girl. They are different from the time they are snatched from the stork's beak. My experience with a little man was coming.

When I went into labor with child number two, I thought it would be another twelve-hour labor. I was reading Kelly her favorite book. She called it *"Stars and Moon"*. It was actually a third grade science book about the rotation of the earth, but Kelly loved it.

I tried to wait until the last minute to call Paul home. I guess I did wait until the last minute. The anesthesiologist was scrubbing up to catch him, and the OB was in the hospital and on his way. The OB traded places with the anesthesiologist, just in time. It looked like an intercepted pass. Mike was born twenty minutes after we showed up at the hospital.

Mike was a maconium birth. He had taken some of the thick fluid into his lungs. The Pediatrician, Dr. Daley worked on him for a while before Paul could hold him. It was scary from our perspective, but Mike was O.K. Things don't always go as smooth in real life as they do on TV.

Mike was my night child. He was a really good baby. Before he was born, he let it be known at 10:00 p.m. he was at his prime. I'd be trying to go to sleep, but the baby would be kicking so much that I would ask Paul to put his hand on my stomach. Sometimes it would calm the baby down.

When Mike was a baby, he would have a crying spell at four in the afternoon that would last about twenty minutes. Then, he would just pass out. We began to realize if I would put him in his bed as soon as he started to fuss, instead of holding him, he was happy. He would fall asleep without the crying jag. Everything we were doing was stimulating him, yet he wanted to sleep. So, at 4:00 p.m., I would put him down, so he would nap. At 10:00 p.m., we would put the little guy in his bed. He wouldn't make a sound except you could hear him playing with his mobile. I'd peek in, and he would be kicking it with his feet.

Paul and I felt guilty because we wanted to be holding the baby while he was awake. That wasn't his style. He would play in his bed until he fell asleep. Sometimes it would be after 11:00 p.m.

Before Mike was old enough to put three words together, he was counting to ten. His vocabulary was always excellent for his age. He knew his months on the calendar nearly as soon as he could speak. I was beginning to think, maybe he was going to be a child prodigy. Right!

We would sing the song from *Annie* (1982), "*Tomorrow*", and Michael would sing along at nine months. "*Tomorrow, tomorrow, I ya, ya tomorrow…day away.*" We needed to have him tested before he could enter kindergarten, his vocabulary tested in the ninety-eight percentile on the charts.

Once he went to school, we found he was an auditory learner, so he paid attention to the flash cards and lessons I would go through with Kelly and pick it up. Anything could be learned if it was spoken enough times, but please don't ask him to write it! Where a person is advanced in one area, there is a deficit somewhere else. With Mike, it was his fine motor skills.

Mike loved to play in the sand box, sometimes for an hour. He could be all by himself in there, while his dad would be working in the garden nearby. Mike really loved the outdoors. We went through as much sunscreen as we did diapers. You never saw a happier baby. He had a huge belly laugh if he got wound up. He was never real interested in toys when he was little. He liked playing in the water or splashing in the mud, climbing and wrestling on the floor with anyone who would let him, like a bear cub. He also liked stripping off his clothes and running around the backyard without his diaper. I had a heck of a time keeping clothes on that kid.

Paul and I had satin waterbed sheets. Mike decided this was his blanket, and he would drag these massive sheets around the house. We cut them, first in half. Then, we cut them into several baby-blanket size pieces. When one was dirty, we would pull out another. Slowly, they became tattered or he would lose one. We would cut the tattered edges off the satin blankets and give them back to him.

As Mike became older and we needed to wean him from his blanket, we would cut it in half once again, each time it went into the dryer. We told him his blanket shrunk, until they looked like handkerchiefs.

It was God, who planned the third child. We wanted three, but planned to space them two years apart. God had another plan. We didn't need fertility drugs with child number three. He was due on my brother, Danny's birthday. Choosing a name was easy!

The doctor warned me, "Since Mike came fast you best pay attention to your body. When labor starts with Dan, get to the hospital right away!" He would remind me each time I came for a visit.

I would have nightmares, Paul pulling to the side of the road to deliver the baby boy. I would be talking him through it, right up to the time he would cut the umbilical cord, and he would put the baby on my chest. I'm sure that's what would have happened if it were a TV program, but again, things are different in real life.

I would make four trips to the hospital before Daniel Paul came. Four times my sisters arrived and sat in the waiting room. Each time they were sent away by the nurses. "False labor" The last time, the doctor gave me a shot, which was supposed to stop the false labor. Kitty and Christy were sent home. I surprised everyone and had the baby anyway!

From day one, Dan loved to be held. Funny, no two kids are the same. Sometimes, I would forget I even had a baby on my hip. He was really a good baby. He was quiet and sucked on his middle two fingers, never needing a pacifier.

Dan was different from my other two because he didn't like crowds. He was not happy when he was around all of his cousins and aunts and uncles. He didn't like it when strangers talked to him in line at the grocery store. Dan preferred the indoors and he loved playing with *McDonalds, Sesame Street* toys. I called him a toy kid. He grew up with *Ghostbusters* (1984) and *Teenage Mutant Ninja Turtles* (1990).

Manipulating things with his fingers was fascinating to him. Paul was working in the backyard, putting something together. Dan took his screwdriver and dropped it in the well.

The plumber was called out twice to pull Ghostbusters out of the toilet. The second time, the toilet had to be pulled, we found Janine, his favorite Ghostbusters in a sitting position, tightly hanging on by her feet and buttocks to keep from flushing all the way to the reservoir.

You rarely saw Dan that he wasn't wearing his Ghostbusters Proton Pack. On days when I was working on my class plans, he could keep himself busy for hours shooting ghosts on the toys at *McDonalds*. Kelly's dollhouse at home made a pretty good firehouse, until he got a real one for Christmas.

It's funny, because many of these traits my children showed as babies stayed with them as they grew. Kelly, who loved music from birth, found her first job out of college, working for *Cox Radio*. She sold advertising time for their Christian radio station. She loved the work but hated the fact that it was commission only and not always friendly competition among fellow workers.

Mike thrived when the sun would shine. He had to have some down time in the afternoon, yet in the evenings, somehow he would catch a second wind. Sleep is and never was a high priority and neither were clothes. Mike, with a degree in film, got his first job working for *Sinclair Broadcasting Company*. He worked strange hours. Mike loves to laugh and he tells a great story, and he never forgets the punch line of a joke. Now days, Mike understands that clothes are not optional!

Dan, the youngest, would have breathing problems in restaurants and need to go outside. We blamed it on his asthma, but once he went to college, we found he was susceptible to panic attacks. He would go with us to family weddings; while all of his cousins were on the dance floor going crazy Dan would pull up a couple of chairs and put them side by side, then take a nap. He still hates crowds. He prefers just one best friend, or a few friends and not the big party. He still hates it when I talk to strangers in line at the grocery store, or anywhere else for that matter.

Kelly and Mike would have big birthday parties; they would invite every kid they knew, yet Dan would ask for one friend and let Kelly and Mike bring one friend too. That way he knew they would leave him and his friend alone!

When Dan was about four-years-old, we went to *McDonalds* and a girl was giving out free balloons to the children. She offered one to Dan and he turned it down. I asked him, "Why?"

His answer was very logical and well thought out. "If I take a balloon and it fly's away I will cry.

If the balloon doesn't fly away, eventually it will pop and I will cry. I don't want to cry, so I don't want a balloon."

Dan is studying International Business and with his logic, I'm sure that he will succeed.

The early morning ritual on weekends was Paul wrestling with the kids in the bed, while I fixed breakfast. The tumble usually didn't end until one of the kid's hurt Paul or visa versa.

As the children got older, the tumble didn't stop. Like little monkeys, they would attack their father any time, any place.

Sarah and Stan, Paul and I, we spaced our kids close together. I had Kelly in '82, Mike in '84 and Dan in '86. Sarah, had Little Bo in '82, Jenny in '84, and Heather in '86. The only difference is

Sarah and Stan kept going. They would add Eric and Bryan, (named after Uncle Bryan) to the list of children in their family.

Our kids often played together at Julie Nelson's home. Julie was in my brother, Bo's class, and was a friend of Sarah's from the old *Marquette School* days. Julie had three children Stephanie, Tommy and Jonathan. Our children all took swimming lessons together at a pool near Julie's house.

Can you imagine three very talkative women with nine children between them, all under the age of five, twice a week, walking to the pool with strollers, towels, cameras, diaper bags and purses? Storeowners would lock the doors when they saw us coming. (just kidding)

The older children were very helpful with the younger ones, so it wasn't too difficult. We spent the entire day at the pool, when we could. Staying home with the children was a luxury not all women could afford. We knew we were lucky so we took advantage of our time with the children and each other; I wouldn't trade those days for anything.

Across the street, on the corner lot, from Paul and me, I had a good friend Raeline. She was one of the few neighborhood women on our block who stayed home with her children. Raelines' husband Bill was in medical school when we met. Bill studied to become a vet, but decided he didn't like it. He went back to school to become a doctor. When Dr. Bill graduated, it was such a relief for Raeline and there was a huge celebration.

Every Halloween she and Bill would have a huge party for the kids in their backyard, because it was close to their son, Matthew's birthday. The kids would have a chance to wear their costumes early. The party had apple bobbing and pin the tail on the donkey. Matthew was Kelly's age, but he was interested in *Star Wars* (1977) toys! Kelly and her best friend Starla couldn't both be princess *Leih*.

They preferred to play on the swing set and pretend that they were both princesses.

Raeline was a busy lady and she helped Dr. Bill get his new doctors offices decorated. She always had dinner ready for Bill when he came home, no matter what time it was. She had an amazing amount of energy, like the energizer bunny. She loved to entertain and even managed to drag Paul and me out a few times for dinner or to the theater. Keeping us up past 10:00 p.m. is a chore; we're not late nighters.

She organized a babysitting co-op with some of the neighborhood women, to give each other a date night on the weekend. Paul and I had enough going on with ballgames, church functions and family events we didn't need a date night. We couldn't wait for an evening when we could be at home.

Raeline and I were often running back and forth from house to house to borrow a cup of sugar or a package of macaroni and cheese. Sometimes we would get together, just to iron clothes in the company of another adult. It was great to have a friend so close by.

Paul's sister, Kathy, and I became very close friends in these early years on Rockford, Place. We spent a lot of time together, before Kathy fell in love, and she married David Detrick. She had a condominium close by, and we would go out to eat and shopping. After she and David married, they lived close to the *Pecan Grove*, just on the other side of *Heller Park*.

Kathy was the most domestic of the girls in Paul's family in her teenage years, sewing and knitting. When I met her in the late 1970's, she was still in school, studying interior design. We would go to the lake with the Huber family about four times a year. Kathy would pull out her guitar in the evenings and we would sing folk songs.

Kathy had a booming career in corporate interior design. She and David waited awhile to start having children. David loved the lake; he purchased a sailboat and wasn't ready at first for children because he was afraid they would get in the way of his weekends.

When they did finally start their family, they took the kids with them to the lake! The children, Dustin and Lindsey looked like little brown berries, always tan.

It was David's job in corporate real estate, which took them away from *Tulsa*. Their children, Dustin and Lindsey would spend the majority of their years growing up in *Dallas*. Dustin played soccer, and Lindsey was a cheerleader. Their trips to the lake became few and far between. Kathy gave up her career in order to stay home with the children for several years. She returned to school and studied Environmental Engineering. Huber's don't allow their minds to sit stagnant for any length of time.

I tease Paul; I think, it was really Kathy I fell in love with first. She was **Cyrano De Bergerac** and coached Paul the first year we were dating, when he was studying at OU, on how to win my heart. Truthfully, Paul needed little coaching. He was charming!

Kathy and her children, Dustin and Lindsey would come and visit us in *Houston*, around Christmas time each year. I asked her to bring their Pug, Bogart with them when they came, so for many years they did. Bogie caught my attention two years before we got our own little Pug, Ginger. Bogie was the reason I chose a Pug for my children. He had a typical Pug personality. He acted as if he could care less what you were doing most of the time unless you had food or a ball.

Anyone who knows a Pug will tell you that Pugs are food obsessed. They'll watch you eat and Hoover up any pieces that you drop, even if it means scratching their flat nose on the pavement to get a crumb. They love to follow little kids around who have food because they know they have increased odds of a bit falling.

Dustin liked to play soccer against the garage door, and Bogart would chase the ball. I don't know what he was going to do with it when he caught it. The ball was almost bigger than he was.

Pugs are the largest of the small breeds. They don't break easy. Bogie would spend the majority of his time trying not to be bothered. He would come if you called him and let you stroke him but required very little attention. He patrolled the backyard and played the watchdog.

Kelly's best friend Starla lived with her Mother and Grandparents, Mr. and Mrs. Miles. They were just around the corner, with one house on the corner lot between us. Starla's mother, Teresa would cut our hair at the kitchen table every six weeks or so. She and I would spend days together listening to and discussing the **Ollie North** Trial while Kelly and Starla played with their My Little Pony's, and Lady Lovely Locks.

Once the girls found each other at about age four, they were inseparable. They loved the garden, loved their dolls. They even had chicken pocks together.

Kelly and Starla had gymnastics together twice a week, then they would play on the toys at the park and wait on Mike to finish his tumbling lesson. Sometimes we would go by Granny's old house afterward, just for the memories. Granny's children moved her into an apartment in Broken Arrow, so she would be easier for them to visit.

Mrs. Miles, Starla's grandmother, loved to garden. She would share her bulbs with me when she divided them. We would talk across the back fence, near Paul's vegetable garden and sometimes I could share some okra or tomatoes.

I had to run to Starla's grandmother Marie's to pick Kelly up after play day. I called and told Marie I was on my way. Dan was napping but he woke up just as I was running out the door. I swept him up and placed him on my hip, and I trotted around the corner. As I was rattling on with Marie,

I said, "I need to run, I left Dan in his bed, napping."

Marie laughed! "Cheryl, Dan's on your hip."

You know, they say children make you crazy. It was just the beginning of my mental illness.

Most days of the week were full of things to do. Wednesday, we called "Dit Day" at Kitty and Russell's house. Dit was a nickname for Christy, short for Ditty. Ditty was what Kitty called Christy when she was a baby, because she could not pronounce Christy correctly. Ray said it was short for, "Dip Shit".

All of the sisters would go to Kitty's with their kids on Dit's day off, and she would provide donuts for the whole gang. We would spend the entire day together at Kitty's, visiting with coffee around the dining room table.

Our children stayed entertained by Kitty's daughters, Katie and Sandy, who looked after them and played with them. Often they would put on plays or perform for us. As they got older, they would use the video camera and record their performances.

When the teachers had a day off, my oldest brother, Bryan, would come too. We would start with the donuts in the morning and order several pizza's for the afternoon. We would give Billy a call at work, to see if he could join us for lunch. Russell would drop in from work every *"Dit Day"*. It was like having a party. Kitty and Russell made everyone feel welcome. Her house was always where we would gather. They had a large dining room with a long table, similar to the one we had on Newport. Her dining table would be the focal point in her home, just as Momma's was when we grew up.

All of the children would run in like little *Ninja Turtles*, (1990) around the table and put more pizza in their mouths than you thought they could hold. After they had their fill, the children would head back to the living room for more play, leaving their paper plates with leftovers on the table for fair game. Little Dan, the smallest of them all would sneak back in and clean all the plates, through what Kitty and Russell thought was a hollow leg.

The oil industry was hurting in the early 1980's. Mostly because of the price of oil and inflation was hitting the housing market. This was affecting the job industry in *Tulsa* severely. Paul's company was on four-day workweeks for several years. This basically, meant that they cut his pay by twenty percent because he was a salaried employee. I was no longer bringing home any income because this happened just at the time I had decided to stay home and be just a mommy.

I took in extra kids after school. That helped a little. There was always the fear that Paul might be laid off from work. They cut their number of employees nearly every pay period. *Dresser Engineering* sold to *Davy. Davy* became *Davy-McKee.* Paul would find a cave to hide in within himself. I felt at a loss of what to say. I'd sit by and watch the wheels turn in his head.

We found ways to make ends meet, or at least not to go too far in debt. We never felt too broke, because we always knew someone who had more and we always knew someone who had less.

Dit would get flooded again; by coincidence, Memorial Day weekend, just like the first flood that damaged her home and belongings. This time, the city of *Tulsa* was in the process of digging out *Mingo Creek* for residence further down stream. The results, her house was full of about six inches of mud. Something to make the clean up just a little bit harder.

Kitty and Russell would go through a period of time that Russell would be out of work in the early Eighties. Money would be tight for them for a while as a consequence. Still, they were highly involved in helping Dit get back on her feet. I remember Billy, Russell and Bryan, climbing under Dit's house to try to fix her plumbing, after the flood had moved her house off the foundation.

One evening, I returned home from choir practice. Paul greeted me at the door with news that Granny had died. When someone is old, it is expected and you try to prepare yourself ahead of time. I was still shocked! It was the five-year anniversary of Daddy's death. I think that Granny died from a broken heart, thinking about my daddy. I will always miss her. However, Granny I carry with me most often in my life today. I'm delighted to be in her presence when I'm in the garden planting, or just enjoying the beauty of the day. She was "Pioneer Stock", as my daddy would have called it. "She was a very capable woman." Granny was full of character, never pretentious, just Granny. I enjoy her company!

Paul, Stan Hoffmann, (Sarah's husband), Tom Egan and Charlie Nichol, (names from the BKHS past), were the football coaches for the new Comet football team. Catholic schools no longer had enough boys to supply each school with their own team. They made one team, for all of the Catholic schools and named it *Bishop Kelley Comet Jr. High.*

It was a sign of the times. More and more, Momma's were going to work. Children were fending for themselves after school. They would have to find rides to practices and games. Football was no longer the number one sport and video gaming was replacing outdoor activity after school.

My sister-in-law, Ann, called me to see if I would volunteer to help teach music at *St. Mary's School.* The nuns were called back to their order and the school was left scratching for help. I hated the idea of kids not having music. Music was something I loved so much and was such an important part of my life.

I did volunteer to teach music. I loved it! I wasn't always sure of what I was doing, but somehow things would fall into place.

One time we had a music meeting and decided we would all focus our lessons on **Stephen Foster?** O.K., I thought, how am I going to make this interesting for eighth graders? The middle school children seemed to be the ones I clicked with the best.

The following weekend I was at a garage sale and rummaging through records, I found one, Steven Foster hits made famous by Jolson.

Perfect, it was a Godsend just for me. Coincidentally, I found exactly what I needed. I had pictures of Paul's Grandfather in vaudeville. We were able to discuss the good and bad in vaudeville, blackface, **Jolson's** fame and **Steven Foster.**

163

My favorite part of the year was when I helped the eighth grade pick their class song and we planned their graduation mass. I felt I was right where God wanted me to be.

One afternoon, I was ironing with Raeline in my living room. I pinched a nerve in my back. Then, another one, the next day, my neck wouldn't move. I was in horrific pain. Paul had to help me with the kids. *The St. Mary's Women's Club* would bring the family dinner. I went to see Dr. Bill and we ran tests. The conclusion was a virus struck my back. I was flat on my back for six weeks and left with an arthritic back for several years thereafter.

I was happy teaching music. Life seemed so perfect. Perhaps God was trying to prepare me for what was coming next. Paul had been quiet and a bit irritable when I spoke to him, as though I was interrupting something.

I discussed this with Momma on the phone. This is when she gave me this advice.

"Cheryl, stay close to home. Work with him in the yard and he'll open up when he's ready. If you're not there when he's ready to talk, you might miss it."

Momma was a wise woman.

I did work with him in the yard, and he did open up. Paul spoke carefully, watching my face for any reaction. We were being transferred to *Houston.*

This was a great opportunity for Paul. We were ready to begin dreaming again. We were just keeping our head above water in *Tulsa,* sinking further and further into debt. Paul had a chance to move up in the company and be challenged again.

He knew this would be difficult for the family and was trying to figure out how to approach me. It wasn't just difficult for me. Paul grew up in the same community I did. *Tulsa* was home. Paul went to *St. Pius X,* (the rival, with all of the school spirit that I admired so much in my youth). His family would go to Mass at *St. Pius X,* when it was being held in a barn on the property where the church now sits. Remember, the church is the people, not the building! The school was up and running before the church was built. Paul's dad, AJ, volunteered his time to put in the electrical wiring in the school.

Paul and I met at *Bishop Kelley High School*, where he participated in football, baseball and student council. He was still involved with the Kelley community through his coaching. We never missed a *Bishop Kelley* Football game on Friday night. Huge numbers of our classmates would be at the Friday night games as well.

This was a life changing decision. Paul understood that. I think he wanted to make sure I understood, before giving my consent.

We put the house up for sale and moved that summer to *Houston*. We were leaving our families and community for the first time! We would experience many firsts.

Kelly started kindergarten at *Ashford Elementary School*, in *Houston*. She had all of her class to our house for her fifth birthday party. Our neighborhood was crawling with young children. There was no lack of friends for my children to play with. All of the mothers in the neighborhood worked. I would join the choir for adult conversation.

I volunteered to help the kindergarten with an opera, *"The Three Nanny Goats Gruff."* I became an officer for the Suffolk Chase Neighborhood Association. I found things to keep me busy, but it wasn't a substitute for family and though I wanted to be happy, I just couldn't let myself be happy without my family and community. I was like a fish out of water.

It's the first six-months, which are the most difficult after a move. You need to get through a few holidays to see if they go to plan. What will your new traditions be? You also need to find a comfortable daily routine.

Paul and I both were having a difficult time adjusting, because we couldn't get past what we had left behind. Paul was working ten to twelve hours a day. We hung on to our OU Football tickets, just in case. I prayed for a way to get back home.

The children would play in the cul-de-sac until Paul got home from work. I'd begin sitting on the curb at about 3:00 p.m. when the neighborhood children got out of school. Sometimes the other parents would join me on the curb for a while when they arrived home. We put orange cones up to warn the traffic to slow, for the children on bikes and tricycles. There were ten children under the age of nine living in the houses in our cul-de-sac.

Paul and I found a new routine once the pool opened. Paul would get home from work; he would watch the children three days a week at the pool, while I went jogging. I would watch the kids at the pool when he ran. Then, we would go home and I'd get dinner ready. Fortunately, the pool was only a couple of houses away. We joined a gym and I would take the kids to the nursery while I worked out.

Paul's folks, Rita and AJ, came to visit. I enjoyed taking them around *Houston*. One afternoon, Kelly was at school, we were visiting downstairs, and Mike and Dan were upstairs watching TV. I heard the boys making a lot of noise and getting excited about something.

"Fire's on the TV! Fire's on the TV!"

They were shouting. I went upstairs to see what all of the fuss was about. The words were correct, but they were in the wrong order.

"TV's on fire!" TV's on Fire!"

Reminded of Kitty's reaction to the car fire in the Catalina, I grab the kids and run for help!

AJ, Paul's dad, calmly unplugged the TV. I don't think I would have handled the situation by myself correctly at all. Once the TV was unplugged, the fire went out all by itself.

Perhaps it would be a good idea to buy a fire extinguisher and a ladder for the upstairs. I thought.

AJ always handled crisis with such calm. He was sure of himself and it gave me confidence in his abilities to handle about any situation. He was a brilliant man and had a well-rounded education in about any subject. He used to say, "If you can read, you can do anything." It's true, for him! There was no job too big. He wore many hats!

AJ helped Paul re-roof our first house. I called my father-in-law, AJ, when my hot water tank overflowed and flooded the house. Paul was out of town at the time. AJ was there in a heartbeat; he could and would fix anything for anybody if you asked! He was so good at reading directions and following them, it amazed me.

My Dan ended up with the same gift. He would help me put furniture together when it took following instructions. To this day, when I have computer trouble, Dan gets the call.

When we lived in *Tulsa*, we went to Mass on Sunday, with Rita, AJ and Paul's youngest brother, Jim. They helped Paul wrestle the kids when I sang in the choir. We would go out to breakfast after church and sometimes Ann and Terry or John and Kathy would join us. I missed that so much.

Life would change drastically in just that one year. Raeline and Bill were supposed to come and visit us in *Houston*, with their children, Matthew, Angela and the new baby, Jonathan in February.

Raeline called. "Cheryl, I'm so sorry, we won't be able to come and see you in February. The baby and I both have the flu."

"Raeline, I have a secret. You can't tell anyone! Word can't get out until an announcement has been made at the office. Paul said I could tell one person. I want that person to be you." I think she knew that I was reluctant to tell her at first.

"Paul and I are moving back to *Tulsa* this summer".

She squealed at the prospect of us being together again.

Everything was falling into place perfectly, except there was one snag. The Catholic schools in Tulsa were full.

Kitty and Russell were serving as president of the Home and School counsel at St. Pius X. The principal, Holly Goodwin, mentioned to Russell, that their music teacher had quit, just two weeks before school was to start. She asked if he happened to know of anyone.

It didn't take long for negotiations to begin. If I could sell my house in Houston, then I would be happy to teach, if they could get my children into the school. I put the phone back on the receiver after my conversation with Mrs. Goodwin, and the phone rang, just as I hung up.

It was the realtor. You guessed it. We sold the house.

Kelly started first grade at St. Pius X, in Oklahoma, while the boys and I stayed and tied up all of the loose ends in Texas. A couple of months later, I got a call from Doctor Bill.

"Cheryl, there's no easy way to say this. Raeline died! Raeline died this morning. I tried to bring her back, but I couldn't." He paused. "I was in the shower when Matthew went to wake her up, but he said that she wouldn't wake up."

I flew to *Tulsa* for the funeral. It was my first time to fly alone. I must confess I got lost on my way to the *Hobby Airport* in *Houston*. I was afraid I was going to miss my flight.

I didn't realize what an impact Raeline's funeral would have on me. She had lived in *Tulsa* for less than three years the church was packed with people, young and old, yet didn't have to ask, I knew how she had touched so many lives in such a short amount of time. She was always doing things for others. I remember going to her house one time, when she was baking cookies for a fundraiser, babysitting for a friend and working on a third volunteer project for her church at the kitchen table.

CHAPTER FOURTEEN

MY NEW HAT, A TEACHER

♫

In 1988, Paul and I were transferred back to *Tulsa*. Life had changed so drastically in just that one year; I had nothing in my life that felt the same. Sarah and Stan were transferred to *Louisville, Kentucky*. Julie Nelson and Kitty had both joined the working world and Raeline was gone.

We were trying desperately to get Kelly into a Catholic school, but all of the *Tulsa* Catholic Schools were full. Kitty and Russell told the principal, Holly Goodwin about me. I was offered a job, to teach music at *St. Pius X*. If I would teach, they would find a way to get Kelly enrolled in their school, even though it was full.

I tried on my new hat and loved it. I was Mrs. Huber, the music teacher, teaching first through eighth grades, just three and one-half days a week. Mrs. Goodwin worked hard with me, to help me gain the skills that I lacked.

We lived a short while in a rent home while my friend Gloria Van Tuyl, helped me look for the perfect home. I'm glad we took the time, because we found it.

The house was a two-story Tudor design. It had four bedrooms, all upstairs. Two living areas and a large kitchen, with a two car garage downstairs. Our new home was forty-five minutes from the school. We lived at 101st and Sheridan, on the outskirts of *Tulsa*, in *Sun Meadow Subdivision*. The lot was nearly an acre, pie shaped and located in a cul-de-sac. It had plenty of room for the kids to run and play. Sheridan, Road was under construction at the time, causing the traffic on HWY 169 to be more like a parking lot than a highway. My commute the first few years, until the construction was done, was forty-five minutes each way.

Paul and I would take care of the lawn ourselves. We both loved working in the yard, and this yard had lots of apple trees, peach trees and various other trees as well. The neighbor had a huge cottonwood tree that would lose its pods in our yard. It took time to pick up all of the debris before you could begin to mow. We purchased a riding lawn mower and it still took hours to mow the lawn. It was actually kind of fun, two hours without any children underfoot. We would fight over who was going to get to mow the lawn.

Paul was working really long hours for the first year we were back in *Tulsa*. It was a tremendous project in *Syria*; one that advanced his career by leaps and bounds. The children missed their dad during this time and I realized he needed to see them as much as they needed to see their dad. I began bathing the children and taking them up to see Paul in their pajamas at his work. Paul would let them play on his computer and read them a story, and then I would take them home to bed. It made a huge difference.

Paul and I were busy driving from field to field, usually in separate cars on weekends. The late 1980's were a busy time for us, but they were also fun. I rarely went home after I dropped the kids at school. I picked Dan up at noon from pre-school, it was not worth driving all of the way home and then all of the way back out to 31st and Memorial to pick up the other two children, just two hours after I got home. Dan and I would either go to Kitty's house, or go to the *McDonalds*. Dan would play on the toys while I worked on class plans.

Paul and I played on a co-ed softball team with our *St. Pius X* friends. Kitty and Russell were on our team as well. The group of friends we made during this time in our lives remained our friends throughout the years and various moves. We still make an effort to get together whenever we can.

I sang in the choir with Kitty at *St. Pius X*. We also belonged to the same Bunco group. We named ourselves M&M Bunco because we always had peanut M&M's on the tables. Twelve women meet once a month for the dice game, friendship and fellowship, and each month they go to a different house. This same group has been together for over twenty years. We've supported each other through every kind of drama, good or bad.

If I needed a babysitter, Katie and Sandy, Kitty's girls, would look after the kids for me. Poor Michael Ed, Kitty and Russell's son, he had to share his toys with my boys and they didn't always treat his toys with the respect they should have. It must have been like having siblings, because my kids were there a lot.

Dan and his proton pack would travel along with me nearly everywhere I went. The chairs in the old music room probably still have his marks. He decided to use the magic marker on them while I was writing class plans on the board. You can't imagine how embarrassed I was when I had to tell Father Dorney what had happened. I felt like I was going to confession.

Once Dan reached Mrs. Shocklee's First Grade, everyone already knew him. I coached his tee ball team with Matt Ingram, whose daughter, Heather, was in Dan's class. Paul helped to coach Kelly's basketball and softball, with friends John Hotaling and Jim Miller. The girls called him "watermelon man", because Mr. Hotaling told them that the ball Paul was throwing was a watermelon. Then, he helped to coach Mike's baseball team with Joel Turner. Our boys also played basketball and soccer.

Paul and I were outnumbered and running as fast as we could to keep up with the kids. Thank goodness, cell phones became a novelty item for the car. My 1988 Town and Country Minivan was getting a ton of mileage back and forth between *St. Pius X*, the ball fields and home.

I treasured the *St. Pius X* Community. I learned a significant amount about raising children, and I learned methods to use working with children with learning disabilities, especially Attention Deficit Disorder.

The principal, Holly Goodwin pushed us to be the best we could be. I was called into the principal's office more times as a teacher than I ever was as a student. I do wish I could have a quarter for every time I had to apologize to the students for using curse words. The other teachers at *St. Pius X* were highly dedicated. It was an exciting time for me.

I taught a couple of years at *Bishop Kelley High School*, two days a week. My nephew, Sean came up with the idea, of a Christmas Program and had Father Muggenburg contact me to organize them. The first year I was a volunteer, the second year I proposed a music program that could be a part of their religious education, teaching them to cantor the Mass.

This was a dream of mine. When I began to learn to cantor at Mass, I was nervous and unsure of myself. The church, hundreds of years ago had such beautiful music. Now, it's difficult to find someone who can carry a tune to lead the congregation. I thought, if we taught children to cantor and brought them up doing it, then they would feel comfortable and understand the words they were singing had power. It's a Spirit that comes from music that can give someone chills or put a lump in their throat. I know music can touch souls. I've seen it touch my Momma's soul on several occasions.

While all of this was going on in *Tulsa*, my momma was feeling ill in *Jacksonville*. She went to the doctor and the doctor was treating her for asthma. Momma kept telling the doctor that the symptoms were similar to those her son, Danny, experienced when he had cardiomyopathy, and there was something wrong with her stomach and stools. The MD sent her to a stomach doctor.

My little sister, Patsy, studied hard and became an anesthetist. She had been working in medicine for several years and was not afraid to speak her mind. She got involved and told the doctor exactly which tests she wanted run on Momma.

The doctor complied, and Patsy and Momma's instincts were correct. In 1990, Momma was diagnosed with dilated cardiomyopathy. She was in heart failure and was placed on a heart transplant list. Momma carried a beeper with her. If the beeper went off, she was to head straight to the airport, where she would pick up a helicopter that would take her to a hospital in *Georgia*, where the transplant would take place.

It was required that Momma quit smoking if she was going to be on a transplant list. She was a smoker for forty years. It wasn't easy, but that's when Momma was the strongest, "when the going gets tough, and the tough get going"!

In support of Momma, all of the family members who smoked cigarettes, quit. Momma was so pleased, she said she would never start back, for fear that her kids would follow suit. The family members that were smokers vowed never to start back for fear they would be giving Momma the green light to give up on life.

Dit took leave of her job as a nurse and left her twice flooded, rotting out house for the bank. There was no way she could sell it in the condition that it was in, and she couldn't afford to fix it. She moved to *Jacksonville, Florida,* to take care of Momma, yet she didn't know what to expect.

She wondered; would Momma's heart continue to fail before a transplant would be made possible?

Would the transplant take place and Momma need help through a long recovery? She felt she was in the best situation to take care of Momma. The rest of us in *Tulsa* still had little ones at home. Punkin and Bo were just getting started with their families.

Dit left her older two boys, Todd and Jess, in the care of Kathie Sullivan. Kathie had been Dit's best friend since high school. She knew the boy's from the time that they were born. They played on the same ball teams with Kathie's nephews and the boys were best friends. Todd and Jess were both in high school now and were highly involved at *Bishop Kelley.* Kathie worked across the street from *Bishop Kelley,* and was the official scorekeeper at the basketball games. She was able to get the boys where they needed to go.

Clint, Dit's youngest, was old enough to hold his own. He would go to live with his dad for a while. Clint was young when his folks divorced. This gave him a chance to bond with his father.

Dink was one of the football coaches for *Bishop Kelley Junior High* now. Clint would help his dad at practice, when he wasn't practicing himself. Dink would see to it that the boys stayed with their present routine while Dit was in *Florida.*

Dit's boys were a lot of fun to be around. My children thought Clint was the greatest cousin in the world. He always acted glad to see them and didn't act as if he was too cool for little kids. He would wrestle around with them and let them climb all over his back. He was a friendly person, very easy to like, and Clint was always smiling!

Jess played football at *Bishop Kelley* and was a very good athlete. He got a scholarship to play football in college. He also played basketball, and his nickname was "sasquatch". All of Dit and Dink's boys could grow hair all over their bodies. Much like their father though, it's tough to keep it on their heads. Jess could tackle as well on the basketball court as he could on the football field.

Todd, the oldest of Dit's boys was athletic as well. God forgot to give him the size to go with his heart, and by high school, he was lucky he didn't get killed. Still, it didn't keep him from trying.

I heard that Todd participated in pep club during the basketball season and would help the crowd noise as much as he could. One game he wore shorts and shaved racing stripes in his legs. Dit's boys were creative in their ability to insight the crowd.

I'll give a further example with Jess, a few years later, when he was in college. It was half time and coach was having a "rah, rah", session with the team. Every week coach would say, "We don't have a superman on this team, we have to work together."

Jess was waiting for the exact moment, knowing the line was coming and when coach said, "We don't have a superman on this team",

Jess said, "Yes we do!" He ripped open his shirt to a shaved chest with a large "S" in the middle of it. The last laugh was on Jess, when coach asked, "Jess, were you looking in the mirror when you shaved that "S" on your chest?"

Ahhhh! However, that's not all. Clint has the winner. He came very close to being kicked out of *Bishop Kelley* for this one. One year for homecoming, following in his brothers footsteps, he let his imagination take it a little too far. He had John Scott Williams, a good friend; shave BK on his ass cheeks. When the time was right in the locker room, he mooned the team.

It would have never gone any further, but there was a photographer in the locker room who thought the picture would be funny. In fact, I heard the picture almost made the yearbook. The school board didn't think it was funny, not a good representation from a Catholic school. Ooooops!

Dit and Dink didn't see things eye to eye as husband and wife, but they were pretty close to seeing them the same when it came to raising teenage boys. They also shared a love and respect for Momma that was extraordinary. The boys did their part and stayed out of any real trouble.

When Dit came back to *Tulsa*, Clint was fourteen-years-old. He chose to stay with his father. She rented a two-bedroom apartment and went back to work. Dit was grateful that she didn't have to mow a lawn or put money into fixing a broken down house.

Kitty was burning the candle at both ends, staying up late and pushing herself. She was a mother of three, going to school to get a degree in Early Childhood Development, and she was working, teaching pre-school, at *Marquette* at the same time. She still managed to get her children, Katie, Sandy and Michael Ed, to and from their sporting events, sing in the choir, and participate in Bunco monthly and various other parish functions. During spring break, she managed to find time to give phoresis.

This was what Kitty and I wanted to do for Lent, a time during our church year, to practice prayer and fasting. In addition to just giving something up, we wanted to give of ourselves in a different way. We went together to the Red Cross. We were informed that if we gave phoresis they would put our DNA into a bone marrow donor bank, just in case someone needed it, we would get a call.

Karen and Charlie's son, my nephew Matthew, on the Huber side of the family, was in need of a bone marrow donor. He had been diagnosed with aplastic anemia, where the bone marrow stops functioning properly, resulting in low growth or no growth of blood forming stem cells.

Kitty and I knew we couldn't match Matt, but perhaps God would help him, if we were willing to help someone else. Two weeks later, Kitty got a call to give blood. She's a rare blood type and answered the call often. During the question and answer period, just before giving blood, the nurse took her pulse. Kitty was missing too many heartbeats. The nurse told Kitty she needed to see a doctor right away.

Kitty found she was in heart failure. She had several tests and the results showed she had cardiomyopathy. Was it hereditary? What are the odds of three family members having this same disease?

Kitty's not even forty-years-old. She has three children at home. One can imagine how difficult this was for all of us. Immediately, we thought we would see Kitty decline the same way we lost our brother, Danny. Could something this tragic be happening to someone so decent and loving?

I found I wanted to control everything she did. Tell her what to eat, what to drink, how active she could be. I was forever trying to slow her down. I sang in the choir with her at *St. Pius X*. The doctor told her to quit choir, but she would not. She quit her job, she quit school, but she could not give up choir.

Much as I reacted when my dad was ill, I couldn't focus at work. I had a difficult time even driving the car. I would forget to get off the exit on the expressway or I would make a wrong turn. The anxiety was making me crazy. I had a panic attack, which landed me in the emergency room. I should have stopped working and stayed home at this time. I can see that now. I was too involved and couldn't see what the stress was doing to me.

At the time, I was still teaching at *St. Pius X Catholic School*. We were all going to confession for a special holiday. I went in and asked for guidance from my priest. Few people know that priests are actually educated in psychology and can be very helpful. There's more to confession than confessing sins but asking for guidance.

Father said something that made perfect sense to me. "Only Kitty can make the decision on how much quality vs. quantity of life she will have." Cheryl, "You need to let go".

"Let go and Let God". Momma used to say that all the time. This is the first time it made sense to me.

I came out of the confessional and there were students standing outside laughing. I had taken so long with the priest they had to move all of the students to another line. They thought I must have had a long list of sins.

Father was right, I made a conscious decision to let go of all of the anxiety that I was carrying around with me. I put it in the hands of God and Kitty, because they were the only ones that were going to make a difference. I prayed for acceptance of whatever. God had a plan we're just not privy to that plan!

Momma was getting better. They had removed Momma from the heart transplant list because she was improving so much. Never underestimate Momma and her positive attitude. She never gave up hope.

Later that year, my momma had a fall getting out of the shower. She broke her ankle so bad that they had a difficult time putting it back together. The doctor said that her bones were like mashed potatoes because her osteoporosis was so bad. They tried to put screws into the ankle, but there was nothing there. They gave Momma a walker, but said that she would never walk again without it.

That Easter Momma had visitors. Bo and his wife Donna came for an Easter egg hunt with their beautiful daughter, Laura. Punkin and her husband, Jeff, came with their son, Tommy and baby Christy. They were all dressed up in their Sunday best.

Momma was dancing with the grandkids, Laura and Tommy, in the kitchen. She had a broom, pretending to be *Snow White*, (1937), singing, *"Whistle while you work"*. She wasn't using a walker. Momma was never one to be defeated.

I would teach music until 1993. During that time, Paul went to *Harvard University* and got an accelerated business degree. It required three months away from home and no communication between us except once a week he could call, and once a month, he would come home for three days.

Some families would not be able to make the sacrifice. One of Paul's friends whom he met at *Harvard* had to leave because his wife couldn't handle it and filed for divorce. Military families go through things much rougher than this, I would tell myself.

Our country had been through the first Gulf War and some of our friends spent a lot of time away from home. In our case, it was definitely worth the sacrifice. Paul was very appreciative of our support. Most importantly, when he came home, he listened even better than he did before he left. He had been exposed to other people from other countries. They approached business from a different perspective. He had broadened his mind and his approach to everything.

Paul said the experience away from home also helped him to focus on what was important in his life. His appreciation for our little family was at the forefront.

Paul survived yet another buyout and the name of the company changed. *Davy McKee* became *John Brown* and *John Brown* was bought out by *Kvaerner*. He was now working for *Kvaerner-John Brown*. The pond kept growing and Paul continued to grow with the pond. We were transferred once again to *Houston*.

Before we left *Oklahoma*, Kelly had the flu, and she was complaining of chest pains. When I took her to the doctor, they felt that given our family history, it would be a good idea to get a look at her heart, so that they would have a baseline and watch for changes as she grew.

The results came back and the doctor was concerned. He felt it would be a good idea to have her looked at more closely in *Texas*. Her left ventricle appeared to be enlarged. Her doctor gave me the name of a doctor at *Texas Children's Medical Center* in *Houston*.

In a large family, you have to learn to share the good times and the bad times. For instance, there are more births, weddings, and graduations, and then you must deal with more divorce, illness and death. The lessons that have had the greatest influence on my life are the ones that were most painful.

All of the years that I had children in the household were special. It got better with every year. The years from 93-97 were no exception. We loved our home in *Katy, Texas*.

We lived in a subdivision called *South Lake Village*, in *Cinco Ranch*. The children on the other side of I-10 called it "*Cinco Rich.*" You didn't really need to be rich to live there. That was the perception people had. We had a two-story home with a swimming pool in the backyard.

We lived down the street from a beach house with a sandy beach, which was actually a part of a swimming pool that looked like a real beach. There was volleyball net for sand volleyball available to all who lived there. The water in the pool gradually got deeper, the further you walked into the pool. Then, there was a rock barrier and a lake on the other side, so it looked like the pool was a part of the lake.

Across the street from the lake, was a park, with tennis courts, toys and a jogging trail that went around a second lake. It had a beautiful fountain, which would light up at night. There was a second fountain in the body of water on the other side of the street. We were allowed to fish and boat in the lake. The boathouse had paddleboats and sailboats that belonged to the neighborhood. They were free, as long as you took lessons and followed the rules.

This was a planned community. It was multicultural. The one thing we all had in common was that education was extremely important to us. To walk and jog the lakes was near three miles. The schools were among the best in the state. Ninety-five percent of the students would go on to college, according to the statistics provided to us when we moved there. That's where we wanted to live.

Our community also had several other swimming pools and various parks scattered about. We had our own security and gardeners to keep the flowerbeds looking nice. It was like living in a dream world.

The last year that I had spent in *Tulsa* left me exhausted. Working at the two schools while Paul was off to *Harvard* was a bit too much for me to handle. There was a great deal of emotional trauma, handling Matt's health issues on the Huber side, Momma and Kitty's health issues on the O'Brien side, and now worries about my Kelly left me drained.

I wasn't proud of the hectic lifestyle we were living. It was difficult for me, but I think it was also taxing on the kids. Finding time to get homework done and eat properly was becoming impossible. I didn't know how to slow it down, but it was spinning out of control. I was growing impatient with my students, my kids and responsibilities at work, feeling pulled apart.

I could not have done it all if it weren't for family and friends helping me. Julie Nelson and I found ways to work together. She would take Mike with her son, Tommy, to baseball and I would take Kelly and Julie's daughter, Stephanie, to softball. Then, I would run Dan where he needed to be. We didn't live close together, so we would meet at *St. Pius X*, a fast food restaurant, or a ball field.

It was difficult to make the move, yet *Katy, Texas*, was the best thing that could have happened for all of us. I thought of myself, like looking from the outside at my life on a TV screen. One picture was before the move to *Katy*, and in the second picture, I was getting the children out the door for school in the morning, after the move.

One screen would be a picture of me screaming at the kids, forty minutes on the road, in traffic, for forgetting their book bag or homework. There was no going back. I had to be at work.

The other screen would be me walking the children to the bus stop in front of the house, greeting their friends in the morning, with little Ginger on her leash. If they forgot their homework, they could run back to the house and get it. Nobody was stressed or losing their temper.

CHAPTER FIFTEEN

THE BUS STOP KIDS

♂☺♀

My children could pick up the bus right in front of our house. Their friends would all live in the same neighborhood. I would not have to drive all over creation every time they had a school project that required a partner. It was heaven.

We purchased our first dog while we were living in *South Lake Village*. She was a full-blooded Pug. We named her Gingersnap, but we called her Ginger. Ginger was beautiful. She wasn't cheap. She came from a long line of champion show dogs. Ginger was a fawn Pug, with a slight bee sting over her Pug nose. She stood a little duck footed but had a perfect cinnamon bun tail. Her markings over her eyes, in the middle of her forehead, were a perfect diamond and she had a dark area on her back from her head to her tail. She had the cute little black velvet mask and ears that Pugs are known for and big eyes.

Ginger would snore when she slept and she could rattle the whole house. We kept her in the utility room, and we trained her eventually, to stay in just the kitchen and den. Pugs shed and I didn't want the hair all over the house. The kitchen and den were not carpeted, so it made the hair a little easier to clean up. Ginger was right there with us when the kids were doing homework or watching TV.

There were two little Russian girls at the bus stop every morning. They would walk with their grandfather. Grandpa Alex is what we called him. He spoke no English. I spoke no Russian, but he would bring treats for the dog and we would walk together after the bus left for a short while. You don't have to speak to be friends. Dog lovers will bond regardless, even if the only thing we have in common is the dog.

Paul had a cashmere sweater, which I purchased for him for Christmas, which he never wore. Paul said he didn't like sweaters. I asked him if it would be O.K. to give it to Grandpa Alex. Paul didn't care, so I wrapped the sweater in just regular wrapping paper, and I took it with me to the bus stop on the corner. Grandpa Alex was dressed up in his veteran's uniform with a pin on the collar. It was a Russian holiday of some kind. He was very touched by the gift.

A few days later, I found Russian dolls and hand painted bowls and spoons resting in the tree off my front porch. My friend had returned the kindness with a gift from his homeland.

Those little Russian girls never got help at home with their homework because their mother couldn't speak English. I would go to the awards ceremony at school in hopes to see one of my children walk up to get an award. Those little girls were wearing the floor out between the podium and their seats.

Grandpa Alex and I would clap as they passed and the girls would smile with their shy little grins.

When Grandpa Alex and his wife were headed back to *Russia* because their visa was going to expire, I put together a scrapbook of pictures of *"the bus stop kids"* and everyone signed a card for them. Then, I put together a basket of toiletries for them to take back to *Russia*.

Before he left, he painted a picture of a cat and had it framed and sent to me through his granddaughters. I had no idea that Grandpa Alex was an artist. I thought it was nice to find out something else about him before he moved away.

The granddaughters would bring one more gift to me after Grandpa Alex left. It was a newspaper article about Pug dogs in Russian. The girls had to read it to me. The gist of which was that Pugs were good lap dogs and would instinctively warm the arthritis of the elderly. I still have the article as one more memory of my old friend.

Isn't it interesting how people can find a way to connect, even without being able to speak the same language? We underestimate our ability to communicate through more than words. Sometimes, it's enough to share the same sunrise.

Most mornings, after I would see Grandpa Alex back to his house and Ginger back to the kitchen, I would meet my friend Kathy

Rahn in front of her house. She and I would walk three to five miles everyday. Kathy was also a retired teacher, with a husband who was an engineer and she had three children, a girl and two boys. We had a lot in common.

Kathy and I enjoyed shopping together or going out to lunch. We did some volunteer work in the gardens at the school, and sometimes we would play golf. We remain friends today. Kathy's son, Rory, met at our bus stop and there was one other house, which was on the corner and sat between my house and Kathy's. That house belonged to John and Rhonda. Their children and mine would become very good friends.

Lauren and Johnny were beautiful children, both with red hair and freckles. They were intelligent too. I remember Lauren helping my momma with the crossword puzzle one morning, when Momma had come to *Houston* for a visit. Momma couldn't believe how smart Lauren was.

I would help Johnny and Lauren with their homework, much as I did with my own children. Lauren loved to go over her spelling words. I think she liked the attention she would get from Kelly or me when we studied with her. She especially liked spending time with Kelly. Kelly was older and seemed almost like a celebrity to Lauren.

Lauren and Johnny's parents were going through a divorce. Their Momma was sick. I would feed the children most nights of the week, and sometimes I would send home food to Rhonda, because I knew she wasn't eating.

It was a blessing their dad, John, ended up getting custody of the children. He was a good person. John would walk the children to the bus stop in the morning. He had a woman that came in and helped after school, and she would cook dinner and look after the children until he got home from work in the evenings. They spent a great deal of their time at our house after school, playing with my kids. I loved them as though they were my own.

John was a member of the Knights of Columbus and after the divorce; he remained involved in the church. He met a young mother of two and they began dating. Jennifer was her name. She became his new wife and a mother for the children.

When John and Jennifer married, they were moving to the east coast. I was convinced that the reason God had moved me to *Texas*, was to help these children through this transition in their lives. Still, I hurt deeply knowing they would no longer be a part of our daily lives.

John, Jennifer, and the kids were leaving for their house-hunting trip. I was praying in the den, having a bit of an anxiety attack. I had just said goodbye to the children and I wanted God to send me reassurance that Johnny and Lauren were going to be O.K.

Bam! I heard something hit the window. "Dan, look outside, if that was a bird, it might be stunned."

Dan came in with a blue parakeet. "I think this is Johnny and Laurens bird." He said.

As it ended up, the bird got out when they left on their house-hunting trip and they didn't have time to catch it. I kept the bird until we could get it back into the house, where it would be safe.

Then, I convinced myself that this was the sign I was praying for, God was listening. We are not alone in this world. I felt a little like *Mary Poppins*, (1964). I was there to get the children through a difficult transition in their lives. Johnny and Lauren were going to be O.K. I provided a safe haven, for just a short time in their lives. It was time to let them fly.

CHAPTER SIXTEEN

WE'VE COME A LONG WAY SINCE THE HORSE AND BUGGY

♥

Kelly was in the sixth grade at the time when we made our move to *Katy, Texas*. She started middle school, taking a separate bus from her brothers the first year. Our little girl was growing up and by the middle of the year, she would ask me to stop walking her to the bus stop because the kids were teasing her. It was rough for me to let go. The children became independent much too soon for me. I didn't want to cut the umbilical cord. I enjoyed quizzing her on her spelling words and helping her memorize lines for plays. "Why do things have to change?"

Early that fall, I took Kelly to the Pediatric Heart Association, and her appointment with Dr. Grifka, at *Texas Children's Medical Center*. Going to the doctor is an all day affair if you live in the big city. When we lived in *Tulsa*, it was a couple of hours out of your day.

If you're from *Tulsa, Oklahoma,* driving in *Houston* can be a little intimidating. Driving in the city would make my shoulders, back and neck sore, from all of the tension. I would find myself squeezing the steering wheel to the point that my knuckles were white. There was concrete everywhere I looked, and bridges and overpasses going in all directions. Then, when I would reach the medical district, it was building after building and hospital after hospital.

The *Abercrombi* building was our destination. Parking lot number 11. Five stories of the building was nothing but parking lots. You don't want to lose your car in that mess. I wrote down all of the information I could think of to be sure I could find the car again upon my return. The cost of parking was five dollars or more. The whole experience was frightening. I just tried to stay focused on the directions given to me and somehow we arrived at the location, which we were intending to go.

We sat in the entry of the Pediatric Cardiac Unit and watched the parade of worried parents come in and out while waiting for our turn. The waiting room had a large aquarium full of beautiful salt-water fish. It was entertaining for the children and adults as well, yet brought a peaceful feeling to the room, providing a place for the eyes to focus.

There were toys in the corner and several children playing quietly. Most of the parents sat with a blank stare and tried hard not to make eye contact with any of the other people in the room. That is not generally the way for Texan's to behave. They usually love to talk.

The nurse called Kelly's name. We followed the clean white shoes down the hallway and she led us to a small room. Kelly and I went through the typical routine for a new patient and amid the mindless sequence of activities, came the family history.

"The family history usually can't fit on one page." I told her, with a nervous laugh.

Then I began to rattle off all of the afflictions from both sides of the family. When the Dr. appeared a few minutes later, he seemed to be curious, or concerned, I wasn't sure which, about our family history. He asked me if I thought the family would be interested in participating in a study of dilated cardiomyopathy.

It was an answer to our prayers. This had been discussed in our family on many occasions. Not everyone in the family had insurance. This would be a way for them to be looked at without having to pay excessively (through the nose). If this disease were hereditary, it would be nice to know who needs to be watched closely.

Dr. Grifka placed a call to Dr. Towbin, at *Baylor College of Medicine*. Next thing I know, Dr. Towbin is coming to meet me. He hobbled over on crutches because he had a broken ankle. Dr. Towbin wasn't a big man. He looked like a thirty-year-old college professor, with hair on his face and curly locks on his head. He was a good-looking man and very kind. You would never know if you met him on the street, that he was such an important person, but he was. He was someone intelligent, who could speak to you at your level without making you feel like he was being condescending.

185

Dr. Towbin took a formidable amount of time explaining the medical study. His conversation with me included hand drawn diagrams of the heart. He explained how the disease could progress. A weak heart muscle enlarged to compensate for the inability to pump blood to the organs. As the heart grows weaker, the heart grows larger until it reaches a point that the valves leak and it can't beat properly.

I agreed to talk to our family members to be sure they were interested. Then, promised to help get all of the information from family members etc…I would work together with Karla, one of the members of his team.

Funny thing, Kelly's test results came back normal. (The ejection fraction was on the low side of normal, but it was normal.) Her heart was fine. I was relieved. Still, we would have never been set up with Dr. Towbin if we had not gone through this reality check. It was worth the worry everything seemed to happen for a reason.

We had a blood letting party with my momma's family in *Louisiana*. All of her siblings lined up and we had a nurse draw their blood. Then, I would refrigerate it and bring it back with me to *Texas*. We did the same with my siblings in *Tulsa*. We shipped the blood from Patsy and Shelton's children in *Georgia* and Bo and Punkin in *Florida*. It was all coming together.

Then we had a three-day weekend, and all of my brothers and sisters living in *Tulsa*, came to *Houston* and brought their children. There were fourteen of us in all who would have our hearts looked at on that day. All of my children had been looked at by this time.

Our home was large but we didn't have that many beds. We had everyone bring his or her sleeping bags and had a massive slumber party. It was actually a lot of fun. I would introduce my family to *"Fuzzy's Pizza"* that weekend. **David Letterman** touted *"Fuzzy's"* to be the best pizza in the US, when they had one flown in for *Late Night*.

It took three vans to get all fifteen of us to the hospital the next day. I had been there a number of times at this point; often I would get turned around. It was easy to find the medical district, because of some twin buildings on the street next to *Texas Children's Hospital*, but it was hard to find the right building if you couldn't see the skyline.

I had my brothers and sisters follow me, so they wouldn't get lost going to the hospital. I should have used a map. We didn't have GPS back then. I got turned around at one point, but then spotted my twin buildings. Yea!

Because this was a three-day holiday weekend, the traffic in the medical district wasn't bad. I pointed to the twin buildings on the horizon and said, *"Follow me!"*

No one followed. They just honked the horn, pointed and laughed. I was headed the wrong way on a one-way street. *"Ooops*! I hate when that happens."

This was holiday when the clinic was closed. That way Dr. Towbin's team could have all of us come in and have echocardiograms done by the same doctor, on the same machine, looking for similarities, and discrepancies. He knew exactly what he was looking for, and he was getting baselines on all of us.

We kept each other well entertained in the waiting area. There's never a dull moment with our family.

Over the next few years, they watched certain family members closely, looking for signs of the disease. Genetically, Momma, Kitty, Kitty's daughter, Katie and my sister, Patsy, had DNA that lined up exactly. These were the family members who would need the closest monitoring of signs and symptoms of the disease. This was still not an exact science and others with similar DNA would be watched closely as well.

Kitty and Russell's daughter, Katie, came down to *Houston* with Erin Bender, one of her *Bishop Kelley* friends, for spring break the following year. Katie and Aaron had been great friends throughout most of their childhood. They drove from *Tulsa* to *Houston* together. It was about a nine or ten hour drive. I can imagine that they had the radio blaring the entire way.

The girls had the opportunity to stay long enough to enjoy the *Houston* weather. We visited *Galveston* and took the ferry across the water, feeding the seagulls. The girls worked on their tans and collected souvenirs. We tracked sand into the car and drove back to *Katy, Texas*. It's only about a two-hour drive from our home to *Galveston*. Well worth the drive.

Katie had more than her mother's heart. She inherited Kitty's broad smile, big blue eyes, her cute figure and her long beautiful blonde hair. My children looked up to Katie but feared her just a little as well. She was their babysitter when they were young. She could be strict if she had to be, in their words, "*bossy*". Katie was used to being around children a lot. She and her sister, Sandy, were often amusing children in their living room, while the parents would be visiting at Kitty's dining room table.

Michael Ed, their younger brother, was too young to baby-sit. He was more like a friend for my kids to play with. He didn't like being "bossed" by his sister, so they bumped heads a lot. They had nearly as many cousins on the Otterstrom side of the family as they did on the O'Brien side. Kitty's home was just as open to the Otterstrom Clan as it was to the O'Brien Clan. It put Katie and Sandy both in a position of authority at a young age that matured them beyond their years.

I went with the girls when Katie went for her heart tests. It was good that Katie had Aaron with her when she visited with the doctor. Katie would need the company for the drive back home to *Tulsa*. The news was disturbing. The test results showed that Katie was in the beginning stages of the heart disease. It hits each generation earlier than the generation before. They told Katie that she may never be able to have children, because if might weaken her heart and take her life.

Kitty and Russell's oldest daughter, from the time that she turned seventeen-years-old, would steadily get worse. Katie would drive to *Houston* and have a check-up every six months. Dr. Towbin's team eventually informed her that she needed to get a doctor in *Oklahoma* and get on heart medication.

Michael Ed, Kitty's son, his heart beat sloppy but he was never truly diagnosed. Still, the doctors felt, given our family history, it would be wise for him not to participate in football. Pushing the heart would not be prudent. Michael joined a theatre group and kept his interests at a lower activity level.

In his twenties, he tested it a little, trying to see what his capacities were. He had hopes of joining the service, but they turned him away. Then, he tried to be a Fireman, perhaps in denial of his limitations. The body will only do what it can; eventually he gave up on the idea.

We've come along way since the horse and buggy, and modern medicine has come along way as well. What the doctors found, which was to our advantage, is that the medical condition in our family was moving much slower than in most of the cases they had seen. Since the disease was moving slow, the body was learning to compensate. Many families don't have enough family members alive by the time they realize the specific disorder exists.

We had plenty of visits from family over the years in *Katy* and we were sure to have a great time. When Billy came, we went to NASSA. I locked my keys in the car with the car running in the parking lot. Billy had to use a coat hanger to get them out.

Galveston was a hot spot for most of our visitors. We took them for a free ride on the ferry, to feed the seagulls, off the back end of the boat. We packed picnic lunches and ate on the beach and watch for porpoise. The kids would go for a swim and we'd eat burgers when we became famished and ready for dinner.

Still, no time was more memorable than the time we had our slumber party and visited the *Children's Medical Center*. We drank beer and told our stories for the one hundredth time. We had a new audience because John was over, from next door. We were all in brilliant form and had John in stitches.

I would call Momma on Saturday morning for several years, and we would share a cup of coffee and converse. She had been complaining of feeling weak and was having difficulty breathing. She went to her heart doctor; she thought it was her heart making her tired. The doctors in *Florida* had changed her medication and she was part of a study, where some people would be on a placebo. She told her doctor her symptoms. He assured her that her heart was fine.

Momma would go home, only to find that the problem was getting worse. She went back to the doctor, and still, he didn't feel her medication was the problem. He began by running tests on the heart.

It didn't take long to figure out that the problem was somewhere else. Tests revealed a spot on Momma's lung the size of a fifty-cent piece. More tests were necessary to see if it was cancer. Momma had not smoked a cigarette for ten-years, but she had smoked for forty years prior to that.

Momma was in the hospital, waiting for the results to come back when she told Punkin if it was cancer, she wanted to go like Aint Jo. Momma was at Aint Josephine's bedside when she passed away. She had hospice care and went quietly, with little suffering.

For the next two weeks, I reread *Jonathan Livingston Seagull*, **Richard Bach**, *The Prophet*, **Khahill Gibran** and *Christ among Us*, **Anthony Wilhelm** and books about the life of **Mother Teresa**, *In Her Own Words*, and *No Greater Love*. I went through my Bible study books and reread my Bible. I spent a lot of time in prayer, preparing myself for the worse and still hoping for the best.

The results of Momma's tests came back, and Momma had lung cancer. The doctor said it was already in advanced stages!

I called daily to check on Momma. Each time I called, it sounded like they were having a card party. Momma was enjoying herself. She even made fun of herself because she was seeing fairies dancing on the wall. Her medication was making her hallucinate.

All of my siblings had raced to *Florida* to spend some time with Momma. I felt it would be sensible to wait until they were all back home. I would go and stay with her after the rest of them used up their vacation time. Maybe I would even get some "one on one" time with her. I had imagined this was going to drag on for a while.

Two weeks later, I was on my way to *Florida*. The flight was a bit bumpy coming in. *Jacksonville* was being hit by tropical storm, Josephine. I stepped off of the airplane and made my way down a narrow tunnel toward the gate. Two of my brothers, Ray and Billy, greeted me. After a typical O'Brien greeting with big bear hugs, my brothers informed me that Momma had a "really bad night." The explanation, which followed, was grim. She had been on a downhill spiral for a couple of days.

They didn't tell me over the phone the last time I called. They just told me she was resting. They knew I already had my flight arranged and would be there soon enough. Still, they didn't want me to be surprised when I showed up at the house and saw Momma totally incapacitated.

Momma's bedroom was really cold. The windows were open, even though the tropical storm was in full force. There was a fan blowing in Momma's face. She felt like she was burning up. Her fight for oxygen was wearing her out.

I had come from *Texas* and didn't bring a sweater. I was expecting *Florida* to be as warm as *Texas*. They had the air conditioning cranked down as low as it could go. I know it had to have been below sixty in her room. I had to get a sweater out of Momma's closet.

Momma teased me. "You can't wait until I'm gone before you start taking my stuff"!That was Momma's way. Make light of the situation.

Momma asked, "Are all of my ducks in a row?"

That was her way of asking if all of her paperwork and insurance papers were in order. She had lots of help getting those things organized, because of her heart scare.

My brother, Billy, did a wonderful job helping Momma put it all together, her last will and testament and living will. Between the two of them, they had left no stone unturned. Momma went through it all with me. She had me type it up the last time I had visited her in *Florida*, and the neighbor notarized it for us.

I sat at Momma's bedside and sang songs softly. We prayed together and I rubbed lotion on her feet, an informal reflexology, since I've never really trained for it. It helped to relax her and she liked that a lot. I rubbed her head at the temples and combed her hair. These were all things, which I thought might help her relax and forget about her pain.

At one point, I remember thinking this would be the way to go. Bryan was at her head, stroking her hair, Kitty was stroking her arm and I was massaging her feet. We were singing our choir songs and old songs from our past, some in two-part harmony.

When we sang "Sunrise, Sunset", from *The Fiddler on the Roof* (1971), our momma got tears in her eyes. Just like Momma, only music could touch her heart that way. This is the song we sang for Punkin and Jeff's wedding, and she cried then. Momma loved it when we sang.

When Father came to give Momma her last rights, I wasn't sure how cognizant she was. The priest would ask me questions and I would answer them. He asked if all ten of Momma's children were present.

I answered, "All but Dit."Dit had gone home earlier that week.

Momma jumped! "Where's Dit?"

From then on, every 15 minutes or so, Momma was asking to see Dit. We don't really know why it was so important to Momma that Dit be there. Maybe it was because Momma knew Dit had a sense of humor and would keep things light. Maybe, it was because she

191

knew how hard closure would be for Dit. Whatever the reason, it was imperative at this point.

Our husbands got together and made arrangements for Dit to come back to *Florida*. She ended up on the same airplane with Billy's daughter, Diane.

I remember De and Sheena in the kitchen, cooking Momma's last meal. It was a thoughtful thing to do, typical of De. Momma had requested Thanksgiving turkey, green beans and cranberry sauce for her last meal.

What a lovely way of looking at death. I imagined, "this was in thanksgiving for the life she lived and a thanksgiving for the life to come."

Ray's son, Ed, (Daddy's namesake) brought his guitar. His rendition of the **Eagles**, *"Hotel California"*, I remember the best. The music was soothing and you could tell that it pleased Momma. Billy came in and sang some songs. Then, I asked Momma if she would like us to have Christmas early. She loved the idea! There were nine of the ten, gathered at her bedside and several of the grandchildren as well. We sang every Christmas carol we knew, as she slept.

In a way, you could say we sang her to sleep. Momma never spoke again before she slipped away, but we saw tears in her eyes a couple of times, and wondered if it was Momma's typical tear up for a song, or just a natural occurrence. We would never know the answer to that question.

The very moment Dit came into the house, she ran to Momma's bedroom as we all rushed her towards the door. She came in drenched, from the rain. The storm was blowing violently when they came in. Momma took her last gasp of air in Dit's arms. Dit kissed her and hugged her tight.

"It must have been the onion bagel!" Dit said through her tears.

"Anyone else want the kiss of death?" She held out her arms and we all laughed and cried at the same time.

That's the way Momma would have wanted it. She was keeping it light!

Suddenly, the sun came out. The rain ceased. There was an eerie calm in the air. We were in the eye of the storm.

We called *Louisiana* to tell Momma's family that she had passed. Charley answered the phone. When the words reached his ears, he said, "We knew when tropical storm Josephine passed through *Jacksonville*, Aint Jo had come to get Alva."

Hospice was there to help us with the details. We took Momma with us to *Tulsa*, to be buried at *Calvary Cemetery*, next to Daddy and Danny. The difficult task of taking care of Momma's home and property would fall on Bo and Punkin. Bo was the executor of the estate. (Punkin and her husband, Jeff would eventually sell their house and buy Momma's.)

We had a prayer service in *Jacksonville* for Momma. I think I was so numb, I don't remember it well. We sang all of the songs ourselves, and family read all of the readings, as we did for Daddy.

Punkin put together a collage of the family. Then she pulled my heart right out of my chest when she played a song that I had never heard before, which became a huge hit, by **Celine Dion**, and written by Diane Warren, called, *Because you Loved Me.*

Because you loved me
For all those times you stood by me
For all the truth that you made me see
For all the joy you brought to my life
For all the wrong that you made right
For every dream, you made come true
For all the love I found in you
I'll be forever thankful
You're the one who held me up
Never let me fall
You're the one who saw me through, through it all

Refrain:
You were my strength when I was weak
You were my voice when I couldn't speak
You were my eyes when I couldn't see
You saw the best there was in me
Lifted me up when I couldn't reach

You gave me faith 'coz you believed
I'm everything I am
Because you loved me

You gave me wings and made me fly
You touched my hand, I could touch the sky
I lost my faith; you gave it back to me
You said no star was out of reach
You stood by me and I stood tall
I had your love I had it all
I'm grateful for each day you gave me
Maybe I don't know that much
But I know this much is true
I was blessed because I was loved by you.

Refrain:

You were always there for me
The tender wind that carried me
A light in the dark shining your love into my life
You've been my inspiration.
Through the lies, you were the truth
My world is a better place because of you

Refrain:
Refrain:

We all rode back to *Tulsa* on the same airplane. I ask you, why is it when you get together with your siblings that everyone drops back into the rolls that they played in childhood? I'm sure that the stewardess wanted to choke us before we left the plane.

I remember Punkin, flicking a pea, from her plate, across three isles to hit Bryan in the head. He would turn around and she would look away. Then, she would giggle and do it again. She was a 35- year-old woman, flicking peas at her fifty-year-old brother.

There we were, just a day later, in *Tulsa*. We had visitation at the funeral home for Momma. Time was spent mostly visiting old friends of the family. Some traveled all the way from Louisiana, to pay their respects. We had our Cousin Jay, Uncle Jack and Aint Evelyn's son, who was a preacher, say a few words and lead us in a prayer.

The next day was Momma's funeral Mass. We had it at *Christ the King Church*. Our parish church from our childhood. It could not have been more beautiful. The *St. Pius X Choir* I sang in with Kitty in the early 1990's sang from the choir loft above us. It was touching. The music was beautiful. How special they would take off work and make the time to be there for us. Hundreds of people filled the church. Once again, it was the *Catholic Community* of *Tulsa*, and our extended family that brought comfort and support at the time we needed it most.

We went to Kitty's house and sat around her dining room table. We spent the day reliving our stories of the past. Visitors were coming and going all day long, bringing food and friendship. Toward the end of the evening, there was a young boy, probably about five-years-old, who had been playing with our children throughout the day. Most of our guests had cleared away.

"Who is that?" Kitty said.

"I thought he came with Kelli Powell." Sarah guessed.

"No I thought he came before Kelli, and Kelli's gone." Someone else said.

Kitty's knee jerk reaction, "We better feed him, he's been here all day and I haven't seen him come in for even a drink of water."

Kitty brought him in and stuffed him with everything she could think to give him. Then, cake and cookies added to a full stomach, as we tried to get information from him to see where he belonged.

It appeared that he came from the apartments down the street from Kitty. He saw all of the kids playing and decided to join the party. He didn't say much, but we got his first name.

I went with several of the other brothers and sisters and eventually found a family who had been looking for the child for several hours. I think they were relieved to know that he was O.K. Still, they were really mad at him for being so far from home.

Once again, the hat was passed. One more story tacked on to the list of tales to share at the table. It's appropriate under these circumstances the hospitality carried on from one generation to another. What a suitable ending to the life of the *"Queen of Hospitality."* Kitty accepted her new role with honor.

She is Mother
Wm H. O'Brien (Billy)

She is Mother.
She is The Womb.
She is the night light in my
Room.

She has unending patience
And unwavering morals.
She remains impartial
When settling quarrels.

She listens intently
Without making a sound.
Then delivers a message
That is short and profound.

Her moves are well planned
With attention to detail.
She overcomes obstacles,
Determined to prevail.

Her healing ability
Is hard to explain.
But, somehow her compassion
Seems to take away pain.

Though fate has been cruel,

She showed no resentment.
In fact, in her presence,
You can feel her contentment.

She loves unconditionally.
Her only concern
Is whether or not
She is loved in return.

She is worshipped!
Her honor is defended
If you insult a man's mother,
He is personally offended.

She is a part of us,
As we are a part of her.
She is the heart of us.
She is Mother.

CHAPTER SEVENTEEN

LONDON BOUND, 1997

✝

Paul and I had discussed the possibility of being transferred to *London*. We knew that the opportunity would eventually present itself. Paul's career had already gone as far as he could go in *Houston*. I doubt I would have agreed to go to *London* if Momma was still ill. The timing appeared to be in our favor when Paul's company made the offer.

Still, the decision was difficult to make. We were happy and I don't like to rock the boat when things are going well. I was waiting for some revelation, anything that God or man could do to help in our decision to make this move.

Talking with my Aint Leona about the subject, I said, "I wonder what Momma would have done?"

My momma's sister looked at me with my mothers brown eyes. "I know what your Momma would have done. She would have followed Ed to the end of the earth."

We were leaning toward choosing *London*, as long as the kids were accepted into the *American Community School,* in *Cobham, England.* While I was praying, a robin flew in through the back door. I had to use a broom to scare the bird back out through the same entrance. Birds are a reminder, that I'm not alone when making my decisions.

To those who have faith, you don't need signs, but the signs are always there. Sometimes we ask for them in order to be reassured. To those who have no faith there are no signs.

I was relaying my story to my friend, and she challenged me. She was a woman of faith, but she was not comfortable with the concept of asking for signs. Not all people are!

In the Bible, dreams often were messages, yet today we don't listen for a message in our dreams. In the bible, birds would sometimes play a part in some of the best-known stories. When Christ was baptized there was a dove ascending into the sky and a voice from the heavens that said, "This is my Son with whom I am well pleased"! Noah knew he was going to find land by the dove with the olive branch. Why can't we look for signs as well?

Perhaps I'm just a little crazy!

My sister-in-law, Kathy, was visiting from *Dallas* to say goodbye before Paul and I moved our family to *London*. She and I were making the three mile walk around the *Cinco Lakes*. I told Kathy of my story of the blue parakeet with Johnnie and Lauren and of the recent visit from the robin. I told her of my disappointment when my other friend didn't take the sign seriously.

Then I said, "Maybe, instead of a robin, it should have been a blue bird". The moment that those words came from my mouth, a blue parakeet flew from the area across the street and landed in the tree beside me.

I would not have seen the parakeet if Kathy hadn't said, "Did you see that?"

I have to say, it gave me a bit of a chill. The hair on my arms was standing straight up as I tried to coax the blue parakeet onto my finger, but it never came out of the tree. Just for clarification, parakeets are not a common bird for *Texas*, unless they're in a cage.

Weird Huh? I wonder how many other people have stories like these, but keep them to themselves for fear that the world would call them crazy? I feel the connection between man and nature is much closer than we are willing to accept. If it were a regular blue jay, I would have thought nothing of it, but a parakeet.

Our children had not really started high school yet. Kelly was going to be a freshman. She had been accepted into *St. Agnes Catholic School*, in *Houston*. She had gone for only a few days before our decision was final. We were waiting on the school in *London* to accept the children and they did. Things were finally coming together.

Paul and I came to the conclusion, moving to *London* would be a chance of a lifetime. This will be an education money can't buy.

Kelly began as a freshman, Mike, in the seventh grade and Dan was in the fifth grade. It wasn't going to be forever. It was supposed to be a two-year stay. It was time enough to experience something we might never experience if we didn't take advantage of this opportunity. Not just Paul and me, this would give other family members a chance to experience a part of *Europe* as well, if they wanted to come for a vacation.

In our lives, doors open, but if we don't have the courage to walk through, we might miss opportunities. I've always believed this, yet, sometimes it's difficult to walk through. It's easy to see what we're leaving behind, and it's not so easy to see what's ahead. Still, I know I'm not alone, and that's what gives me courage.

Flying coach with three children was not the best way to travel. Then, somehow, I lost all of my good costume jewelry. It was strapped to my waste in a fanny pack that disappeared somewhere between the airplane and customs.

When we arrived to *London*, we had ten suitcases between the five of us. Still, we managed to get all of the suitcases to the *Wheatsheaf Hotel-Pub*, where we were going to be staying until we could get settled into our house.

The *Wheatsheaf* was an old English pub and our room was to be located above the pub. It had a lot of character. The outside looked like it was Tudor. Inside, there was short carpet; more like a rug than the thick carpet we had back home in the states. It was dark in the pub. There was not much lighting and the walls and floor were dark colors, mostly shades of red and brown. It smelled musty and full of smoke and mildew.

Our room was not ready when we arrived at the hotel. We filled the small waiting room in the lobby with our suitcases and spread out across the entry, jet lagged and exhausted, smelling a little ripe by now and stuck in a tiny non air-conditioned room.

When our quarters were finally ready, we went upstairs, dragging our suitcases behind us.

We flew in during the month of July and *England* was having an unusually hot summer. There was no air conditioning in our room. I'm certain that most of the time in *London* they didn't need it. The windows were open; perhaps there would be a breeze in the evening to cool things off.

Staying above a pub on a Friday evening with the windows open and live music until one o'clock in the morning was now a new experience. If there was a breeze, I didn't feel it. This was one night that I didn't want to experience twice. I was exhausted and the jet lag was beginning to get to me.

I told Paul I thought it would be worth sleeping on the floor at our rented house before staying another night above the pub.

He agreed, so we went shopping for bedding. The kids picked out their own sheets, pillows and duvets for their rooms. We picked up alarm clocks and various other necessary items for the kitchen.

When we got to the checkout at *John Lewis*, with several hundred pounds in merchandise, our credit cards would not work.

"Is this material for a **Chevy Chase** movie or what?" I said, with a fake laugh. The kind of laugh you have, when you've topped the stairs and are climbing into the seat of a roller coaster. Things were not going smoothly, or as Paul would say, "the tea leaves were not lining up."

I was beginning to panic, but Paul could here it in my voice. He always knows how to handle me in stressful situations. We took the kids to the food court at the mall and found a familiar place to eat. I never thought I would be so happy to see a Burger King!

Everyone calmed down once we filled our bellies. Paul assured me he would call the bank in the morning and everything would be just fine. We explored the town a little and found our way back to the hotel for another sleepless night.

A car picked us up at our hotel. We loaded the three kids and ten suitcases into the car and we were ready to begin our adventure. Our driver dropped us at our house in *Woking, Surrey*. It was across the street from *Horsell Commons*. The commons was an area much like a national forest would be in the states. It was full of pine trees and the ground was covered with ferns. When the sunshine streaked through the pines, the long shadows were cast across the ground and it was surreal.

Ours was a new house, red brick exterior, with a clay roof.

Paul said, "The construction is outstanding." This was the civil engineer coming out in him. "This house was built to last a long time." Our taxi driver was ready to leave. Thank God, Paul had the foresight to ask,

"Do you have a map or something to help us find our way around?"

The real estate agent didn't leave us anything. No maps, no instructions at all.

The driver left us with his A-Z map of *London* and the surrounding area. Paul convinced him to stay long enough to circle our location on the map, where our dog Ginger was staying in quarantine, where the school was located and the train station so that he could get to work. Then, we were on our own.

The house was very nice. It was a two-story house with five bedrooms. The rooms were small, much smaller than we were used to in the states. All three of the kids had their own room. Kelly would have the guest bedroom. It had a bathroom, so she wouldn't have to share with her brothers. She had the largest closet too. I think she may have had the best room in the house. Through the window, you could see the back garden. There was a cypress tree in the back, which must have been over two hundred years old. It was majestic.

The boys' rooms were barely big enough for their beds and a dresser. Their closets were small, but they didn't need as much room for their clothes. Mike and Dan were glad to have their own bedrooms and that they didn't have to share. They would share a bathroom between the two of them.

The master bedroom was great. The furniture the company had rented for us was not up to the standard I was expecting and I would have to work that out over the next few weeks. I was beginning to relax. We were going to be all right.

The last bedroom was for the computer to be set up. This would be where I would spend a lot of time. I was totally computer illiterate, but would learn enough to get the computer and printer up and running by talking to the technicians on the phone, in what seemed to me to be a foreign language. There were days I thought I might throw the computer out the second story window. I had no confidence in what I was doing at this point.

The kids showed me how to send e-mail. Up until this move, I was afraid to turn the computer on. I would have some friends back in *Texas* who would stay in touch through the internet. Not many of my friends or family were computer savvy but the world was changing rapidly.

Our children's school required the kids to have a computer. A lot of their homework was done on the computer and sent directly to the teacher or was saved on a disk they would have to take with them to class. The school was on top of the changes happening in the world and I was certain that the kids were going to get a good education at *ACS Cobham.*

When we picked up the company car, it was a Sunday. Paul had planned it that way so there would not be a lot of traffic. Paul would have an opportunity to drive on the left side of the road for the first time. No one had gassed up the company car and it was sitting on empty. Paul had no idea where to find gasoline, especially on a Sunday, in *London.* He was not a happy camper. I'm sure someone at work got an ear full.

Our shipment was six weeks away, with the majority of our belongings. We had an air shipment coming with just our essentials that was two weeks away. For now, all we had was what we could carry in our suitcases.

What do you do with three kids and no TV or entertainment? That was our next, new experience. It was time to get the imagination working. It was only one generation ago, that TV, radio and air conditioning didn't exist. How difficult could it be? I thought.

Kelly designated this, our "Brady Bunch (1969) moments"! We played charades and cards. The kids played with the movie camera, dance, and they sang songs. They did everything they could think of the first weekend we were there. It was going to be a long six weeks!

Anyone who tries to tell you that the British people are not friendly to American's, did not share the same experience we did. Our neighbors were quick to come to the rescue.

One of our neighbors loaned us a small TV. They allowed us to use it until we had time to get a TV of our own. Another neighbor loaned us pots and pans and took us to the grocery store and to the kid's school. She showed Paul how to get to the train station, so he would be able to get to work. We were finally settling in.

If you've never been through an international move, it's hard to describe what it's like. You don't know how to bank, you don't know how to grocery shop, because you don't recognize the brands. You don't know how to drive. The stress levels can rise rapidly.

Now, the language is called English, but it's not the English we are used to. A fag is a cigarette. A stove is a hob. A boot is the back of a car. A jacket is a sweater, and a toilet is a loo!

If you're being held in a queue, you are waiting in line and if you are pissed, you are drunk. If someone pissed on your chips, you're having a really bad day. These are just a few of the examples of how different our language really is.

Paul's company would pay for the children to go to the *American Community School, in Cobham, England.* The school had students from 67 different countries represented there. It was located about 40 minutes from the house, given the traffic situation.

I felt it was stressful living in the *UK.* When I needed to get away and let go of some of that stress, I would walk across the street. I was blessed to be across from the *Horsell Commons.* It was quiet enough to help me find peace when I needed it most.

I found out later, this is where **H.G. Wells** sat while writing the scene of the aliens coming to earth in his famous book, *War of the Worlds.* I would spend many days walking in the commons and exploring the area surrounding them.

Two weeks after we arrived in *London,* **Princess Diana** died in the fatal car accident, with a drunk driver, going at excessive speed. The British people found this news very hard to take. I must admit I shared their grief. What a waste of a beautiful person with still so much to give.

Her boyfriend, Dodi, was buried just 13 miles from our house. People were taking flowers to *Kensington Palace* and it was all anyone could think or talk about for several days. I was glued to the television, watching the drama play out, as the British people were demanding an explanation as to how this could have happened.

The day of **Princess Diana's** funeral, we stayed home and watched on television. It would have been quite an opportunity to be a witness to such a historical event, but I was not ready yet, to venture out on my own in *London.* It was strange how quiet everything was on that day. There were no cars in the streets, or traffic of any kind, it was just silent outside. The British people had a true day of mourning.

Diana's death was followed by the death of my heroine, **Mother Teresa of Calcutta**. I was disappointed that **Mother Teresa's** death was over-shadowed by the Diana incident. I guess Mother Teresa would not have wanted all of the attention anyway.

We spent the first six months we lived in *Surrey*, visiting our Pug dog, Ginger. We found the nicest kennel we could find, and still, I felt awful putting her through it.

We intentionally chose the house we did because it was close enough to the kennel I could visit daily. Sometimes I would stay for a couple of hours and just read a book. Mostly, Ginger wanted to play tug of war with her toys. There were some days that were really cold and I would bundle up and cuddle with her.

The way the quarantine was set up, Ginger had a room, which was about 8ft by 8ft inside and another room that was 8ft by 8ft outside. The room had a chair that Ginger could sit in or under, and the chair had a light over it that provided heat when it was cold in her room. She had her toys and her blanket from home.

The people who ran the quarantine were very kind and they played with her whenever they had the chance. Who could resist playing with a two-year-old Pug?

The kids and Paul would go on weekends to visit. Only three could be in the area with the dog at one time so we would split into groups. We would bathe her and let her play in the water in a separate room on occasion. Thankfully, Pugs sleep a lot. Once we wore her out, I'm sure she spent a great deal of time sleeping. We couldn't wait to get her home.

Most days I would spend time being a tourist. I filled a great deal of time searching for Ty Beanie Babies. Collecting the little stuffed animals gave me something to focus on while I explored the shops on the streets of *London*. At some point, I lost interest in exploration and collecting. Suddenly, finding a friend and something to belong to seemed more important. I'm a people person!

Kelly got involved and made friends easily. She was a cheerleader, played volleyball and basketball. She would go to professional soccer games. She loved being able to get around in *London* by the trains and subways. She had the opportunity to visit *Scotland, Paris, Spain and*

Austria. She pouted some at first and tried a little manipulation for a while. It works well on me, but Paul didn't fall for it.

Once she met Monica Hamrick, she didn't have time for pouting. The two of them were inseparable. Monica and Kelly were fun to be around even if they were doing nothing. They were both happy teenage girls with all of the energy one could have.

Kelly, Monica, Margaret, (Monica's mom), and I spent one winter day in Covent Gardens, window shopping and enjoying the basking and entertainment in the streets. You could smell nuts roasting on the fire in the crisp clean air. It began to snow, large flakes the size of goose feathers. We stopped in and bought hats, gloves and scarves, and continued with our afternoon of female bonding.

One evening, we dressed in our fanciest clothes and went into London for the premier of **Walt Disney's** *"Anesthasia"*. We hailed a cab, so we wouldn't have to walk in our high heels from the tube station.I felt like a celebrity when the cab dropped us out in front of the theatre in our fancy clothing.

It was very crowded, as people gathered to see who might show up for the premier. You never knew whom you might see in London, just on the streets, if you kept your eyes opened.

Kelly and Monica went through their Confirmation classes together. Confirmation is one of the seven sacraments in the Roman Catholic Church.

(The seven sacraments are; Baptism, Eucharist, Reconciliation, Confirmation, Marriage, Holy Orders and the Anointing of the Sick.)

Margaret Hamrick, (Monica's mother) was Kelly's sponsor. I was Monica's sponsor. We were there to answer questions as they went through their classes and to stand up for them at the ceremony as a witness.

Mike and Dan joined a sail boating club. It was cold out and the weather was miserable so they often had to cancel. Mike played basketball and volleyball. There was absolutely nothing for Dan to do. The school didn't offer sports for his age group. They had tons of homework compared to what they had in the states. The boys went on a ski trip in *Switzerland* while Paul and I were in *Rome*. Mike had fun, but Dan was seriously depressed.

Mike was uncomfortable on the bus when he was in grade school back in *Katy*. The public school kids would pick on him. He was shy and quiet and got his feelings hurt easily. If they picked on him long enough, he would lose his temper and which just made matters worse. Mike made the mistake of saying, "Momma, said to turn the other cheek", when one of the kids was picking on him. That made the ridicule worse. His self-esteem was pretty low when we moved to *London*.

Mike was uncomfortable on the bus in *England*, for another reason. He gave himself a nickname of Bubba, but the kids on the bus gave him the name "Boner". You can guess why. Seventh grade is an awkward age for boys.

No longer mama's boy, "now, he was cool".

It was a popular senior boy who gave him his nickname. Suddenly, all of the upper classmen seemed to know who he was, and they would tell Kelly to say "hi" to "Boner", when they would pass her in the hallway.

When Kelly told me, I scratched my head, "What a strange world we live in."

Mike got the roll of the *Wizard* in the middle school play, *The Wizard of Oz* (1939).

This was a huge production. There was a lot of involvement from parents and upper classmen as well. They had a professional director and choreographer unable to work in *London* because they didn't have working Visa's. They volunteered their time for the play. I got involved with the recording of the sound in a school play and supervised the students on the soundboard.

The thing that impressed me most was how easily Mike memorized his lines. He behaved admirably and did a fantastic job. I was really proud of his accomplishment. He was a natural on stage and didn't seem nervous at all.

Kelly and Monica helped with the make-up and costumes for dress rehearsals and the actual performances. It was really fun. We tried to get Dan involved, but his heart wasn't in it. He would stay after school with us at first. Then, he asked if he could just take the bus home.

I became a member of the church council, choir director and, helped with several church fundraisers. This gave me things to do while the children were at school. On the weekends, the kids helped as well. We had a **Princess Diana** "Beanie Baby", bear. We donated it to the church and sold raffle tickets to help raise money for the church organ. We managed to make about $3,000.00 dollars.

My best friend was an eighty-year-old Scottish nun. Sister Mary Agnes had more energy than most children I knew. She had once been the Head Mistress of the all girls' school in the area.

Sister Mary Agnes was Father John's helper at the parish. She typed the church bulletin and played the organ at church, and she managed the majority of the church fundraisers. She was an amazing woman. Highly spirited!

I had a fantastic time when Sister Mary Agnes turned eighty. The parish had a birthday party for her. They had bagpipes lead her in a parade from the parish hall to a special place they had rented for her surprise party. There was dancing and a live band. It was awesome!

Father John was a Scottish priest. He was very funny and excellent with children. He was a little old school compared to the priests back home. He scolded Kelly for wearing a skirt to church that was too short. Another time he got onto her for wearing toeless shoes. He often would get onto families for grocery shopping on Sunday. Even though he lectured us on occasion, we loved him. He would bring the altar boys and ushers chocolate bars and he would joke around with the kids. He teased Sister Mary Agnes all the time. He was a fun person to be around and my children wanted to be involved as a result.

Mike and Dan would usher and help take up the collection at the offertory. Kelly, her friend Monica, and Monica's brother, Bobby, would sing in the youth choir on Saturday night. After Mass, they had their Confirmation classes. Amazingly, they liked being around the church. The children were doing double duty. We went to church on Sunday together as a family so I could lead the adult choir.

This was something, which surprised me because our kids were never that involved before, even when they were in Catholic Schools. I think they were happy to be with so many of their school friends who also belonged to the parish. They never complained about going to church.

On Wednesday, every week, I had an outing. I would drive to *Guildford* and park my car at the car park. Then, I would walk to a church near the *High Street* and participate in BSF, Bible Study Fellowship. This was a non-denominational bible study group. There were women from several countries and several denominations. It was a great way to get educated and see things from a different perspective.

Sue was a woman I met through the school. She was also a member of the Bible Study Group. Sometimes we would ride out to *Guildford* together. Somehow, I got the feeling that we were meant to know each other. It was a feeling I can't explain, even today.

Sue's father was ill, and he was slipping in and out of a coma. Sue's father had not recognized her for several weeks and she was afraid that she would not get to say goodbye. She asked for prayer, and I added her father to my prayer list. I understood Sue's feelings concerning her father, because I had gone through the same with my Momma, just that same year.

On a Tuesday evening, after completing my homework for the next day's class, I prayed for Sue's father, and I fell asleep with him on my mind. I had a dream that night; I rubbed his feet, as I did with Momma. Though I did not know what he looked like, I dreamed of an older gray haired man with wrinkled skin and frail bones. I dreamed he came out of his coma and recognized his daughter and remained awake.

When I got to the church, I told Sue of the dream. She thanked me for my prayers.

The following Wednesday, Sue told me my dream had come true. Her father woke and recognized his daughter. She was able to say the things to him that she feared that she would not get a chance to say.

I'm not a healer. I kept my mouth shut but felt anxiety that he might now decline rapidly. Sometimes people seem to rally just before they get worse. I'm glad I was an ear for her, but I didn't want her to think this had anything to do with me. Prayer works!

Poor Dan, he was unhappy the entire time we lived in *London*. Fortunately, for Dan, it didn't end up being a full two years. We went home after one year. Paul was offered a position to run North and South America for *Kvaerner*, in *Houston*. We returned to our home in *Katy*. Kelly would miss *London*, but the boys would be much happier in the states.

CHAPTER EIGHTEEN

HOSPICE, WHY?

†

The time was July, 1998. The five of us were sitting on an airplane for a total of 13 hours. Our plane was in need of repairs, and rather than take us off the plane and let us sit in the airport, they just left us sitting in the stuffy airplane. Poor Ginger was stuck in the cargo hold. I was terribly worried about her, yet there was nothing I could do. Thankfully, someone checked on her and told me she was doing fine.

Each time we moved, for me, it would be like starting over. What I came to realize is if I tried to recreate what I left behind, it did not work for me. Instead, I would keep my eyes open for new growth or opportunity. Trying on hats until I found one that fit, is what I called it.

On the airplane, in the pocket of the chair in front of me was a leaflet with information about hospice care in it. I began to read. "Whoever left this, left it for me," I thought.

Hospice is such a noble service. No person should ever have to die alone, or afraid. My love for **Mother Teresa** and books I had recently read about her life inspired me. Perhaps, because she had just passed away that year and her pursuits were fresh on my mind, is why I was interested. If I can do it for my own mother, couldn't I provide some kind of comfort for a complete stranger?

I thought to myself, "If this is meant to be for me, then God will put it in my path."

Paul received a call from a headhunter in *Tulsa*. He was happy where he was, but Paul was willing to listen. It was an opportunity to go home, to *Tulsa*. We struggled with the decision and finally decided if we could get Kelly into *Bishop Kelley*, and the boys into *St. Pius X*, Paul would accept the opportunity and we would sell our home in *Houston* and move back to *Tulsa*.

I phoned Jenny, my life long friend, to let her know we were returning to *Tulsa*. I told Jenny about my dreams and the information I saw on the airplane. I was wondering what it all meant.

Jenny said, "I'm a hospice volunteer"!

"No way"! What are the odds? I thought.

Jenny gave me the phone number of the hospice, which she volunteered for and the name of the volunteer coordinator, Barbara. I phoned Barbara right away!

There was a training class, which would be starting that very week. I began my hospice training before I unpacked the house. I felt strongly, God put this in my path and it could not wait.

If there was any doubt whether I was on the right path, little coincidences kept reassuring me. I went to an estate sale in *Tulsa*, two weeks after we had settled, and over the mantle was a huge watercolor of *Guildford, High Street*. I purchased it for my new home, a reminder of my bible study classes, Sue and her father.

At one point Kitty questioned me. "Why not wait until after you've finished the move and things slow down a little?"

My response, "God didn't wait to put it in my path." I still feel the same to this day. Otherwise, I would have never met Mr. Mac. He was my first hospice patient and the experience is dear to me.

The assignment was simple enough. Drop in and feed a patient in the nursing home during the lunch hour. Mr. Mac was weak. He could no longer feed himself. He had family members who would come in during the evenings to feed him. They had used up all their sick days and could no longer come at lunchtime. The nurses were too busy to spend the time necessary to keep him comfortable.

On my first day, I proudly pinned on my hospice name badge. Then, I set out for work, certain that this was God's plan for me. I would drive to a nursing home, in *Sapulpa, Oklahoma*.

There were a number of patients scooting about in the entry of the nursing home. I had to push a button for someone to let me in the front door. Later, I would be given an alarm code to use, as I would come and go.

211

Some of the patients would ignore me when I came in. There were others who I would come to know well. They were harmless, but could be pests from time to time.

Jackie would stop me each time I came in, to see if I brought any cigarettes or chocolates. I told her I didn't smoke, but she never took that for an answer. If she would get caught trying to pick my pockets or dig through my purse, the nurses would scold her. She would follow me around hoping for attention. Sometimes I would stop for a visit.

There was a TV in a large open room, which was the focal point near the entry. In the far left corner of the entry room, there was a birdcage with a *blue parakeet*. I had to laugh to myself. *"I must be in the right place!"*

There were not as many people in this area as I would find around the corner, in the smoke hole. I walked to the nurse's station down a long narrow hallway that was on my right and I was given the procedure for signing in my volunteer hours.

Entering the quiet room, I introduced myself to Mr. Mac. He was frail and weak. He couldn't sit up, so the nurse showed me how to raise his bed. As I sat at his bedside, I assured him we would soon be good friends. I held his hand while he slept and fed him when he was awake. In my quiet time, I prayed for the strength it would take to make hospice my passion.

While sitting at his bedside, I noticed blue birds sponged on the wall in the bathroom. Imagine that, "I'm not just in the right nursing home I'm in the right room. I'm with the patient that God had chosen just for me."

In my hospice training, they teach you to watch for certain signs, which reveal when death is imminent. Renal failure, not eating, shallow breathing, lack of circulation in the hands and feet, etc… Not in every case will it be the same, but with the elderly, sometimes it's a little more predictable.

I began to spend more than a few hours a day with my new friend. I looked for ways to help him spend his waking hours and I would sneak out when he fell asleep. I brought up my boom box and we would listen to **Patsy Kline,** because his daughter told me she was his favorite. The closer he got to the end, the more hours I would spend with him. I had assured him at this point, he would not be alone and he had nothing to fear from death. I would arrange my time around the time his family members came to the nursing home so they could have their privacy.

I would sing to Mr. Mac and rub his feet and calves. Just like my dream. He was too weak to talk. Sometimes he could answer a question, yes or no, by blinking his eyes. Sometimes, Mac would squeeze my hand, as if he was reassuring himself that I was still there.

A period of three months passed. I needed surgery on my shoulder for a bone spur and it could no longer wait. After the surgery, I went to the nursing home and with my arm in a sling, I would lay my head on the bedrail and rest my arm on my lap, with my other arm holding his hand as he slept. I could tell Mac was nearing the end. All of the signs were present. It was 1:00 a.m. the last time I remember him making any sound or squeezing my hand. At 3:00 a.m., I left to go home and told the nurse I would be back first thing in the morning. At 5:00 a.m., just two hours later, I got a call; my friend had expired.

The time I spent with Mr. Mac was a restful time for me. It was much like a walk in the garden or a walk on the beach. I'm a high-strung individual, one of the well-known "Type A" personalities. I found visiting the elderly slowed me down. It gave me time for prayer and peace. I didn't feel guilty for just sitting. I think I needed hospice as much as it needed me.

Driving to the nursing home, I wondered what it would be like to meet the family. They were all very kind and appreciative of the time I spent with their loved one. One of the Grandchildren showed me a picture. "You should have known him when he looked like this. He was so strong"!

What I realized is; I loved him in his weakest state, not who he once was, but I loved who he was at the time I met him. I was called to be there at Mac's special moment. There was nothing in his past necessary for me to know.

Understand we only use first names in hospice. Everyone deserves his or her privacy. I could not tell you the last name of the majority of my hospice patients. I can tell you, each of them changed my life in profound ways. Still, for the purpose of this book, I changed even the first names to protect the families and the privacy of my friends. I want to share the lessons they taught me or convey the messages I carry for them.

My big brother, Danny's decision not to dwell on dying but on living fully until he died was what I wanted to bring to my hospice work. I choose to dwell on the beauty, which is life, with those who were dying. I looked for ways to make today look a little better. I tried to think of things my patients could look forward to in the short term. I encouraged families to spend quality time, available to them only if they could bring themselves to look for just one last memory.

It's a strange thing we humans do. We tend to separate ourselves before we have to. Like a defense mechanism to cut off the emotion prior to death, thinking it will lessen the blow. I recognized this in a large number of hospice families after just one or two meetings.

My part in being a hospice volunteer was to bond with the person in the room. Not the one that was, but the one that is. There would be no pain in my face, because I was there to pray, to sing, to read and to laugh with my new friend. It would be hours of peace for me. Hours of being free from seeing the faces of those without hope for the hospice patient.

The times together were generally short, but the friendships were intense. Some people have a lot to say when they know that they are dying. Sometimes, patients have nothing to say. They just want to squeeze your hand, but they leave messages, or lessons to carry with you..

Some patients say things they want to say to the family members but, can't because of the emotional drain it would bring upon both parties. I have a better appreciation of what priests and preachers go through when they visit the ill, or give last rights.

I leaked many tears in those days. I was excessively affected by emotion, yet not really sad. I felt blessed and grateful to be present at such a special, (yes, I said special), time in their lives.

God led me here. Somewhere within me, I have been given strength to deal with the sorrow. When I speak of my time as a hospice volunteer, I speak of it fondly. I want others to experience through me, a little of what I have found. Perhaps, others will have the courage to step up and volunteer with the elderly and the terminally ill, because of something I have been able to communicate to them.

This year, the baby boomers have reached the age of retirement. All of our hippies are entering a new phase of their lives. The next twenty years are going to be truly difficult for the medical community. There are going to be too many patients and not enough helpers.

I was asked to visit with a patient and sing to her in her last days. When I went to see Miss Ann at her home, it was so quiet it seemed odd to me. Her children in the other room talked in whispers, so they wouldn't disturb their sleeping mother.

I stroked her arm as she rested quietly. A couple of times she peeked to see who was singing. Her children loved the quiet songs I sang to her. I think of her home as quiet, still whispers or a soft breeze in the air.

Ms Ellen, she was a grandmother of many. She was staying with her daughter, the mother of eleven children. Not a bed in the back of the house where it was quiet, she was in a bed in the playroom with the grandchildren playing under her feet. Toys were strewn about and there was little silence. Our visit was full of laughter and stories.

The difference between Ann's last days and Ellen's last days were that of night and day. Ann's were like early mornings in the garden, when the birds are just beginning their song. Ellen was the garden in the fall at dusk, during my family barbeque, with a swing set full of kids and a flock of birds overhead.

There are no rules. I suspect they lived their lives in a similar fashion to the way their lives ended. There are many colors in life's garden and they're all beautiful.

To people of many faiths, life is but a stepping-stone into another life. Ms. Kay passed; I walked out of the door to the family home with our preacher and a sister of the deceased.

"Would you look at that? There's a rainbow!" I pointed toward the horizon to those who were with me. "What a beautiful gift. A rainbow is God's sign of cleansing and new life."

Kay's sister dismissed the rainbow and began to tell me the scientific definition of a rainbow.

How can those with no faith have hope? I wondered.

Then I thought of how I would feel if I presented such a beautiful gift and received no acknowledgment. Like a child who brings their mother a rose from the garden, only to be ignored. I hope I am never so blind that I dismiss a gift so precious.

I would be willing to bet we do it often. Here is the lesson I carry with me from my short time with Kay. Keep your eyes open to the beauty that surrounds you and say, "thank you".

There was a break in my hospice work for a period of time. My X-brother-in-law, Dink, had peritonitis. His boys took him out to dinner for his birthday, which was just two days after mine. That night, his intestine burst and there was poison throughout his body.

Dink landed in ICU. This strong, sturdy giant of a man nearly died several times. I don't think those caring for him in the hospital expected him to make it. Twice when I was in his room his heart stopped and they called "code blue". His family was called in to say their goodbyes on more than one occasion.

I decided instead, of staying with a stranger, I would spend my time in ICU with Dink. Three hours a day minimum, I would sit at his bedside, making sure he was getting proper care. I had been trained and, I could assist if he needed turning. He was too out of it to know I was there. Still, I noticed his blood pressure would come down and his pulse rate would slow a bit if someone were in the room with him.

Dinks sister, Mary, would spend hours with him as well. Various other family members would pop by, yet none of them had the time available I did, to sit and sing, read a book or put lotion on his feet.

Though, lawfully, I guess we were no longer related, this was Todd, Jess and Clint's dad and my old friend.

This was *"Dinky Duck"*, the guy who played with me when I was three -years-old and made me giggle and laugh. Dink loved babies, but he and Dit never had a little *"Amy"*. He wanted a little girl to go with his three boys!

Dink was like a brother to me. He sat across the card table on more occasions than I could count. We watched *The Longest Yard* (1974) over and over again and laughed every time. Dink coached my boys in football and played softball with the family ball team.

We cried over the same loved ones who had gone before us. Danny, Granny, Grandpa, Momma, Daddy, Norma and others. Dink was a young man still and strong as an ox. He began to get better and we thought we were going to get him out of ICU, but he caught one of those super bugs, which are plaguing the hospitals. No anti-biotic could touch it. Again, I think the hospital staff thought he wouldn't make it. The days were long.

I would clean his mouth out with the lollipop stick that had a sponge on the end, and I would feed him ice cubes when he needed them. As he began to get stronger, once again, I would help him move his feet and hands, and we began to rehabilitate his shoulders. Then, he got the strength to roll over, sit up and stand. He was taking one-step at a time. Slowly but surely, to everyone's surprise, he was bouncing back again.

Dink had an incredible will to live! The ordeal took three months out of his life. He had no recollection of what happened during that time. It left him with a bedsore the size of a frying pan. When he was released from the hospital and allowed to go home, he would need a nurse to come to the house, pack the wound, and change the bandage.

A friend of mine from the choir at *St. Pius X* would volunteer to go to Dinks home twice a week to change his bandage, until he could get things set up with the proper nursing outfit.

Our Catholic community came together with a fundraiser, a potluck dinner. The idea was to collect enough money to help fix plumbing and sewage problems at his house, and to make sure that his home was sanitary when he left the hospital. Then, he began the long process of rehabilitation. He had to learn to speak, to sit, and to walk again. Dink used every bit of the strength he had to survive, both consciously and unconsciously. He was not ready to go!

Despite all of the discomfort and pain Dink endured, his message was clear. The result of his will to live was this. Within less than a ten-year stretch, Dink saw each of his son's marry. Jess and Jill would marry. Todd and Cher' Raine's union brought about two grandchildren, Austin and Cooper and Clint and Stephanie brought Grandpa Dink two boys, Kyle and Luke, and then, as if by a miracle, most recently, they had a girl. Her name is Lily. How I wish I could have been there when Dink held his granddaughter for the first time. Knowing Dink, it must have been one of the happiest days of his life.

When I went back to my hospice work, I was placed with, yet another survivor. It was Belinda's mother's hope keeping her alive. Belinda was my youngest patient. She lost her brain function and couldn't feed herself, or even swallow. She was being fed through a tube in her stomach. She couldn't recognize people and was rarely stimulated by much going on in the room. Sometimes a helium balloon might give her entertainment for a while. Still, she was breathing on her own. Her mother wasn't ready to let go of hope.

I didn't feel it was my place to take away that hope. I would try to get to the nursing home before her mother, so I could wash her face, brush her teeth and comb her hair. I would put makeup on her and try to make her look presentable before her mother came.

Her family would sit at her bedside and watch for any signs of improvement in her health. Her state of life was a result of self-destructive behavior. She was 39-years-old, and had twelve-year-old daughter.

Belinda lived past her six-month hospice. She was transferred to a nursing home in another county.

I observed her mother's suffering and I learned through Belinda, "there are some things worse than death." "Self destructive behavior hurts many more than the person lying in the bed. Belinda wasn't suffering. I don't think she was really there, but her family was suffering". In this particular case, I was there for them. She had a butterfly tattoo on her breast. I keep a butterfly garden for Belinda to remind me to pray for her often. I pray too for the family. One day the butterfly will be released from the cocoon through their prayers, tears and suffering.

There are some people you meet who make an impact on your life by just being who they are. Ms. Alice was one of those people. This elderly woman had the most beautiful red hair I had ever seen. She never had a hair out of place. She took great care of her skin and her room was organized and decorated. Ms Alice was thin and frail, but she carried herself upright and with grace.

By coincidence, she lived most of her life in a home near *Tracy Park*, just off 11th, and Newport. That means I must have passed her house hundreds of times over the years, when I lived at 13th and Newport, traveling back and forth to and from the park, and yet, our paths had never crossed up until her last days. Not that I remember. I'm sure I trick or treated there and I may have picked a flower from her garden a time or two. It's hard to know for sure.

Ms. Alice loved gardening and her favorite color was pink. I would take pictures of gardens and bring the pictures to the nursing home for her to view. Her favorite flower was pink roses. Alice would close her eyes, and I would describe to her in great detail, the beautiful scenery of the park and we strolled through our imagination in the gardens, smelling the roses and jasmine. Sometimes I would bring roses from my garden to enhance the experience.

I would come in the mornings to see Alice. She needed help getting dressed. Sometimes I would read to her, or we would do the morning puzzle. With her perfect hair and makeup, she wore a lovely scarf around her neck because she wanted to be presentable when she showed up in the cafeteria for lunch.

This particular nursing home was nicer than most that I had been to. There was a park across the street with a jogging trail, which surrounded a golf course. The nursing home had a large picture window the patients could look out.

The dining area was set up more like a restaurant instead of a cafeteria. Each of the tables had a white tablecloth. Silverware would be on the table with a clothe napkin, not paper. The food was prepared and served by hospital staff, but it was done in a manner more like a restaurant. It didn't feel at all like a nursing home.

Alice was a woman of strength and dignified grace. Throughout her illness, her faith never faltered. We would pray together often. Her decline was much faster than I had imagined, but she was 96 years old. I never heard her complain about much of anything.

One of my own children was suffering from depression during the time I was with Ms Alice. She helped me get through some tough times.

She had a brother who killed himself. She would remind me over and over again, "Cheryl, do not be too hard on him. Let him go at his own pace." She would always ask for a report on how things were coming along at home. She would remember to ask about each of my children. Polite conversation was something at which she excelled.

Often, I think God put her there for me and not the opposite. I began taking photography classes with my son. I would bring the pictures to Ms. Alice, after the pictures had been presented to our class. We would discuss the art. I would miss helping Alice dress in the mornings.

To this day, I always keep one flowerbed for Alice's pinks. It's a quiet place for me to remember her. She was a wise woman.

Here I am, ten years after my short period with Ms. Alice. I will never forget her. She touched my life in profound ways, and she made a difference for my son as well. We can never know how many lives we touch. We can never know what we might say to make a difference in the life of another. She was still making new friends and giving wise advice at the age of 96.

CHAPTER NINETEEN

YOU'RE NEVER TOO OLD TO MAKE A DIFFERENCE IN SOMEONE ELSE'S LIFE

♥

It was my friend, Ms. Alice who first taught me, "You are never too old to make a difference in someone else's life."Sitting in my garden of pinks, I pondered this life long lesson. "Life's direction is influenced or changed by experiences with pain, illness and death as much as anything else."

From my older brother, Danny, I learned how important it is to "live until you die." He never wasted a day, once he knew they were numbered. He moved forward, seldom looking back.

Through the numerous moves, I learned "you can't go back, so move forward and when doors open walk through. If that hat fits, wear it." Opportunities present themselves and those who take advantage of those opportunities will prosper.

From my experience and anxiety over Kitty's illness, I learned; "only the person who is facing the illness can decide quality versus quantity." I thought that dwelling on her illness would kill us both.

Stress is a killer.

From my first year of hospice work with patients Ann and Ellen, I found, "There are many colors in the garden of life and they're all beautiful. There's no right or wrong way to go out in this world."

We cannot expect everyone to deal with his or her mortality in the same way.

Through Ms. Kay, I learned the valuable lesson, "keep you're eyes open to the beauty that surrounds you and thank God!" and "If it's happenstance, I would rather not know."Life's beauty is there for all of us to experience, rich or poor, in sickness and health. We can choose to acknowledge it or we can overlook it. I find it to be proof of God's love, because love is the only thing that brings that kind of joy.

"Life is worth fighting for!" Dink, my X brother-in-law, taught me one of the most valuable lessons in life, not through his words but through his example. His life was full of pain and suffering, yet he fought hard for each moment. This fight brought him the happiness of seeing his grandchildren.

Belinda, my survivor, taught me, "There are some things worse than death". I will continue to pray for her, and I pray for her family.

Each of these lessons will be fully experienced with my next hospice family and then some. Like all volunteer work, I go into, thinking I'm doing something nice for someone else, the reality is there's a high I get from doing things for others. The kindness I have to offer begets a lasting friendship, beyond death.

It was a hot summer day, the first time I met Ms. Margaret and her husband Frank. I drove to a brick home on the south side of *Tulsa*. It was in an area called *Shadow Mountain*, located on a hill in *Tulsa*.

Most of the houses were built in the 1970's for the upper class and upper middle class families in the area. The homes were well maintained and the streets and sidewalks were clean. The area was cloaked with restaurants and fine shopping centers on the corner lots entering the subdivision.

I drove to the home and parked in the street, in front of the house, near the curb. There I looked over my paperwork, in order to understand exactly what to expect, before I entered the home. I locked the car and made my way up the driveway, toward the front door. I tended to be a little nervous when I approached, but most of the time the nervousness would go away, once I entered the dwelling.

I rang the bell, yet noticed that the door was cracked open. They were expecting me, and I heard them holler from the rear of the house to come in. When I entered, I was greeted by the nurse. She introduced herself and led me to the kitchen, where I was offered a seat.

There were three elderly people visiting over a strong cup of black coffee at the table. I would join them in the kitchen. There at the table, I met Frank's brother, Ralph, who had traveled to see Margaret and say goodbye. Margaret was my hospice patient. Their guest was from *Shreveport, Louisiana*. They each had a thick *Louisiana* accent. Because Momma's family was from Louisiana, I knew the accent well. It was heartwarming to hear the southern draw. The more we visited the more we found we had in common.

Margaret and Frank had lived in *Great Bend, Kansas*. That was where my daddy was from. The old homestead was in *Great Bend*, until the family moved to *Oklahoma* during the dust bowl. Until this day, I had never met anyone from *Great Bend* who was not family. The population in those days was under 10,000. The last census had the population near 15,000.

Margaret loved sports. She especially loved the Jay Hawks. I knew that would give us plenty to talk about, because her Jay Hawks were having a very good season in basketball, and their football team was not to be overlooked either.

Frank was not quite eighty-years-old. He had a fabulous laugh. (His laugh, I still miss today.) He was a great conversationalist. He was in a wheelchair, so I don't really know how tall he was, but I would guess him to be six feet tall. Frank had one of his legs amputated. Other than that, he looked in relatively good health for a man of his age. I observed he had a difficult time maneuvering the wheelchair on the shag carpet in the living room, but I did not say anything.

Margaret was frail, also in a wheelchair, and she was approximately eighty-years-old too. Her health was much worse than Frank's. Her mind was not clear. She was confused most of the time. She was very sweet and never seemed cross.

For a first visit, I came away with a really good feeling. There were so many things we had in common, I felt like we were already familiar with one another. It was like meeting members of my own family for the first time.

We fit together perfectly.

The second visit, the following week, I met the two daughters, Libby and Jane. They were both in their 40's. They had never married. Both girls were living at home helping to care for their ailing parents. There was a full time nurse who stayed in the home during the day when the daughters were at work.

I did not like the way that Frank talked to the nurse. He treated her like a second-class citizen. He would order her around instead of asking for something. There seemed to be some attitude here. Not just with the nurse, with the daughters as well.

Franks relationship with Margaret was beautiful. He looked after her and saw to it that she received the attention that she required. He spoke to her respectfully and held her hand gently when he spoke to her. Sometimes he would flirt with her, like they were teenagers, and she would flirt back. They were cute together.

Frank and Margaret had a son, Peter, who predeceased his parents. Peter was buried in the cemetery not far from the home. There was one other son, Glen. He was married and lived not far away with his wife, Lisa and two daughters. Peter was the sensible one in the family. The rest of the family seemed too emotional to make logical decisions. As a result, he often looked like the bad guy when important decisions needed to be made.

I was fortunate because I owned a 1998 Oldsmobile, Silhouette Van. It would come in handy when I took Frank or Margaret on an outing. Frank wanted to go with us to talk to the doctor when I took Margaret in for her check up. The van came in handy when we ran an errand or went on an outing to the park. One evening we went to dinner together at one of their favorite restaurants. The employees at *Charleston's* knew the couple well. When they saw us coming, they prepared the room, removing the chairs so they could fit the wheelchairs up under the table.

Usually, our outings were more for Frank than they were for Margaret. Sometimes Frank seemed like a caged animal. He needed to get away from the house, even if it was just for a little while. I noticed he would come up with an excuse; he needed to run an errand almost every time I came. I didn't mind. Anything I could do to help the family function in a more relaxed manner would be helpful. Sometimes the household seemed to be tense. I was there to help in any way I could.

Frank and I nearly always made a trip to the bank, then a stop for something not on his diet, like ice cream or a hot dog. He was diabetic, but couldn't wait to break his diet. Each of our outings always ended the same. We would take a drive over to the cemetery and look over the family plot; to be sure things were taken care of properly.

On Saturday's when I visited the home, I spent most of my time with Margaret. We would watch football in the fall and basketball in the winter months. When her wheelchair was no longer comfortable, we would put her in a chair in the living room and watch the games together.

In the springtime, I bought my son, Mike, a Pug . Her name was Lola, *"she was a show girl"*. Pugs are really cute dogs, and as puppies, they are even more precious. Ginger and Lola got along well. She made a nice addition to our family.

Mike brought Lola over to play with Ms. Margaret one day. I think she wanted to keep little Lola. The girls said normally Margaret was not fond of dogs, but in her new youthful ways, Margaret and Lola bonded. We sat in the back garden and watched the puppy play.

The time I spent getting to know the family was my time for gathering information on how I could be helpful in making the next few months, weeks or days pleasant for Margaret. I sensed she would benefit from something to look forward to in the near future. The couple had their fifty-sixth wedding anniversary coming up. Perhaps we could make that special occasion a goal, and we could plan a party.

The sadness over Margaret's impending death weighed so heavy, you would have thought she was already deceased. It was obvious that she was the strength of the family, and with her nearly gone, there was nothing left. The glue that was holding the family together was gone.

I told Frank of a plan to bring the family together. He informed me his daughters were not speaking with the son, and it might not be possible to have them all in the same room together. I explained to Frank, that it's common for siblings to be at each other's throats when they are going through this kind of trauma. I observed many times when adults acted more like children and reverted back to the positions they held in their youth. I saw it in my family after Daddy died and again after Momma's departure, but not to the same severity.

It took some convincing, but the children were all willing to make the attempt for their mom. Something to focus on besides death and dying would benefit the youthful Ms Margaret. Creating one last memory for the other members of the family of a happy time couldn't hurt. The plan was a celebration, a romantic dinner followed by a dessert and a toast to the loving couple, with their children.

The daughters didn't want any stress. Dealing with daily matters was enough for them. I assured them that I would take care of everything. I went shopping, and I purchased Margaret something special to wear. Frank and I went to the florist and ordered a corsage. I sat with the couple and planned the entire evening.

The menu for this romantic dinner needed to be something gentle on Margaret's stomach. Together, we came to the conclusion the meal would be turkey, stuffing, green beans and bread. After dinner, all of the children would join us for a champagne toast, cheesecake and coffee.

Margaret was excited about the upcoming affair. She loved what I had picked up for her to wear. She was focused on the party and not on her illness, for at least a little while.

It was a beautiful evening. The weather cooperated, so I didn't have any trouble when I arrived at the house, carrying in the card table and chairs. I had boxes of dishes, my tape deck and various other things that needed to be carried in from the van.

We had Frank Sinatra music playing softly in the background. It was the music that Frank and Margaret listened to in their youth. How better to set the mood?

Margaret wore her new jacket. It was a cobalt blue blazer with sequin on the collar and a matching pillbox hat, with a fine net that came over the forehead. She looked beautiful.

Frank wore a white dress shirt, tucked into his pants. Both could stay in their wheelchairs. We used a card table and white linen tablecloth and just pushed the wheelchairs up to the table. We wanted everyone to be comfortable and did not want to put the family through any hardship.

Kitty offered to help me. Thank goodness, because I'm not a very good cook. She and I acted as caterers. We dressed in black pants with white collared shirts, with white dishtowels over our arm.

We set the table with soft candle light and a rose bud in a vase. Frank brought out Margaret's corsage to pin on her jacket. Everything was perfect, including the meal.

The children joined the couple for the planned dessert. We all had a prayer together. The couple finished the bottle of champagne with their son. They were laughing and having a wonderful time together.

When the meal was over, Kitty and I took everything out with us. There would be no mess for the family to pick up. We just left a few leftovers in the refrigerator.

I set up a tri-pod and camera for pictures in the dining room. Frank and Margaret had one more event to remember of their long history together. Hopefully, the children had one more good memory, amid their suffering.

Two weeks after our party, I received the call to go to her side. I encouraged the girls to climb in bed with Mom and give her a cuddle. The girls lay in bed beside Ms. Margaret and rocked her. I'm glad that I was there in time to hold her awhile and say goodbye.

I wasn't the only one to come to see her off. A robin came to the window; several times, it tried to enter the house. This would not be the last time I would see this happen. I don't have an answer for the reason why. Perhaps someone else who reads this will have an answer for me.

I requested to stay on and help the family through the bereavement process. I felt I had connected with this family. Frank tried getting bossy with me, the way he did with the nurse in the past. I told him I didn't have to take that treatment. I was not an employee and I could walk away at any time. He never treated me with disrespect again, I never heard him treat the nurses with disrespect again either. I think he was unaware of how he was coming across.

One time, Frank had a plumbing problem. One of the daughters got angry with him when the toilet overflowed. I guess it wasn't a first time. I stayed and helped to clean up. He was embarrassed and acted like this work was somehow beneath me. My volunteer work for hospice was not for lightweights. I was glad to stay and help. He respected my willingness to handle the tough stuff. He was unhappy, but he was in no way unfair. We became good friends.

My sons, Mike and Dan, were earning Christian service hours for school. It is a requirement before they can graduate, to put in a number of volunteer hours. The boys became lawn workers for my buddy, Frank. They would mow and trim the bushes in the summer and rake and haul the leaves off in the fall. They put up the Christmas lights and scraped snow from the sidewalk in the winter.Frank would sit in a lawn chair in the garage or on the driveway and supervise his workers. I would sit with him on days when I had time.

The boys had a relationship with him similar to the relationship I had with my grandfather. I was proud of Mike and Dan, and I was happy they were learning to respect their elders. Frank was good with the boys.

During the next three years, Frank would go on hospice and survive his decline, only to end up on hospice again. We saw him through some really rough days. He was getting weak enough his daughters could no longer take care of him at home. He would struggle on the carpet with his wheelchair, even when he was in good health. Now in his weakened state, it was time to make a difficult decision and put him in a nursing home.

Frank fought his children every step of the way. He did not want to leave his home. The daughters knew their father well. They expected him to fight them all the way. He was a fighter, that's why he kept cheating death. Frank would "never give up", and the children knew that!

Frank didn't want to go to a nursing home. When I asked him why, He said, "Because they're full of old people".

It was funny, but he meant it. "I hate old people! They can't hear anything that I say and I can't hear anything that they say." Frank said.

His frustration was understandable. He would go through many phases of depression. He was once very active and an athlete. Then, he had to learn to do without one of his legs. He was married to the same woman for fifty-six years, and now he must live alone. His was a sad existence for someone who loved to talk.

Now his life was going through another change. He couldn't live in the house he had lived in for decades. He couldn't drive. He couldn't eat the things he loved.

The nursing home the family decided on was the same one that Ms. Alice was in, with the white table clothes. I was glad it was close to my home and it would be an easy commute for me. It was across the street from *LaFortune Park* and the golf course. I would have thought that to be the perfect location for him. He loved golf. When he was young, he would play golf with his children and grandchildren.

Frank was not happy in the nursing home. He kept begging the children to take him back home. It made me wonder, what is more difficult, to lose your body and not your mind? This sure wasn't the best way for Frank to grow old.

Is it more difficult to lose your mind and not your body? That seems to make life miserable for the families. We would see that among people we met at the nursing home. Some wouldn't recognize their own family members. One girl cried on my shoulder when her mother hit on her husband. Mom saw herself as an eighteen-year old girl.

These are not stories, which happen on occasion. These are the details that happen each and every day. One can't work at a nursing home and be a sissy. It takes a special type of person to handle that kind of work. I have great respect for those who choose to work in the medical field.

Franks family came to the conclusion Frank was not going to be happy. Not as long as he thought there was any chance, if he acted miserable enough, the daughters would let him move back home. His family moved him to a different nursing center, but still didn't let him come home.

It was a brilliant plan. I think he finally realized he was going to have to make a new life for himself. I visited several days a week at first. Then, I tapered off as he began to make other new friends.

Frank took a couple of people under his wing and began to build true friendships with them.

His best male friend was a guy named Billy. Billy had multiple sclerosis. I don't know how old he was. I suspect that, he was about forty-years-old. When I met him, he had spent the past 23 years in the nursing home.

Billy had no use of his body, from the neck down. Still, Billy had a smile that could light an entire room. He showed it to you every time you walked in the door. He had accepted his fate and been through all of his phases of depression long ago.

Billy had a camera at the bottom of his bed. When someone came to visit, he would ask one of the nurses or orderly's to take a picture of the two of you together. He had volumes of photo albums in his room. Each was full of headshots. Billy had lots of visitors every week. Many were from his church.

Billy was pushed out into the lobby twice a week and one of the other patients who played the piano would put on a concert for him. He and Frank became very good buddies. Sometimes they would watch a ballgame on TV together. Mostly, they liked to visit.

Frank's son bought him a bottle of spirits for Christmas. He kept it safely in his room. On occasion, he would go see his good friend Billy, and share a little of the wealth. They had many parties together, just the two of them.

Frank's favorite gal friend was a woman by the name of Patti. She was in her mid-thirties and had multiple sclerosis. Her MS was in the earlier stages, but the MS was progressing rapidly. She had no bladder control. Frank made sure if she was not getting enough attention from the nursing staff, the problem was soon rectified.

Sometimes, I would drop in for lunch. Patti, Frank and I would sit and visit for a while. Then, we would go out into the lobby and visit with Billy.

Everyone knew my friend Frank took care of Billy and Patti. He brought them things and looked after them as though they were family. The result was he felt good about himself because he was making a difference in their lives.

They were making a difference in his life, just by existing. I had learned there are some things worse than death. It must be the mind going before the body, because this example proves, the body isn't necessary to make a difference in the lives of others.

One of the girls who worked at the nursing home was a mother with two daughters. The girls were about eight and ten-years-old. They would bring their softball and gloves and they would play catch with Frank in the back courtyard, sometimes, several days a week.

When Frank gave the girls batting practice, if they missed a pitch, he would make them run to the fence and back. When it was his time to bat, they made him do the same. If he missed, he would have to run his wheelchair to the fence and back.

New Years Eve, Frank tipped one of the orderlies on the sly. He put Patti on his lap in his new electric wheelchair, and he had the orderly push Billy's bed. There was a nice restaurant across 61st, Street. There they would have a steak dinner. It was a New Years treat from their good buddy Frank!

That was the type of guy he was. He had a heart as big as all outdoors. Anyone who met him had to have a soft spot for him. He was easy to talk to about anything.

I attended Frank's granddaughters wedding reception at the *Oaks Country Club*. I was Franks ride back to the nursing home after the reception. It gave his son a chance to stay to the end of the evening.

Frank's heart and lungs were not as good as they once were. He was on oxygen and could only be out for a short period of time.

I got to see his brother, Ralph, from *Louisiana* once again. Years had past since our first meeting, the same day I met Frank and Margaret. I met several other family members at the wedding who I had heard stories about, but I had never met in person.

In May, we drove to the nursing home in my van. We loaded the wheel chair, the oxygen tank and an extra tank just in case the first one ran out of oxygen. It was my son, Mike's graduation from the eighth grade at *St. Pius X*. After Mass, there was a reception in the parish hall. Frank enjoyed spending time with the family. To us, he was family. It was important to Mike that Frank was there to share such a special day.

Paul and I had to move our family to *Texas* once again. It was difficult to tell my friend I was leaving. He was going to be just fine in the new life that he was creating for himself.

In *Katy, Texas*, we bought another house in *Cinco Ranch*. We loved our first home there, and we would love our next home even more. Kelly went back to *Oklahoma* to go to college and the boys went to *Cinco Ranch High School*.

I received a call from Kelly. She was in Tulsa and she stopped by the nursing home to see howFrank was. The nurse informed her that Frank was in his last hours. Kelly phoned Franks family, and she phoned me. Frank had it written in his last will and testament for his family to fly me in for his funeral. My husband, Paul made arrangements for me to fly to *Tulsa* and be with Frank before he passed.

Kelly remained at his side until I arrived. We didn't want him to be alone. I was proud of Kelly for staying with him. Frank was still cognizant enough to know who I was when I entered and Frank's family made it there in time to say goodbye. We were all there for his departure. He went peacefully, yet he never gave up his lust for life.

I was there to sing and to speak at Frank's funeral. All of the hats that I have worn over the years prepared me for this one occasion. I was his spiritual advisor on earth, now he can look over me from the heavens.

A permanent picnic table and chairs was placed in the back garden of the nursing home, under a tree near the location where Frank and the girls played ball. It was a gift for his friends, and something to remind them to think of him, and to pray for him. I hope that a little piece of him remains there for his friends.

Frank was content in his last years. He was making a difference in the lives of others. He had something to feel good about himself. Frank gave up the idea of going home and made the best of the situation he was in, even if it wasn't his choice to be there. Most importantly, he lived until he died.

The same year that Frank passed away, I went to *Louisiana*, to be at Aint Evelyn's bedside with her children, Cindy, Jay and Kathy. She went peacefully, listening to me sing, whether she wanted to hear it or not. Again, later that year I would sit at Uncle Possum's bedside in his last days. I saw no fear. He was at peace with God and man.

The same week Uncle Possum passed, I spent a beautiful day in *Oklahoma* with Paul and the kids at an *OU Football* game.

I think, "Happiness and tears belong together. We are not meant to experience one without the other. We learn this as a baby. It is as natural as crawling, right then left, front then back, and yet, we spend so much of our existence trying to change the natural balance in life."

Purpose for Creation,
By: Wm H. O'Brien (Billy)

Did you ever wonder what you were worth?
Or what you could do for this troubled earth?
If you want your life to be worthwhile,
Try to make your brother smile.
When his heavy burden makes him sob;
To make him laugh would be your job.
Good jobs and good pay make life so nice
But a smile from a friend will top any price.

So strive with me to make life gay;
You'll find out that it will pay.
And as our kids strive through their years,
They won't see quite so many tears.

CHAPTER TWENTY

GENERATION NEXT

†

My mother taught me to find the good in any situation, no matter how difficult it is to find. When my life plays out like a **Chevy Chase** movie, I stay calm. I try to keep it together and then think about how I'm going to tell this story to my siblings, because they are not going to believe it!

Some of my brothers and sisters have an even greater gift of making the best of a bad situation. I keep that in mind and I find the hilarity in my crisis. When a situation is out of control, the one thing I can have control over is how I will allow it to affect my life today. Sometimes, I cry.

Momma was one of the youngest members of her family. She saw many of her brothers and sisters go before her. This is another thing, which is unfair about being one of the youngest in a large family. Now, just ten years after Momma's death, the GENERATION PAST is just that. All of Grandma and Grandpa's (Katie and Sam's) children are now gone. They are still loved and never forgotten.

Daddy's family is younger. Many of them are still with us. We see each other at Christmas, weddings and funerals. We have a reunion every couple of years and try to stay caught up.

We are the generation present. It is those of us who are still trying to make our mark on the world. We will endure the loss of many more of our loved one's along our way, until one day, there are more souls to watch over us from heaven than on earth. They will keep us focused on that which is truly important in our lives, faith, family and country, or community and never the chase for the dollar.

Those I call GENERATION NEXT, are our children and our children's children. I want to tell you more about Kitty and Russell's family! They are a perfect example of generation next.

Kitty and Russell had three children who often entertained my children throughout the years as babysitters and in later years, more like best friends or brothers and sisters. Katie, Sandy and Michael Ed went to *St. Pius X*, where I taught and to *Bishop Kelley*, where my children went, when they lived in *Tulsa*.

Katie and her husband, Mark moved to *Edmond, Oklahoma* for Mark's work. As fate would have it, her sister, Sandy, would receive a full scholarship to *UCO* in volleyball, putting the sisters right there together. Was this coincidence? "The girls felt this was God's doing, not their decision which kept them together."

Katie and Sandy are excited, each of their paths led to *Edmond*. They have hopes of raising their children close together, the way we raised our children together; the way our parents raised us so close to our cousins.

In previous chapters, I remind you, I spoke about the enlarged hearts in our family. The death of my brother Danny, and then Momma, Kitty and Patsy were diagnosed. At seventeen, Katie was the one diagnosed, when she made her trip to *Houston* to visit us at spring break. The doctors said it would be best if she never had children.

With modern medicine and healthy living, the disease was moving slowly enough the doctors thought it might be O.K., for Katie to become pregnant before the disease had time to progress. It would still be considered a high-risk pregnancy, but she could be monitored closely.

Katie married early, at the age of twenty. Though it seems young, Katie maintains that she was soooo… ready! She and her husband Mark didn't intend to start their family right away, but sometimes things are not planned. Life Happens! She got pregnant almost immediately after they got married.

Mark was terrified and not quite ready to be a daddy, yet he turned out to be an awesome father. Had Katie not started having kids when she did, most likely she would have never been able to have three children. Her first pregnancy, with Brendan, happened before her heart disease had time to progress, and her pregnancy and labor went well. She was watched closely and the doctors felt her heart handled things about as well as could be expected.

The second child, Alyssa was a bit too close to taking Katie's life. Katie's heart took a long time to recover after Alyssa and she had to spend a long time in bed. Her doctors in *Houston* and her doctors at home in *Edmond*, advised she and Mark to call it quits. The family was big enough. Any more children would be too much risk.

Once again, God had another plan. Despite all of the precautions Katie and Mark took to prevent a pregnancy, life once again, found a way. I believe most people would have understood if Katie and Mark had decided to terminate the pregnancy, given the fact both the baby and the mother's life were in danger. They made a courageous decision, based solely on their faith and a love for life.

When Kitty found out that Katie was required to stay in bed and only get out if she used a wheelchair, Kitty dropped everything in her life and drove to *Edmond, Oklahoma*. She was there to help in any way she could. Kitty was a lifesaver for Katie and Mark. She moved in with the small family of four, for two months.

Katie and the baby would have some very close calls. The doctors watching them found a balance they thought would be the safest point for both mother and child. They took the baby early. A happy little girl named Kristen.

By this time, Katie's little sister, Sandy, had graduated from *UCO* and married. She and her husband Tradd remained in *Edmond*. They now have two children of their own, Savanna and Tara. The girls are raising their children together, cousins, that are more like brother and sister, much as we were with our children growing up.

Kitty and Russell both sacrificed a lot during Katie's pregnancy with her little miracle child, Kristen. (Her middle name is Elizabeth. It was my mother's middle name.)With help from Sandy and her husband Tradd, who live close by, with prayers and support from Kitty and Russell, and with Michael Ed often holding the fort at home, the family's faith was tested.

They passed the test most people would have failed. This faith will carry them through some tougher times still. The birds will sing and the sun will rise, and they will never be alone in their journey through time.

Katie will need to take very good care of her health, because her heart is not as strong as that of a normal thirty-year-old woman. Still, she does not have to live with a decision, which may have haunted her for the rest of her life. As we know well, miracles do happen, everyday!

Kitty and Russell are wearing the concrete out on the *Turner Turnpike* traveling back and forth between *Tulsa* and *Edmond* to visit five grandchildren.

This was just one example of GENERATION NEXT. Each family will have to endure trials along the way. Life is not meant to be easy and only a fool would expect it to be so.

Our children, Kelly, Mike and Dan, all chose to go to college in *Oklahoma*, in order to be close to the extended family.

Kelly fell in love. She and Aaron Myers were married in 2003. They have chosen to make their life together in the *Tulsa* area, where they bought their first home, and they welcome us for vacation and holidays.

GENERATION NEXT, well, they are our hope. They are the one's who will remember us, and they will keep our stories alive. They will mourn over us. Through their tears and laughter, we will be baptized into another life. They will wear the hats we left behind, that of the nurse, the coach, the teacher, the soldier, the poet. They will feel blessed, as we have felt blessed, knowing in their hearts, they are never alone.

The End

PAUL'S FAMILY TREE
RA AND AJ (Paul's Mom and Dad)
1. Ann and Terry
   a. Terry and Kristen
      i. Hannah
      ii. Ryan
   b. Sean and Mandy
      i. Mason
      ii. Bennett
      iii. Caroline
      iiii. ? on the way
2. **Kathy and ~~David~~**
   a. Dustin and Laura
   b. Lindsey
3. **Karen and Charlie**
   a. Matt
   b. Dan
   c. Andrew
4. **Paul and Cheryl**
   a. Kelly and Aaron
   b. Mike
   c. Dan
5. **John and Kathy**
   a. Nick
   b. Kelsey
   c. Christopher
   d. Patrick
6. **Jim and Julie**
   a. Hailey
   b. Allie
   c. Katie
   d. Jake
   e. Joe

ED AND ALVA O'BRIEN FAMILY TREE

1. Bryan and ~~Debbie~~, Rose
   a. Stacy and Dak
      i. Julia
      ii. Katlyn
      iii. Bryan
   b. Shelly and Joel
      i. Kayla
      ii. Emma
      iii. Jack
   c. Danny and Cindy
      i. Tyler
      ii. Nick
      iii. John
   d. Shannon
      i. Kamryn
2. Danny O'Brien (deceased) 1971
3. Christy and ~~Dink~~
   a. Todd and Cher' Raine
      i. Austin
      ii. Cooper
   b. Jess and Jill
   c. Clint and Stephanie
      i. Kyle
      ii. Luke
      iii Lily
      iv ?
4. Ray and De
   Ed and Stacey
      i. Carter
   b. Sheena and Richard
      i. Riley
5. Kitty and Russell
   a. Katie and Mark
      i. Brendon
      ii. Alyssa
      iii Kristen
   b. Sandy and Tradd
      i. Savanna
      ii. Tara
   c. Michael Ed

6. Bill/~~Dina~~/Lori
    a. Diane/~~Eric~~/Shannon
        i. Weston
    b. Billy and ~~Bridget~~
        i. Erica
        ii Will
        iii Kara
    c. James and Tricia
        i. Melinda
        ii Zack
7. Cheryl and Paul
    a. Kelly and Aaron
    b. Mike
    c. Dan
8. Bo and Donna
    a. Laura
    b. Casey
9. Sarah and Stan
    a. Bo
    b. Jenny and Travis
        i. Jacob
        ii. George
    c. Heather and Trent
        i. James
    d. Eric
    e. Bryan
10. Patsy and Shelton
    a. Brooke
    b. Cooper
11. Punkin and Jeff
    a. Tommy
    b. Christy
    c. Joseph
    d. Katie

www.ingramcontent.com/pod-product-compliance
Lightning Source LLC
Chambersburg PA
CBHW061346280526
45784CB00001B/157